Penang

Sketchbook

The publishers gratefully acknowledge the generous support of the patrons of this book:

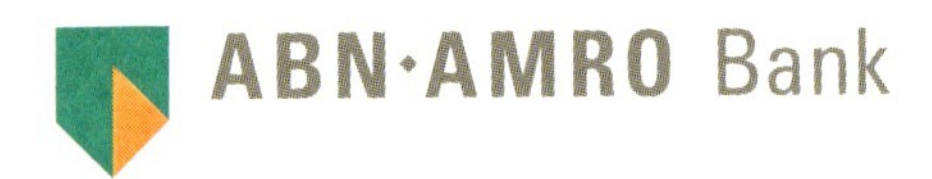

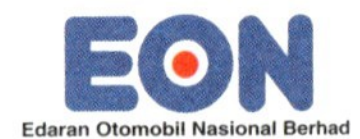

Published by
Archipelago Press
an imprint of
Editions Didier Millet
121 Telok Ayer Street, #03-01
Singapore 068590
www.edmbooks.com

First published 2001
Reprinted 2007

Editorial Director: Timothy Auger
Editors: Dianne Buerger, Marilyn Seow
Studio Manager: Tan Seok Lui
Designers: Lee King Hon,
Yong Yoke Lian, Thievani A/P Nadaraju
Handwriting: Charles P E Yeoh
Production Manager: Brian Wyreweden
Colour separation by
Colourscan Co. Pte. Ltd.
Printed in Singapore by
Tien Wah Press (Pte) Ltd.

ISBN 10: 981-4068-30-6
ISBN 13: 978-981-4068-30-7

Opposite: A row of upper-floor, wooden louvres above green-glazed grilles—a typical façade of early 19th-century shophouses.
Endpapers: Segmented arched toplights framed by modified Ionic Capitals commonly used in townhouses and shophouses.

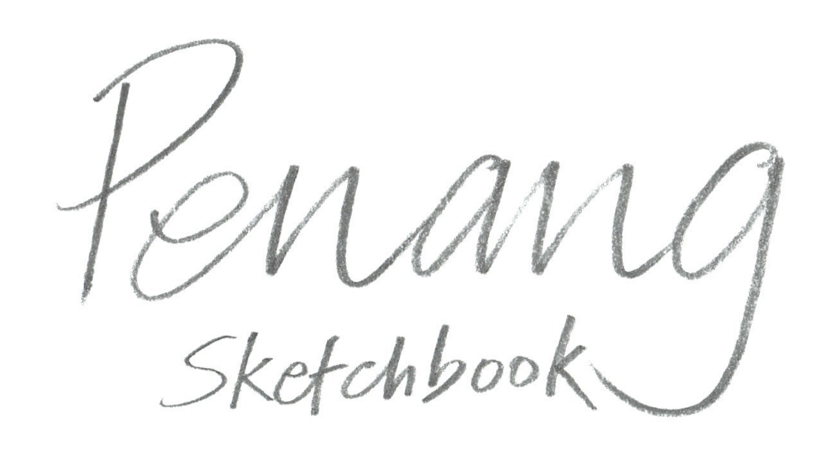

Watercolours by Chin Kon Yit
Text by Chen Voon Fee

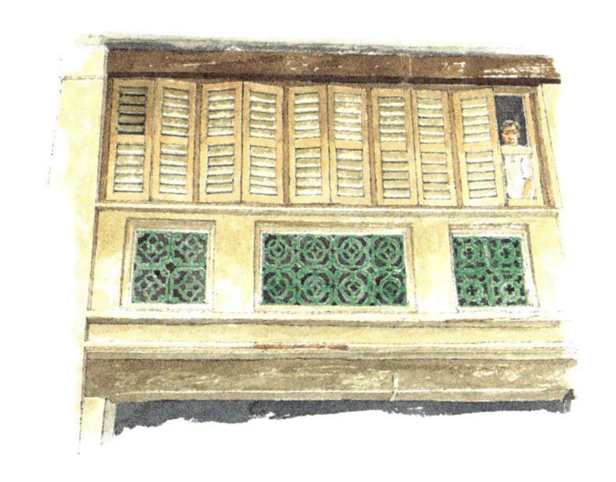

ARCHIPELAGO PRESS

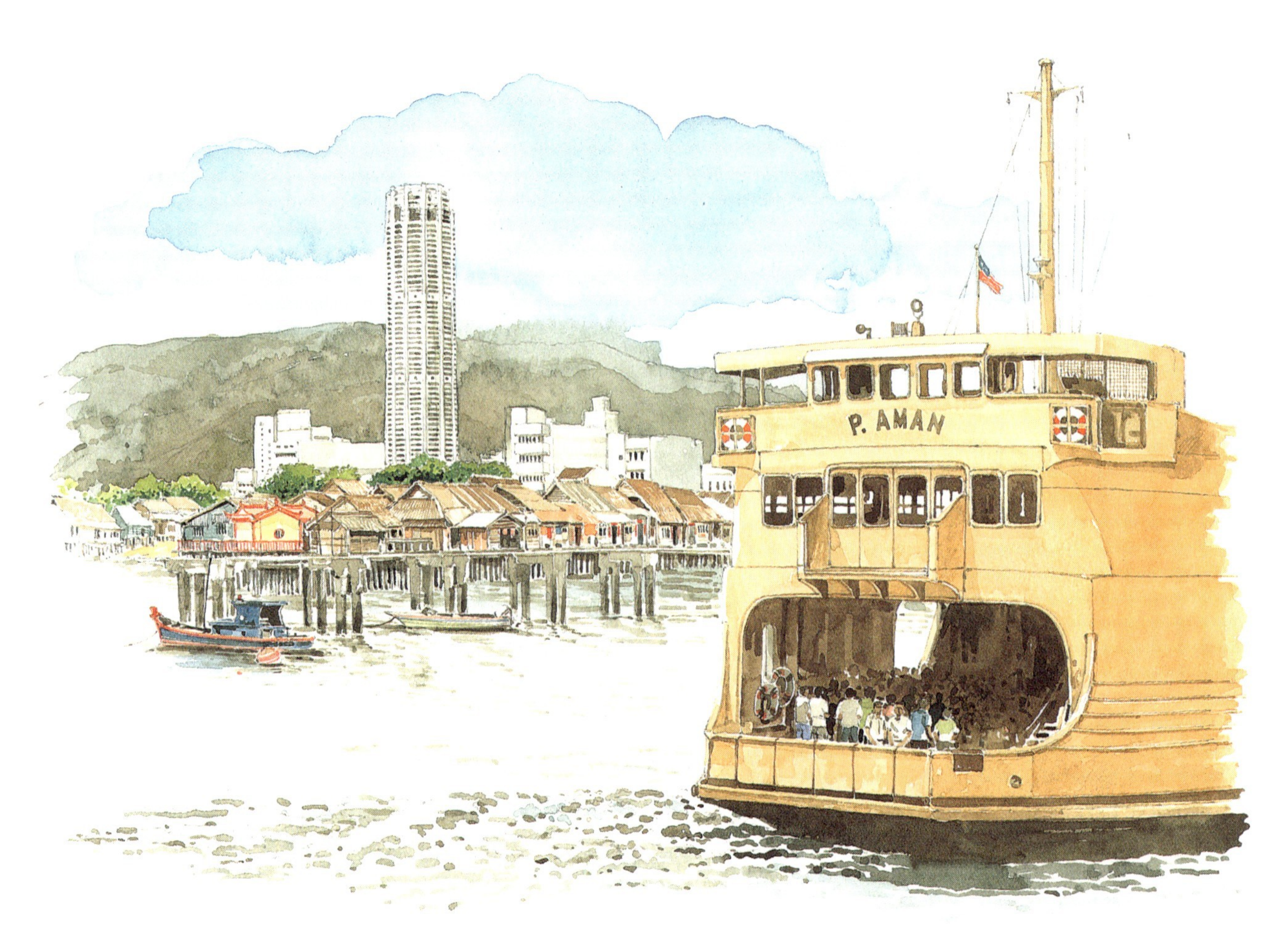

The Heritage car ferry approaching Penang with the Komtar (Komplex Tun Adbul Razak) Tower looming over the century-old clan jetties built right out in the sea along Pengkalan Weld. Ferries brought across from Hong Kong have been conveying people, goods and vehicles across the Channel since 1924.

Contents

The Founding of a Settlement

From ancient times seafarers have plied the Strait of Melaka that links the South China Sea and the Indian Ocean. In an era of European commercial rivalries, this sea lane was a crucial route to the Spice Islands' lucrative trade and beyond to China's ports.

The East India Company (EIC), a British trading company established in 1600 to develop markets for Lancashire wool, had firmly entrenched itself in India both economically and politically, with its ships plying between India and its trading stations in China. It was constantly facing competition for the spice trade in Asia from the Dutch, and after the Dutch wrested Melaka from the Portuguese in 1641, thus controlling commerce along the west coast of the Malay Peninsula for over a century and a half, the EIC's ships had no safe harbour in the strait to refit during the northeast monsoon.

Francis Light, arriving in India in 1765, secured command of a trading ship belonging to Madras merchants, and set up agencies in Acheen, northern Sumatra and Kedah on the northwest coast of the Malay Peninsula. He recognised Penang, an island lying west of the mainland across a 3-kilometre-wide strait, as a safe and suitable harbour for the EIC's ships, and gained the favour of the King of Kedah. Kedah, under suzerainty to Siam (now Thailand), was under intermittent threat by Selangor, a state further along the west coast of the peninsula, and in 1771, the King of Kedah granted '... not only the Qualla of Quedah [Kedah], but the whole coast from this place to Pulau Penang ...' in return for a force 'to assist him against the people of Salengore [Selangor]' (Clodd, page 8).

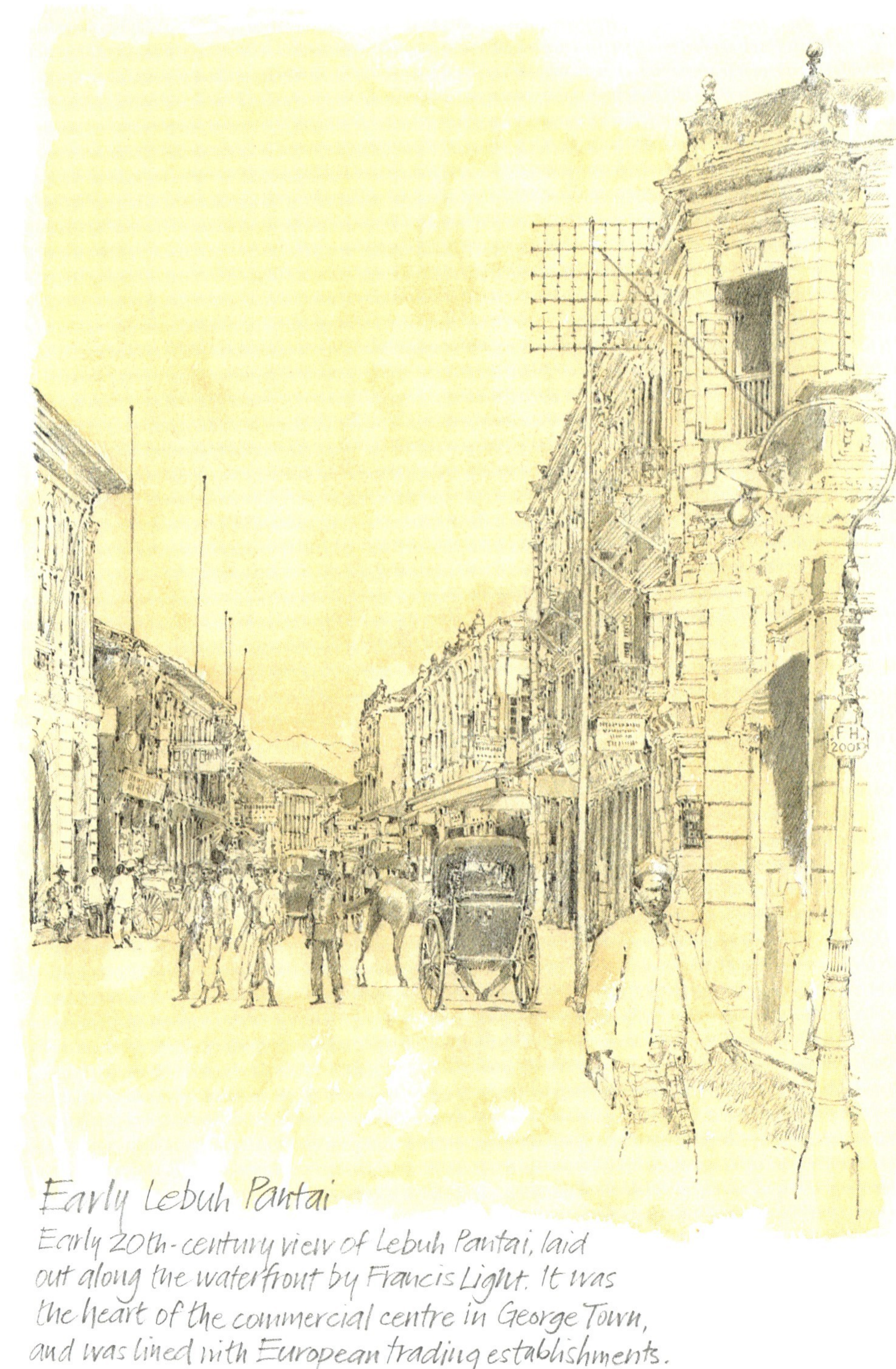

Early Lebuh Pantai

Early 20th-century view of Lebuh Pantai, laid out along the waterfront by Francis Light. It was the heart of the commercial centre in George Town, and was lined with European trading establishments.

It took 15 years for the Madras Council of the EIC to accept the offer, by which time Kedah had a new sultan. Light was finally rewarded for his years of effort and appointed Superintendent of Penang in 1786. He landed at Tanjung Penaigre (Point Penaga), the northeastern tip of the island, on 17 July 1786 and took formal possession on 11 August, christening the new settlement Prince of Wales Island in honour of the heir apparent, the future George IV, although this official name was hardly used even during British rule. The more common name, Pulau Pinang (Areca Island), after the *Areca* palms growing on the island, is still used today. George Town, the name Light gave to the settlement after the reigning George III, remains the name of the island's capital.

Light's first task—clearing the jungle around Tanjung Penaigre and draining the swampland—was formidable. Progress by the Malays whom he engaged was so slow that it was said he loaded a cannon with silver dollars and fired it into the forest to motivate the woodcutters.

The Bengal Government established at the outset that the port would be free to all nations, and traders from the Malay Archipelago and merchants from India, Burma (now Myanmar), Siam and Acheen all came to avoid the monopoly restrictions imposed by the Dutch in Melaka and Batavia (now Jakarta). The port also attracted Europeans and Asians eager to trade under the security of the British flag.

Chulias—Tamil Muslims from southern India who had long traded with Malayan ports and in Sumatra—were the first to seize the opportunity for a new trade outlet by opening a bazaar. The Chinese were quick to follow. In 1792 Light recorded that the population of Penang was 'increasing very fast'.

Captain Home Riggs Popham, a private trader, refitted his ship in the settlement in 1791. He made an exact survey of the island and discovered a new southward channel for navigation. A map based on his 1798 plan (page 92) shows the rectangular grid

Electric Tram
Electric trams were introduced in 1906 and ran until 1936, when the last tramway—the Ayer Itam tramway—was closed down.

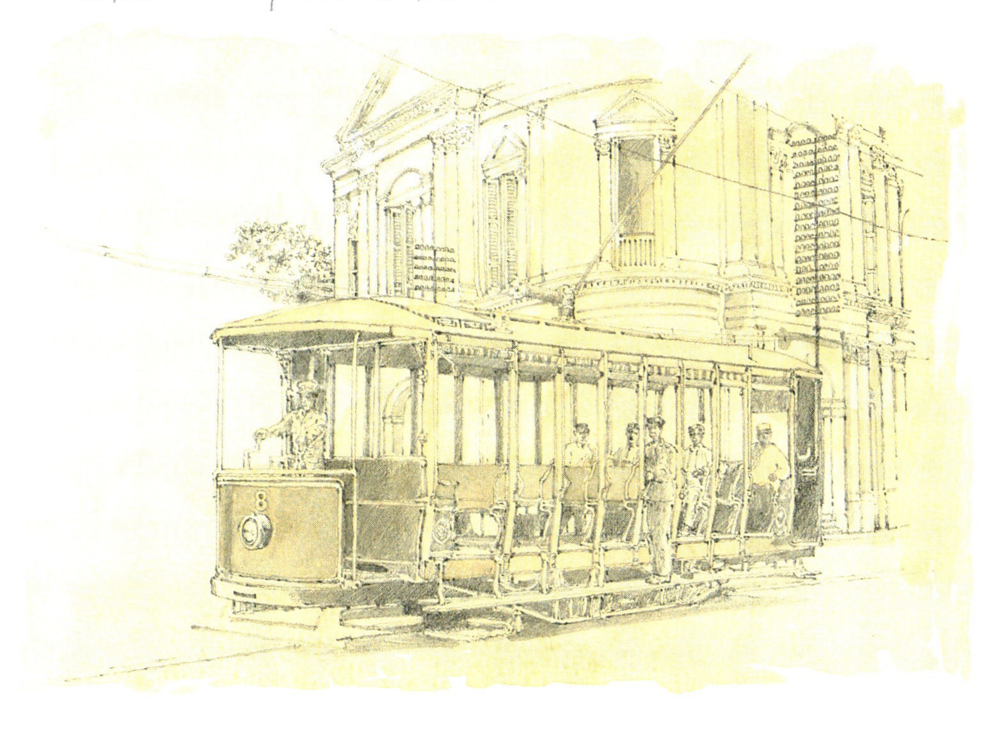

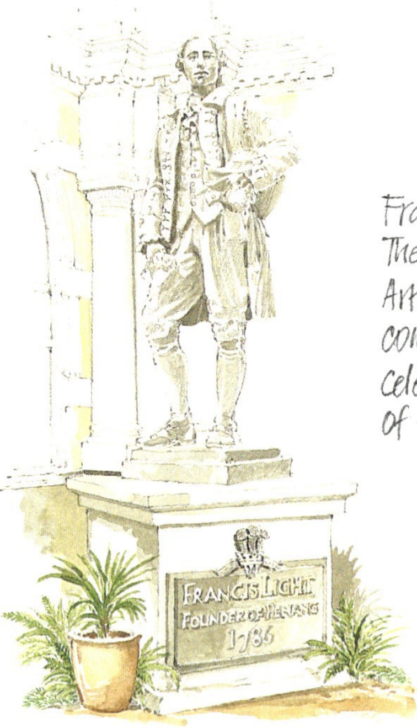

Francis Light Statue
The statue stands in front of the State Museum & Art Gallery, Penang on Lebuh Farquhar. It was commissioned by the Municipal Council to celebrate the 150th centenary of the founding of Penang.

of streets laid out by Light: Lebuh Light (Light Street) to the north, Lebuh Pantai (Beach Street) along the eastern sea front, Jalan Mesjid Kapitan Keling (Pitt Street) to the west and Lebuh Chulia (Chulia Street) to the south. The only road running into the interior was Jalan Penang (Penang Road). The original network, with the names Light assigned to the roads, survives today, except Jalan Mesjid Kapitan Keling.

Light assigned the various streets in the commercial town to different communities: the Malays formed a 'Malay Town' south of Lebuh Chulia; the Eurasians from Phuket and Kedah settled on Lebuh Bishop and Lebuh Gereja (Bishop and Church Streets), with a

Protestant Cemetery
Francis Light's modest tomb carries this epitaph: "Beneath this stone lie the remains of Francis Light Esq. who first established this island as a British settlement. Died 21st October 1794."

Portuguese church standing between the two streets; the Chinese lived and traded from their shophouses in Lebuh China (China Street); and a market lay on the water's edge at the end of Lebuh Pasar (Market Street). Light and his fellow Europeans occupied the entire north beach area: their residences surrounded Company's Square—the present site of St. George's Church—and both sides of Lorong Love (Love Lane).

The first buildings were of light construction: bungalows with attap [thatch] roofs raised on posts after the Malay style. Bricks were used for some buildings. European godowns (warehouses) were built on the seaside of Lebuh Pantai, on posts driven into the mud. The bricks in 'brick bungalows' were most likely used only in the pillars supporting the upper wooden structures.

Light's early achievements were all the more remarkable when viewed against the half-hearted support given to the new settlement by the EIC. Light was instructed not to levy any taxes, and ordered to practise the strictest economy. He had only one assistant for administrative work.

For many years after Light's landing, the Company's officials in India continued to doubt the suitability of the island as a base. However, Light's convictions and energies prevailed. The settlement grew, with the population reaching 12,000 by 1804. Penang became successful as a trading station, though not as a shipbuilding port or as a base for the Company's fleet; these objectives were later met with the founding of Singapore in 1819.

Light died of malarial fever on 21 October 1794, a mere eight years after landing. Two years after his death, it was officially acknowledged that the settlement's 'growing prosperity' was 'due to the remarkable energy with which Light pushed forward its development and to the great trust reposed by the Asiatic inhabitants in his probity' (Clodd, page 70).

After Light's death, Major Macdonald was appointed Superintendent of the settlement. He died in 1799 while away from the island. Sir George Leith succeeded him as Lieutenant-Governor. The most important event in his administration was

Beca and jinrickshaw
Two forms of human-powered public transport in early Penang. The older, hand-pulled jinrickshaw was phased out soon after 1941. Its replacement, the beca, is convenient for getting around the streets of George Town.

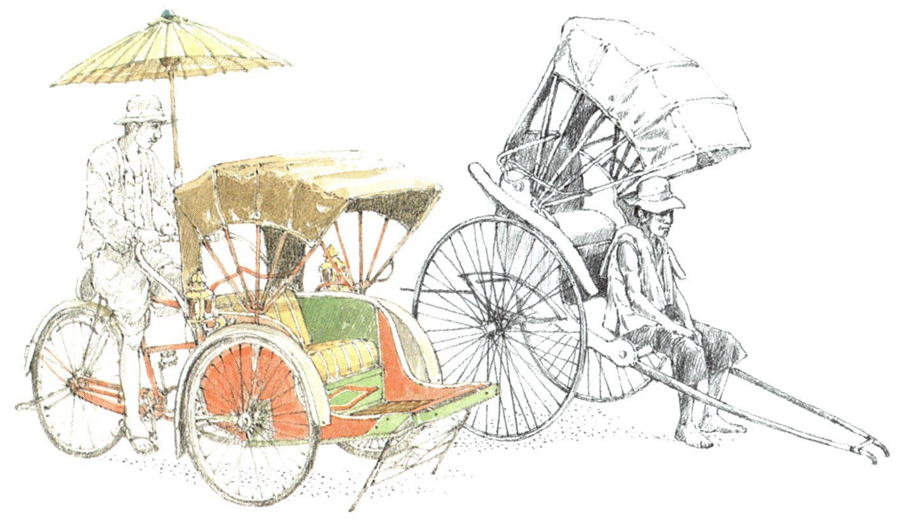

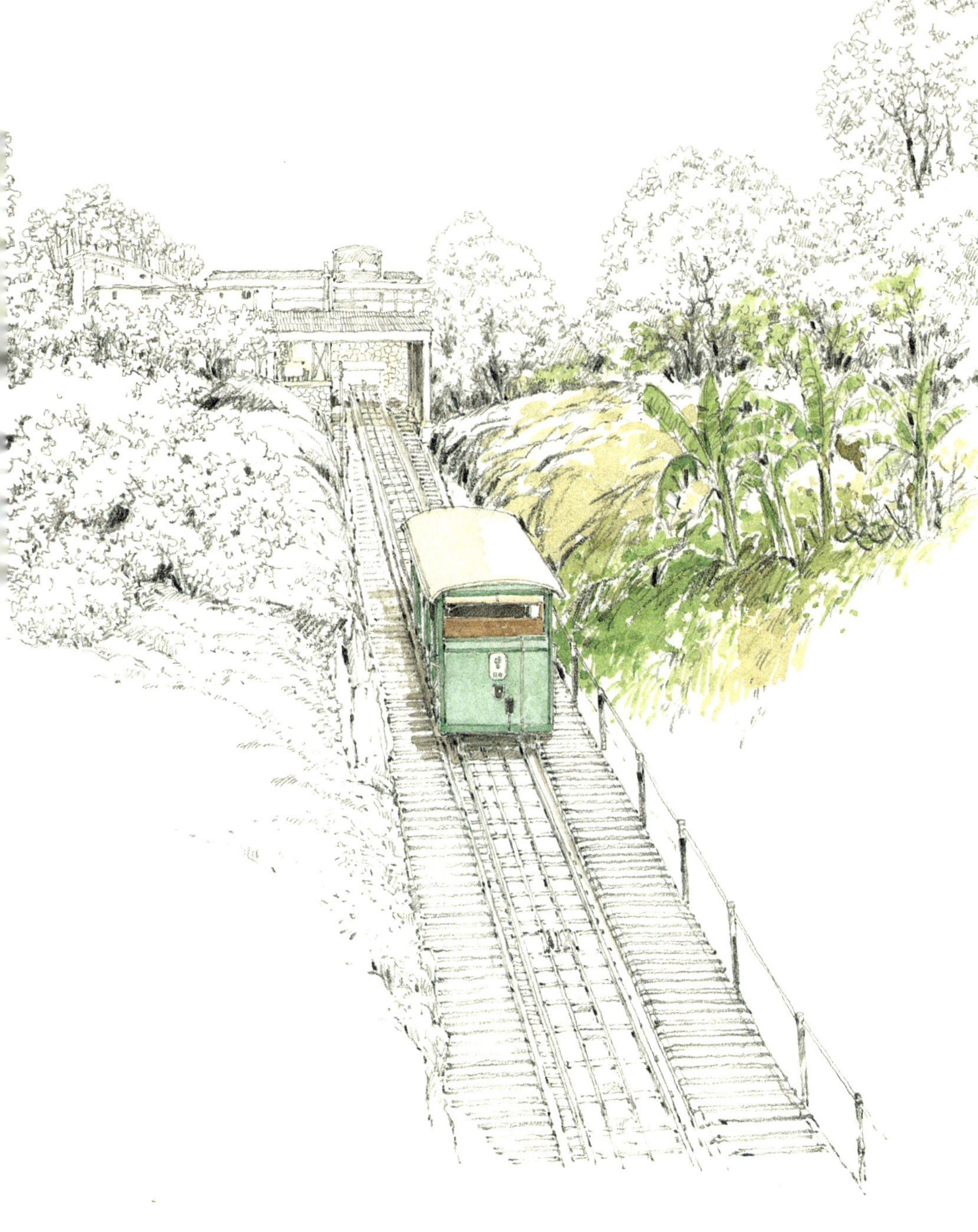

Penang Hill Railway
The original funicular railway carrying visitors and residents up and down Penang Hill had wooden carriages, one of which now houses the Museum Shop on the grounds of the State Museum & Art Gallery, Penang.

the acquisition of the strip of land on the mainland opposite the island. This was the haunt of pirates and a convenient launching place from which to attack Penang, as shown in 1790 when the Sultan of Kedah used it for that very purpose. Following successful negotiations with the sultan, Leith took formal possession of the territory in 1800. He named it Province Wellesley after the Marquess of Wellesley, the Governor-General of India.

Leith was succeeded in 1804 by Robert T. Farquhar, a man of immense energy and ingenious accounting. Farquhar used convict labour to extend the road system and water supply for the island. The convicts were used for most public works, and erected the first large bridge over the mouth of Penang River and six smaller bridges in 1807, and carved out the steep, winding path up Penang Hill.

The year 1805 saw the elevation of Penang into a Presidency under its new Governor, Philip Dundas, whose much-expanded staff included Stamford Raffles as Assistant-Secretary. Penang's status as the Fourth Presidency, on par with Madras, Bengal and Bombay, was a dramatic change from its humble status as a settlement. Commerce increased for the next five years up to 1810. The population continued to grow, reaching 26,000 in 1812 and 51,207 in the next ten years (Wright and Cartwright, page 57).

Singapore's founding in 1819 relegated Penang to a secondary position, its trade diverted to Singapore because of the new port's more strategic location. In 1826 Penang, incorporated into the Straits Settlements with Melaka and Singapore, was the seat of the government. In 1830 the Presidency of Penang ceased, and in 1832 Singapore was made the capital of the Straits Settlements.

Penang's recovery from stagnation was helped by the mid-19th-century tin boom in the world market, the transfer of control of the Straits Settlements from India to Singapore, and the opening of the Suez Canal in 1869. The Pangkor Treaty in 1874 opened up the Malay States to British intervention. With the development of the Malay States and the building of the first railways, Penang was the natural outlet for the products of the northern part of the peninsula, and its trade soared with the rubber boom and the coming of modern communications. The beginning of the 20th century saw Penang at its peak as a regional hub for southern Thailand, northern Sumatra and Burma. Its fortune followed that of modern Malaya's (now West Malaysia) subsequent economic and political development. On the centenary of the formation of Penang's Municipal Council on 1 January 1856, Penang was conferred city status by Royal Charter—eight months before Malaya's independence.

Penang, today, has about a third of the country's historic (pre-World War II) buildings. Its inner city life, fast disappearing in other cities and towns of Malaysia, is threatened by uncontrolled development. Penang's rich architectural heritage and cultural diversity underscore the city's strong claim to gain a place in the list of World Heritage cities, presently under consideration by the United Nations Educational, Scientific and Cultural Organisation (UNESCO).

Nutmeg
Nutmeg, a fruit from the plant Myristica fragrans of the Spice Islands, was eagerly sought after by the spice merchants.

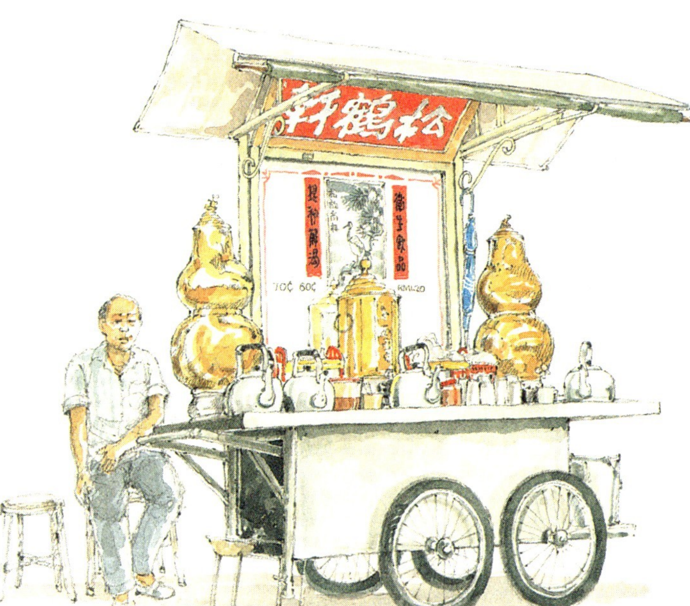

Herbal drinks stall
The popular Chinese herbal tea is sold from mobile stalls.

The Civic Spirit

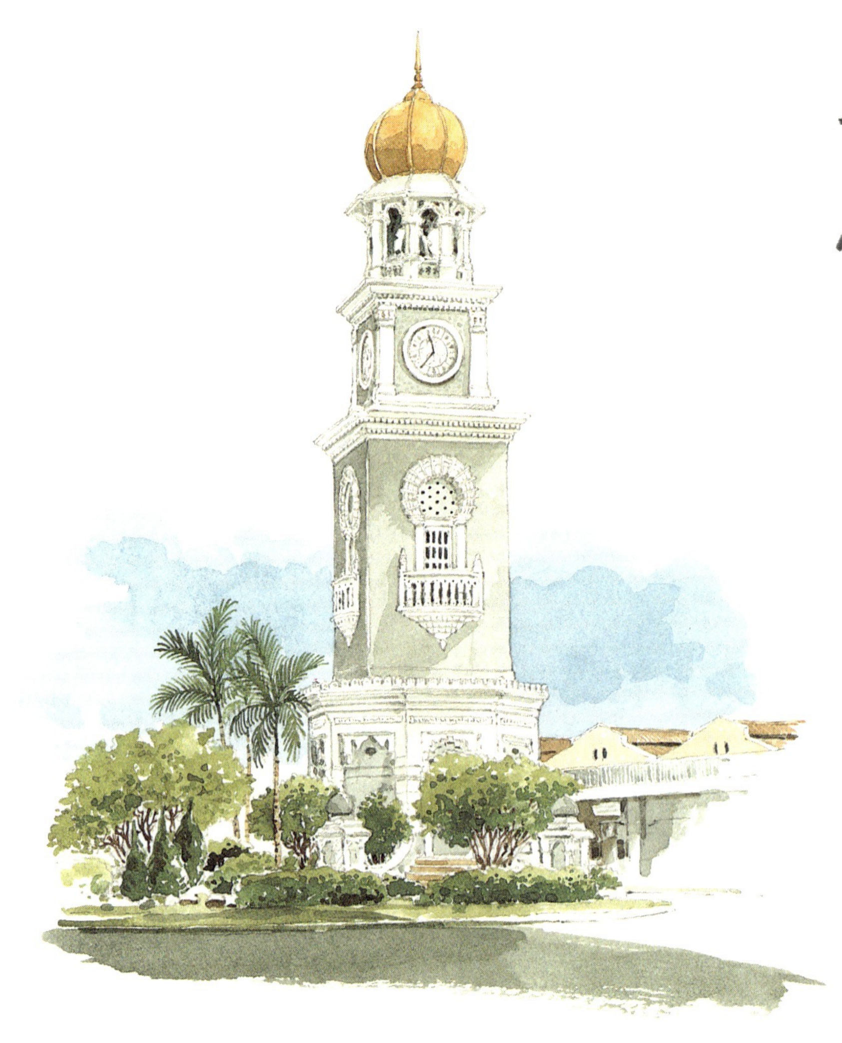

Victoria Memorial Clock Tower
The 18-metre (60-foot) clock tower—a foot for each year of the Queen's reign up to 1897—rises from a landscaped traffic island at Pesara King Edward. It combines strict neoclassical style with ornate Moghul features.

The new settlement of George Town quickly grew up around the stockaded fort Light built on Tanjung Penaigre, a triangular piece of flat land on the northeastern tip of the island, extending west along the north beach and southwest following the old waterfront. In the original grid that Light laid out, each community was assigned a different street. There were no distinct native quarters or European enclaves such as those found in Melaka, Singapore or in Kuala Lumpur, due probably to Light's long and close association with Asians.

There were few public buildings, even after Light's death in 1794. The nucleus of Civic Penang was, however, already in the line up of Custom House, Fort Cornwallis and the sepoy lines. Light's first municipal act was to sink a public well for the town's water supply at the end of Lebuh Light.

Light died within eight years of his landing. In his will, he left a brick 'Bungaloe in George Town' (the Superintendent's house in Popham's 1798 map, now Government House, on the grounds of Convent Light Street) and 'the pepper Gardens with [his] Garden house' (now Suffolk House, on Jalan Ayer Itam) to Martina Rozells, his common law wife. These two buildings are the oldest surviving British colonial structures from the 18th century in the country.

Penang's present civic buildings—the Municipal Council Building, the State Assembly Buildings, the State Museum & Art Gallery, Penang, St. George's Church and the Town Hall—all date from the early to the mid-19th century.

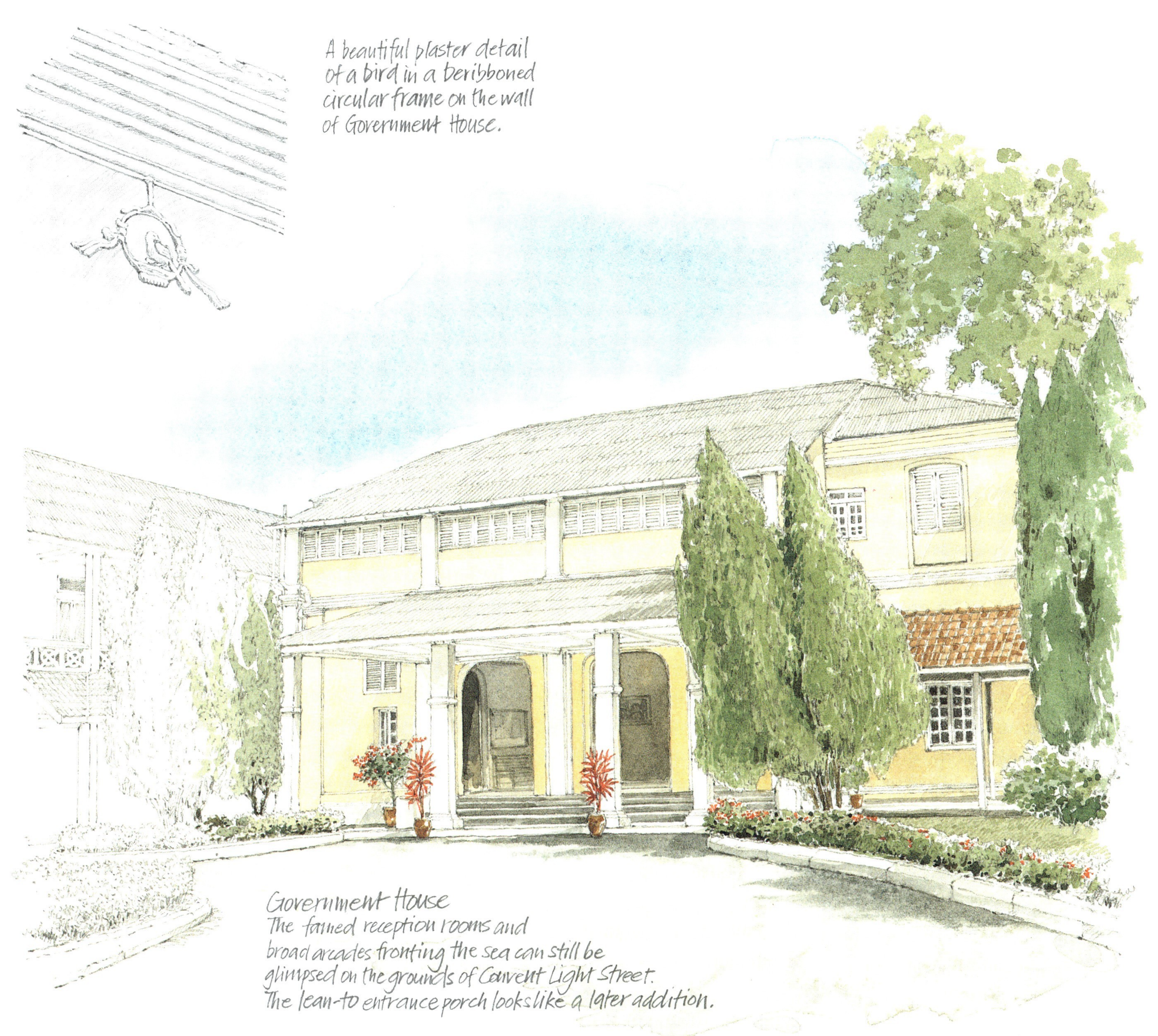

A beautiful plaster detail of a bird in a beribboned circular frame on the wall of Government House.

Government House
The famed reception rooms and broad arcades fronting the sea can still be glimpsed on the grounds of Convent Light Street. The lean-to entrance porch looks like a later addition.

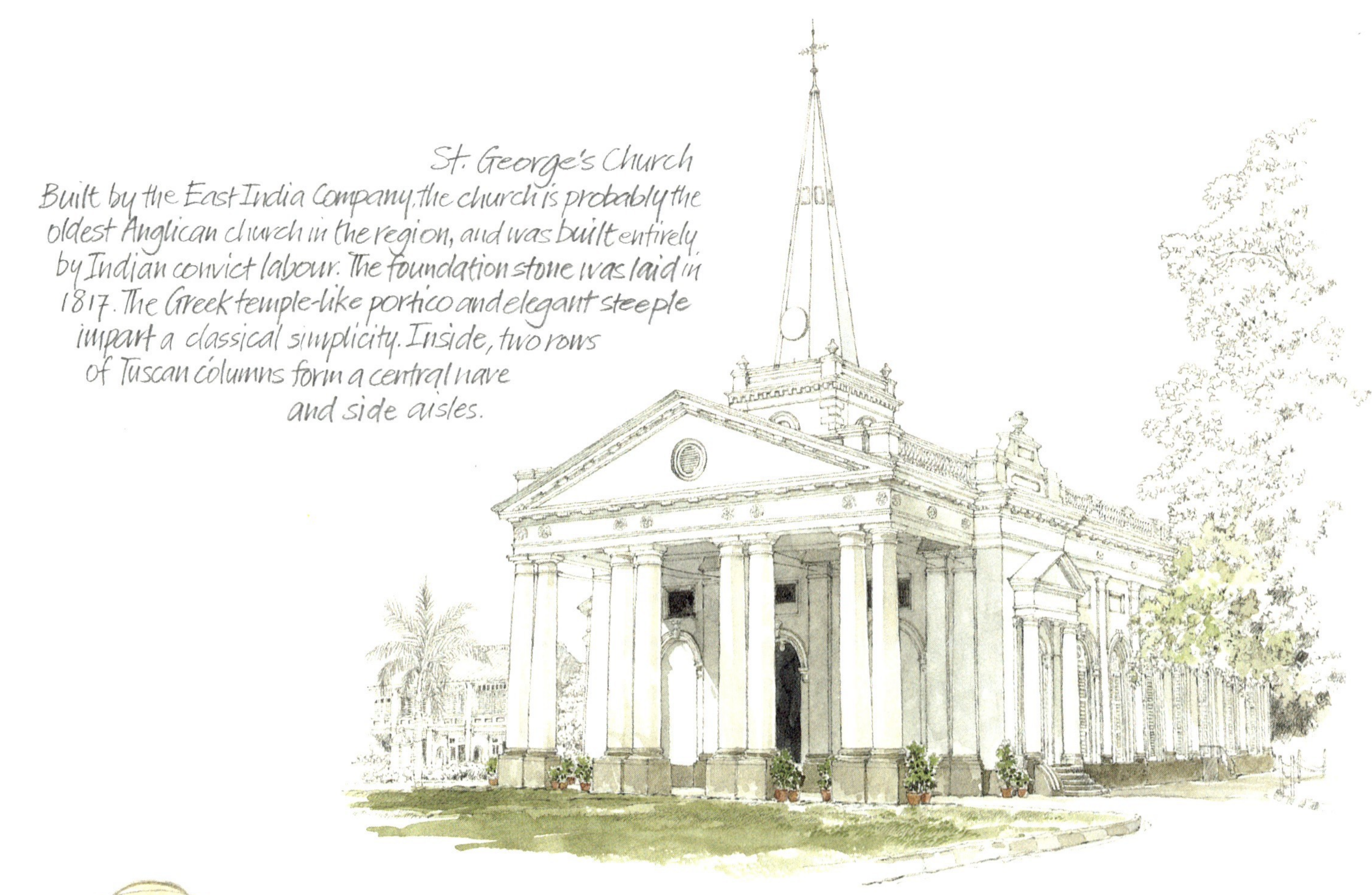

St. George's Church

Built by the East India Company, the church is probably the oldest Anglican church in the region, and was built entirely by Indian convict labour. The foundation stone was laid in 1817. The Greek temple-like portico and elegant steeple impart a classical simplicity. Inside, two rows of Tuscan columns form a central nave and side aisles.

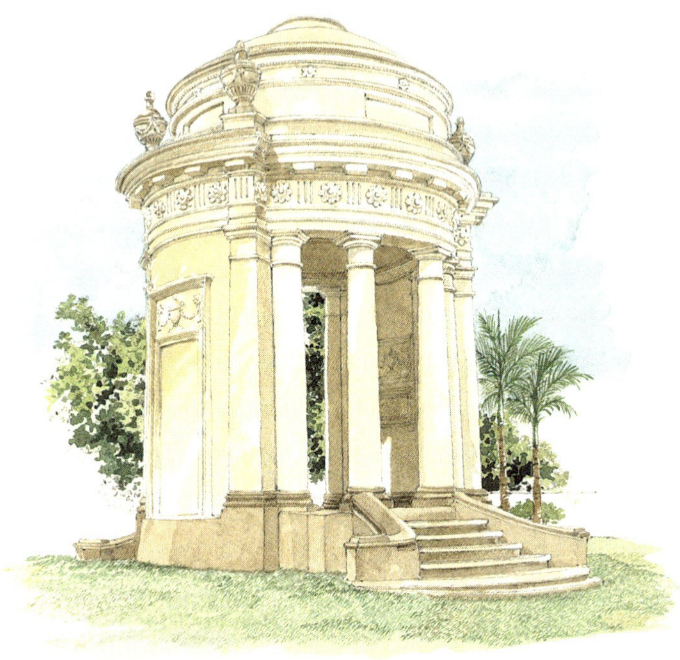

Francis Light Memorial

The circular Greek temple was erected on the centenary of the settlement's founding. The epitaph on a marble plaque in the temple reads: 'In his [Francis Light's] capacity as Governor the settlers and natives were greatly attached to him and by his death had to deplore the loss of one who watched over their interest and cares as a father.'

State Assembly Buildings (Dewan Undangan Negeri)

The buildings are typical of early 19th-century architecture and stand dignified like a row of three Greek temples along Lebuh Light, south of Fort Cornwallis. Their porticoes are linked by colonnaded blocks, all in Tuscan Order, giving the group an appropriately stately character.

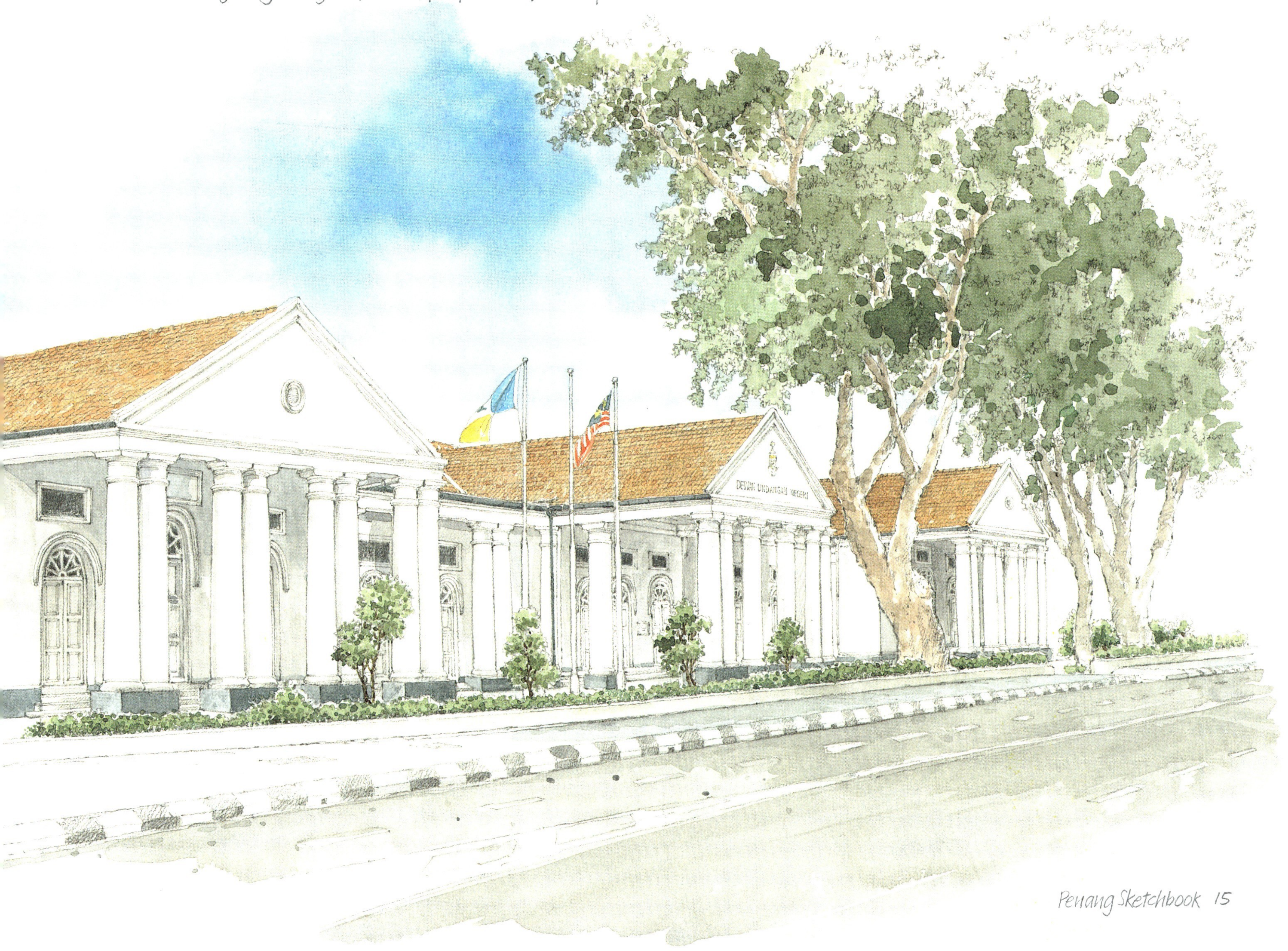

Supreme Court
The grand colonial-style building, erected in 1905, stands at the junction of Lebuh Light and Jalan Mesjid Kapitan Keling. It is symmetrically planned in the form of a cross. The high, central, spacious hall at the crossing is marked by four corner cupolas. Colonnaded verandahs, now filled in with glass and timber louvres, surround the entire building.

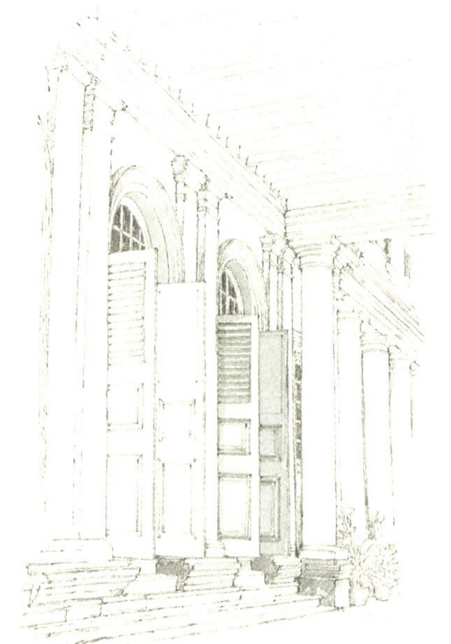

The two entrance doors of the Supreme Court are framed between paired pilasters in the porte cochere (coach port), a typical feature of buildings of the colonial era.

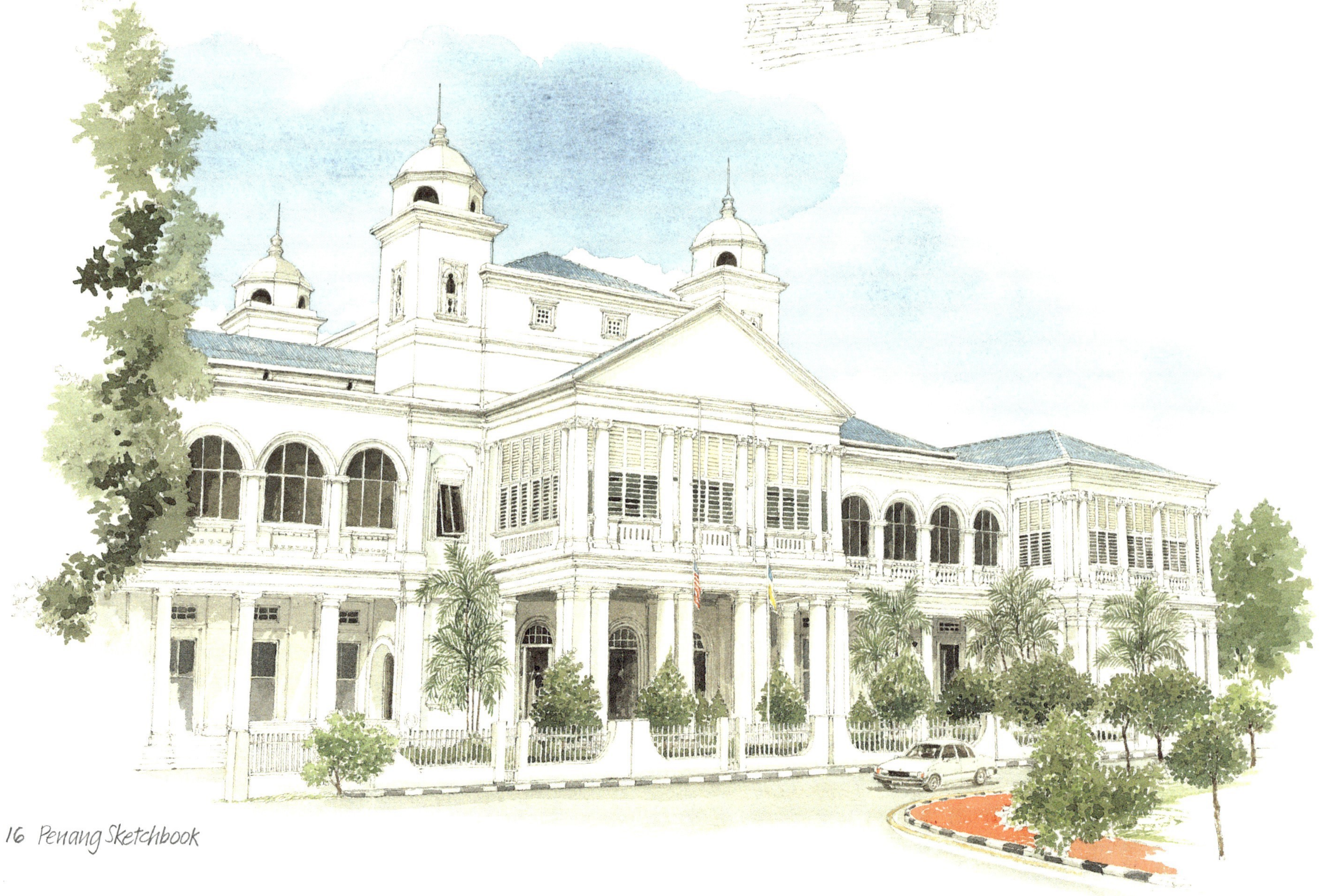

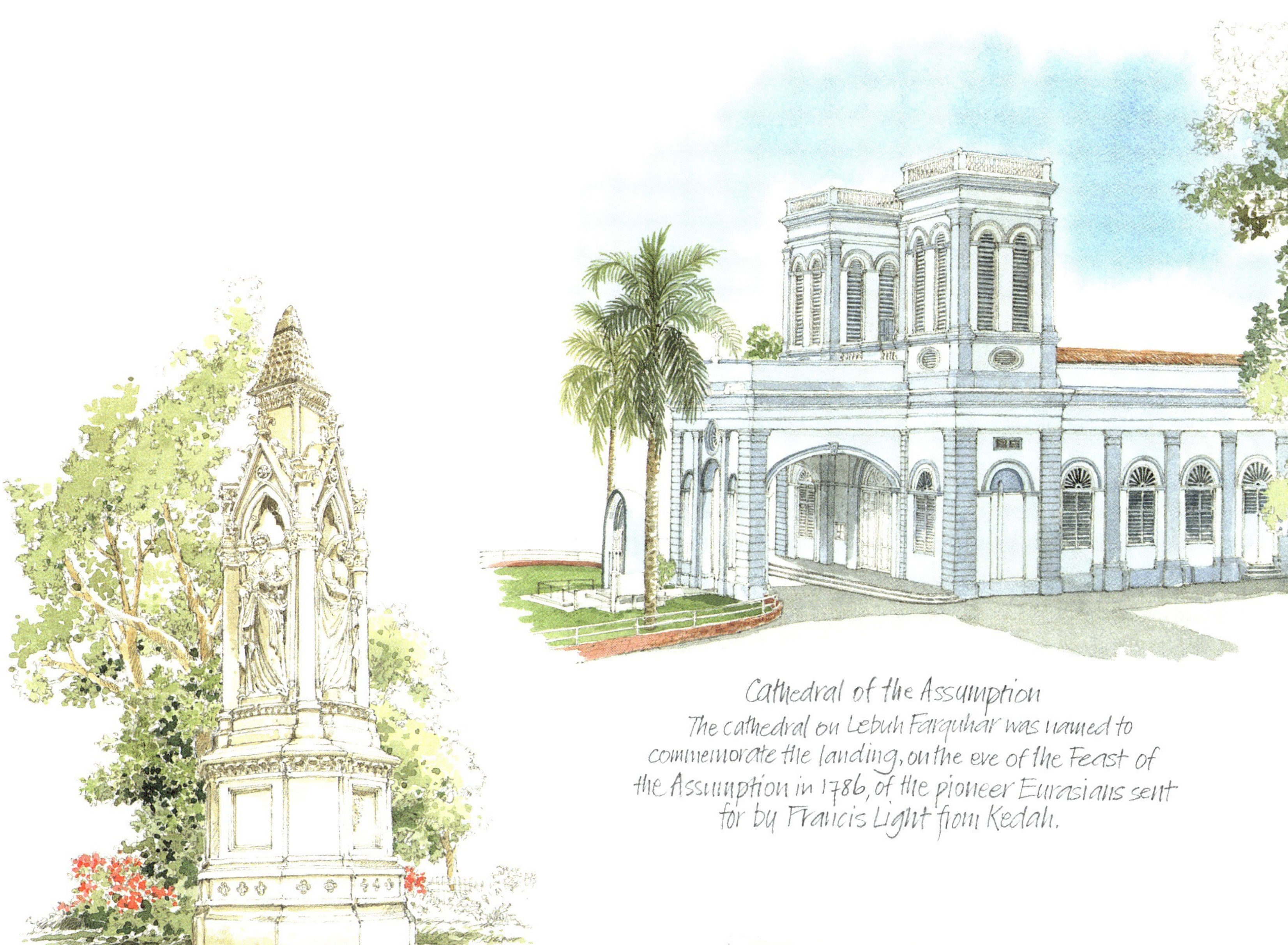

Cathedral of the Assumption

The cathedral on Lebuh Farquhar was named to commemorate the landing, on the eve of the Feast of the Assumption in 1786, of the pioneer Eurasians sent for by Francis Light from Kedah.

Logan Memorial

The gothic-style structure stands on the grounds of the Supreme Court. It was erected in 1869 by the people of the Straits Settlements to commemorate the death of James Richardson Logan.

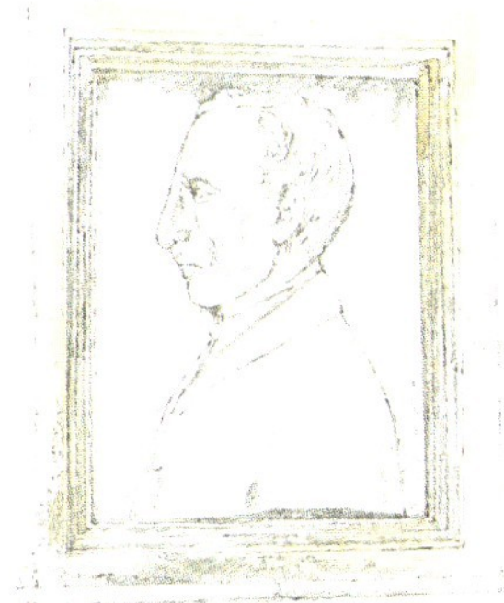

Logan's stern profile is on a marble plaque on one side of the octagonal base of the Logan Memorial.

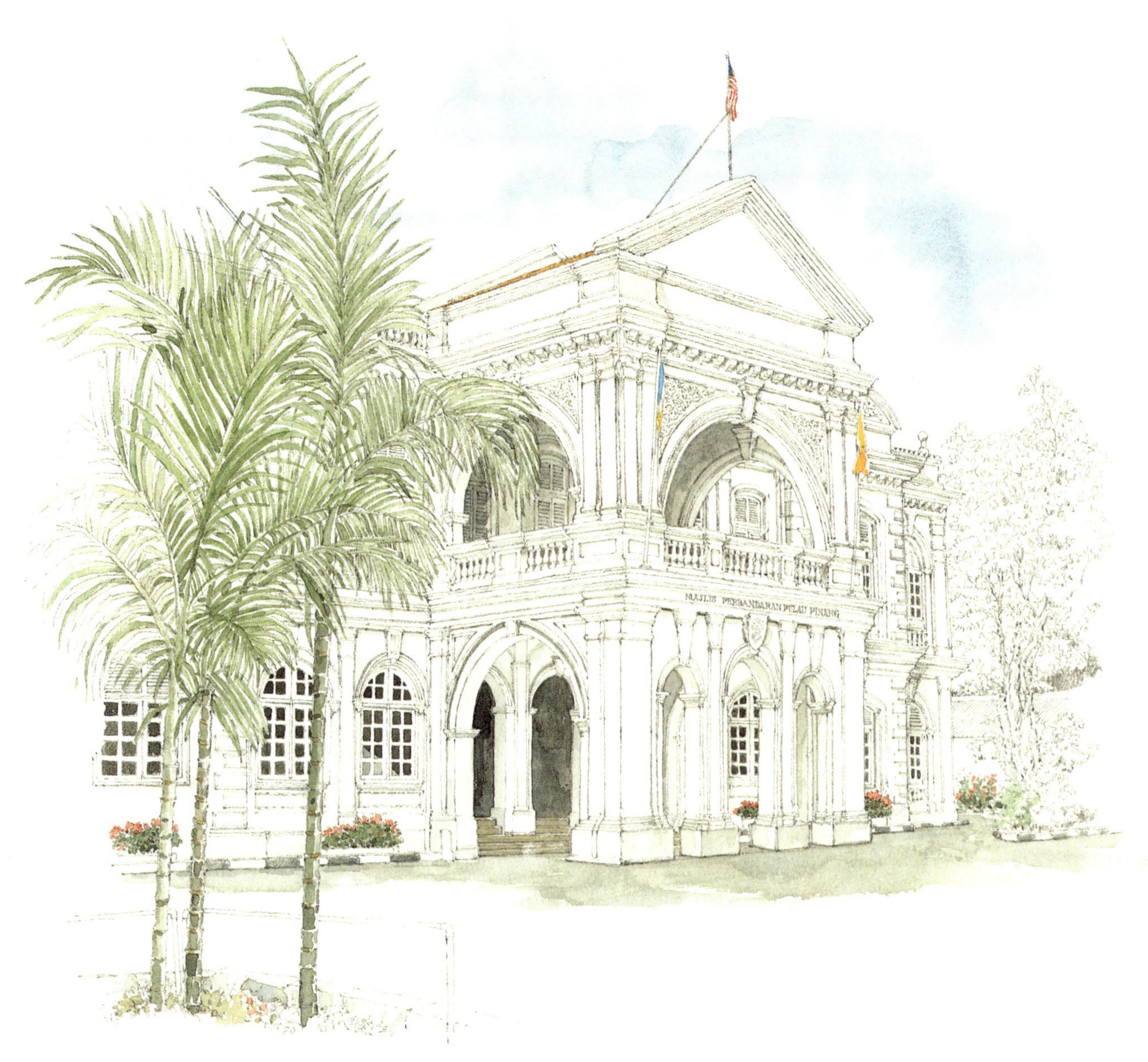

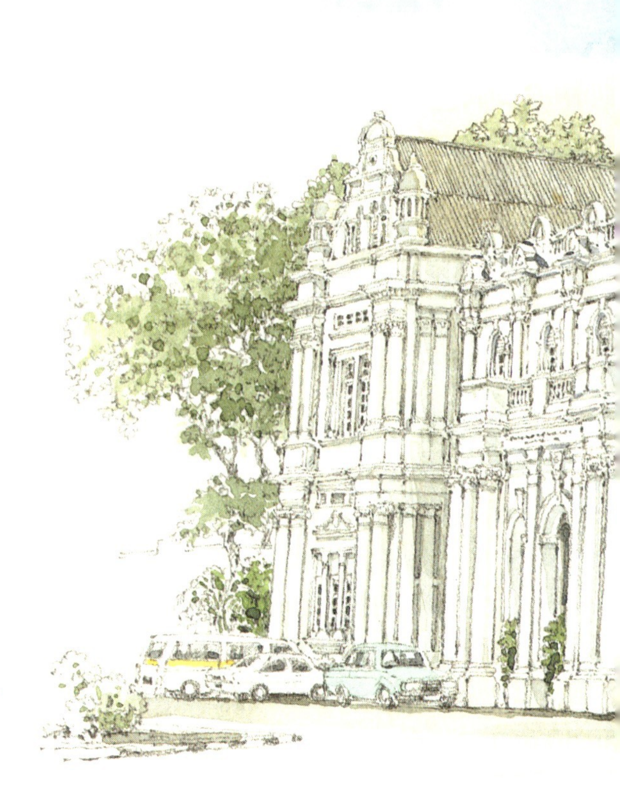

Town Hall

The Town Hall stands west of the Padang or Esplanade. Frederick Weld, the Governor of the Strait Settlements, records his impressions of it in 1880: 'I landed in Penang for a ball and supper, which took place at the Town Hall which I had formally opened a few days before, and which is not only a fine building in itself, but which was, on this occasion, decorated with extreme taste'. The Town Hall was occupied by the municipal offices until the latter moved to City Hall in 1903.

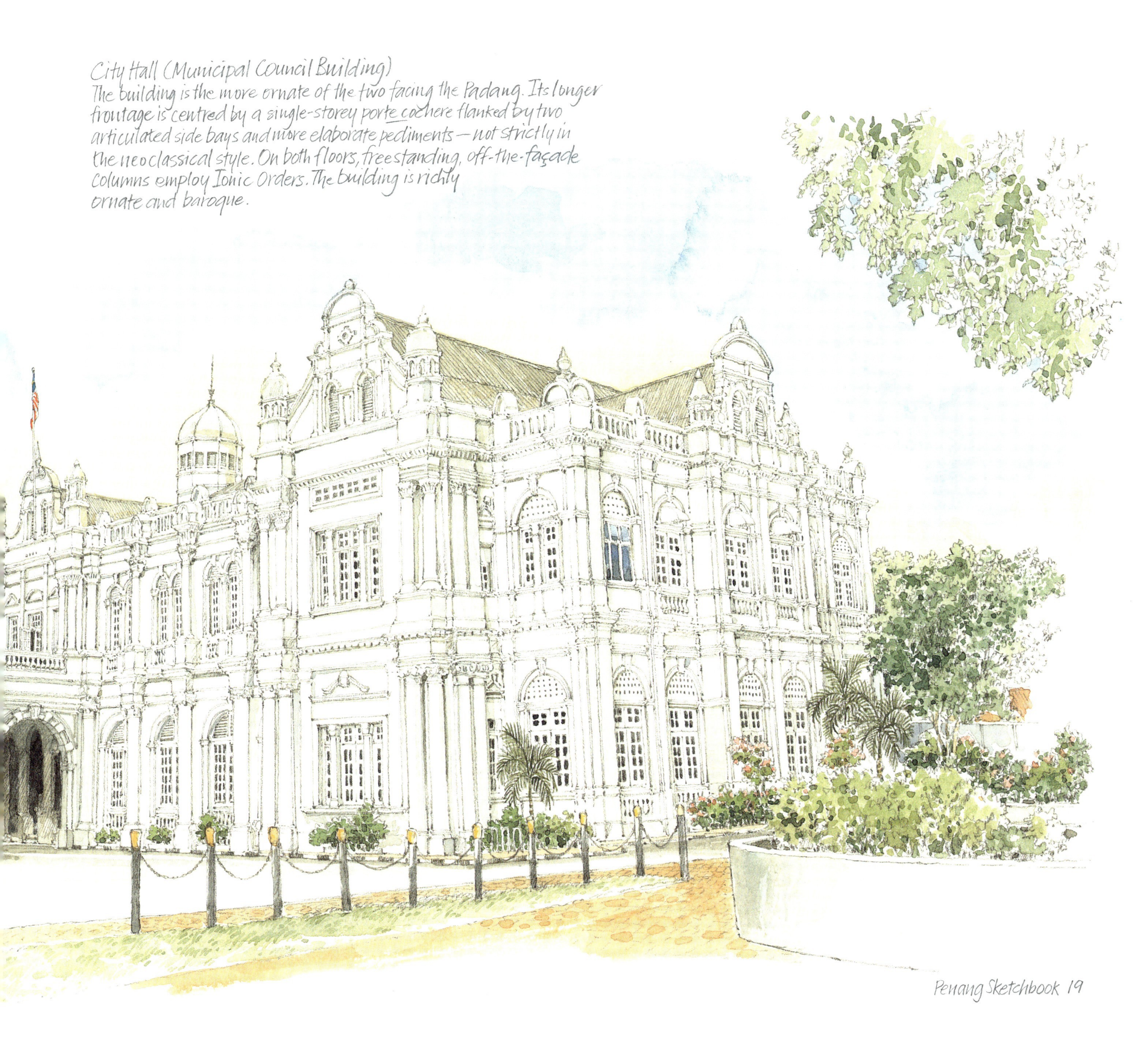
City Hall (Municipal Council Building)
The building is the more ornate of the two facing the Padang. Its longer frontage is centred by a single-storey porte cochere flanked by two articulated side bays and more elaborate pediments — not strictly in the neoclassical style. On both floors, freestanding, off-the-façade columns employ Ionic Orders. The building is richly ornate and baroque.

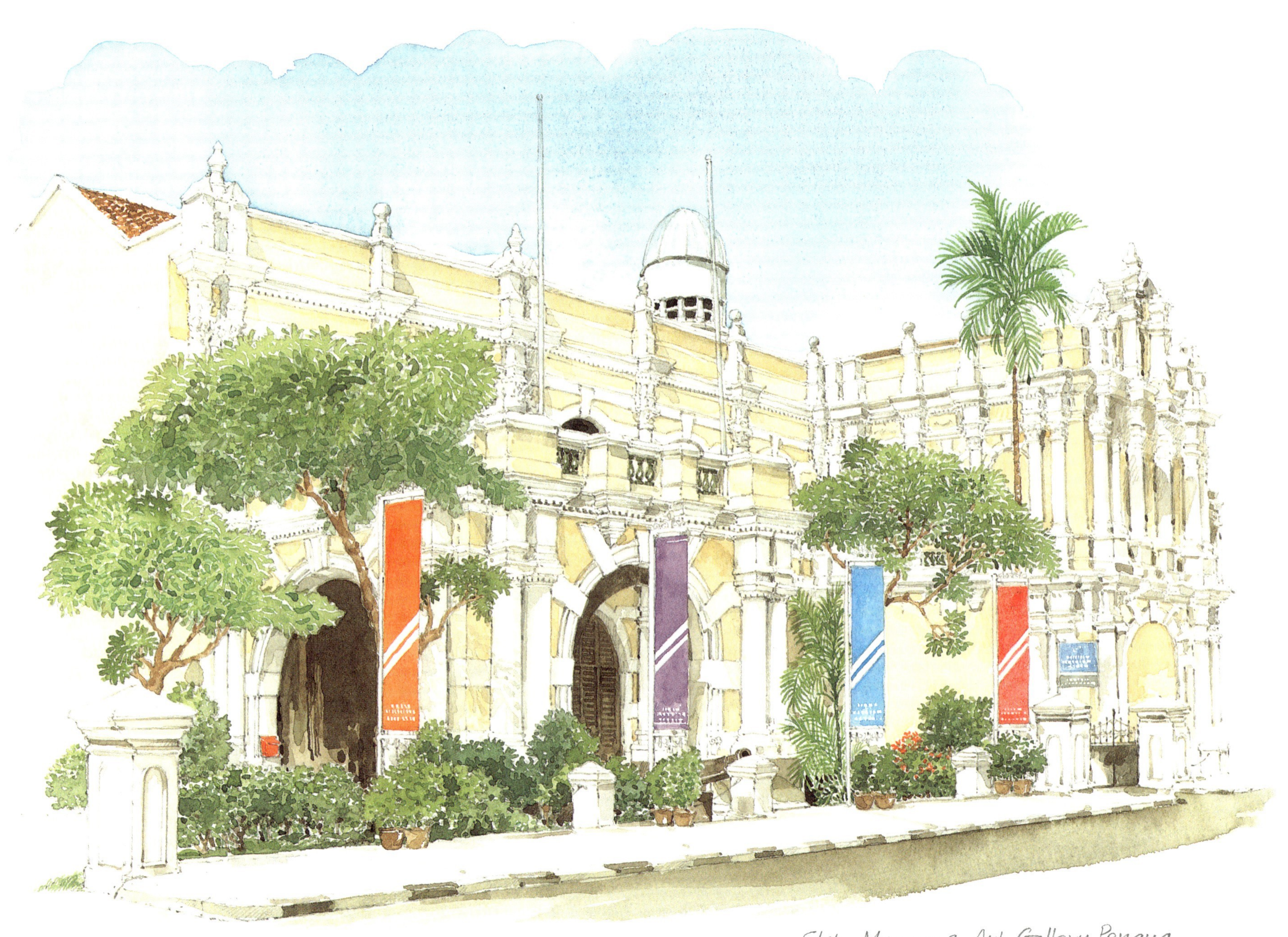

State Museum & Art Gallery, Penang
The museum, located on Lebuh Farquhar, has only the remaining western half of an otherwise symmetrically planned building of the former Penang Free School. Its east wing was a casualty of World War II bombs. Its façade is similar to that of the City Hall: late neoclassical style; an arched porte cochere that carries pronounced keystones; and even a look-alike roof turret.

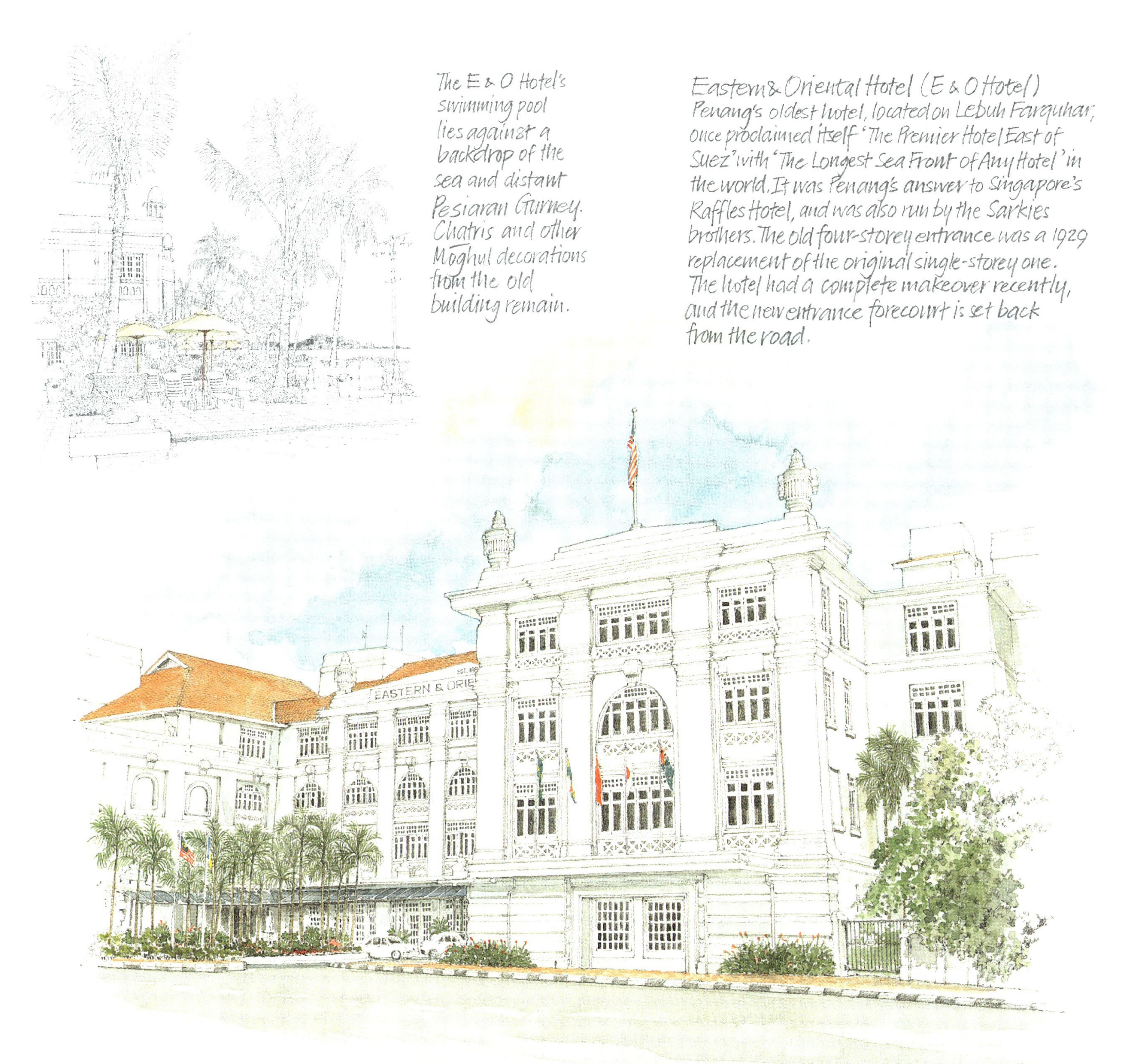

The E & O Hotel's swimming pool lies against a backdrop of the sea and distant Pesiaran Gurney. Chatris and other Moghul decorations from the old building remain.

Eastern & Oriental Hotel (E & O Hotel)
Penang's oldest hotel, located on Lebuh Farquhar, once proclaimed itself 'The Premier Hotel East of Suez' with 'The Longest Sea Front of Any Hotel' in the world. It was Penang's answer to Singapore's Raffles Hotel, and was also run by the Sarkies brothers. The old four-storey entrance was a 1929 replacement of the original single-storey one. The hotel had a complete makeover recently, and the new entrance forecourt is set back from the road.

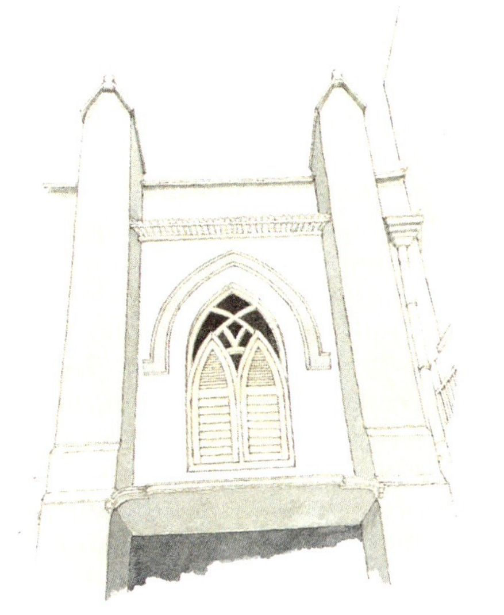

The lancet arched window of the disused chapel, located between buttress-like piers, has a pattern of timber intersecting arcs. The fringe roof shading is a later addition.

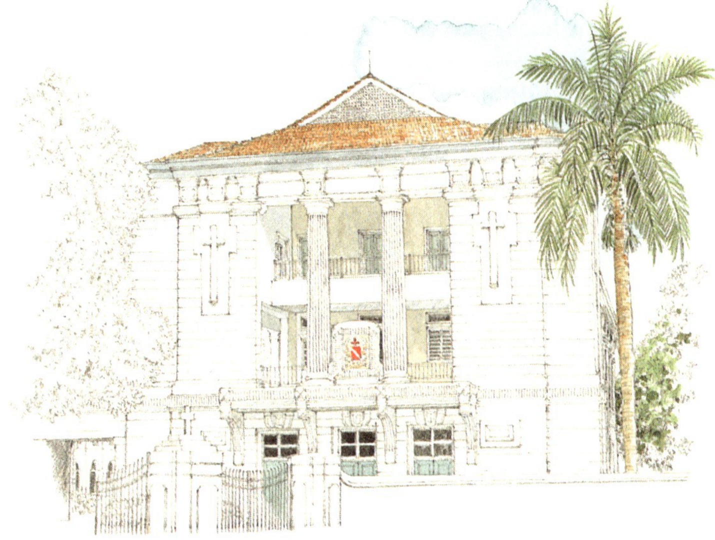

The imposing three-storey School/Exam Hall and classrooms block is a later building mixing giant Doric columns with Art Deco grooved bands and raised blocks.

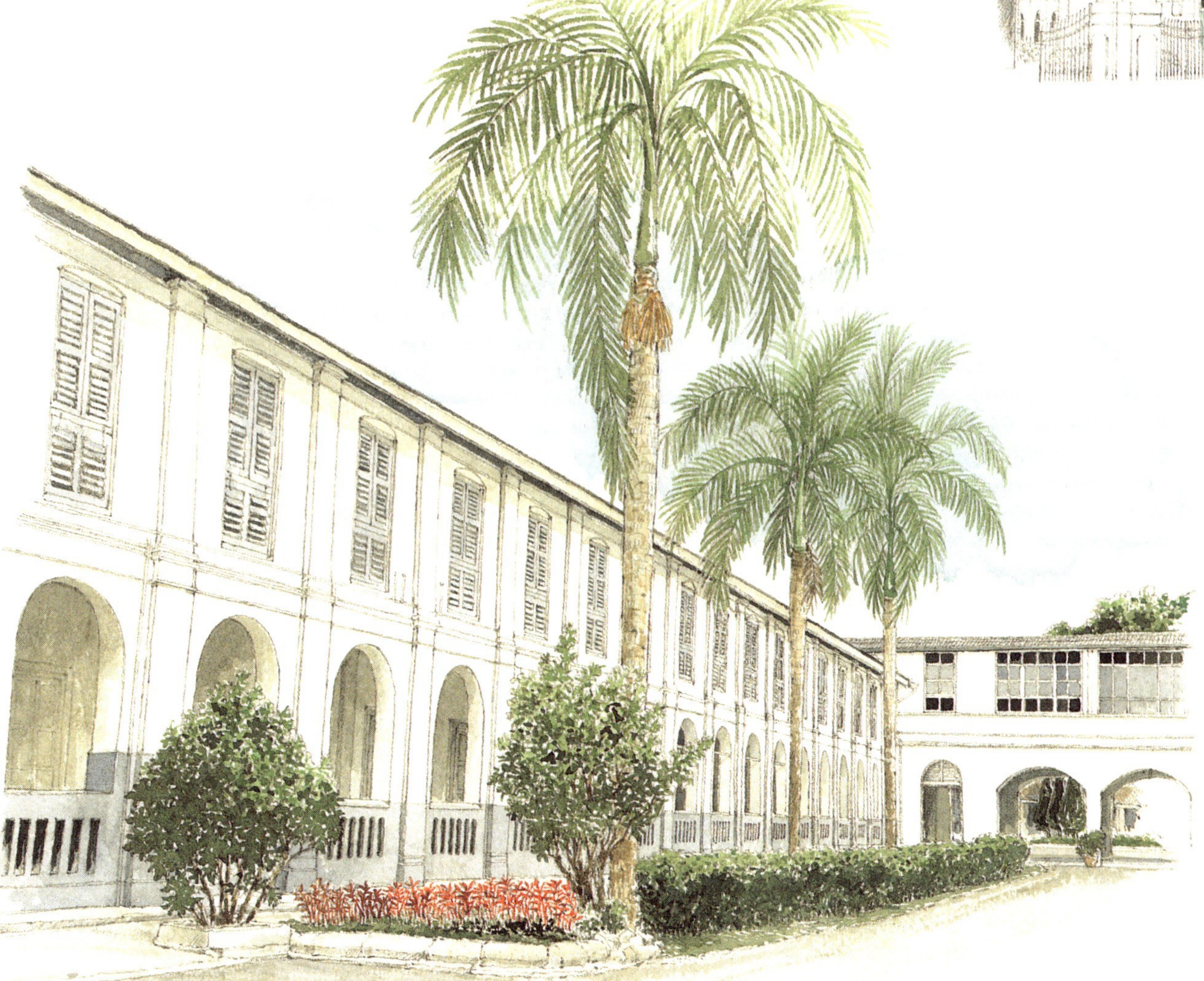

Convent Light Street
Penang's oldest girls' school was founded in 1852 and established on Lebuh Light in 1859. A plain arcade and wooden louvres in the long primary classrooms block impart an austere simplicity typical of colonial seminary architecture.

ABN AMRO House

The 1905 Dutch bank is designed in the neoclassical style typical of prestigious buildings of the colonial period. Its asymmetry is due possibly to its restricting corner site. Stability and strength, qualities appropriate to a bank, are amply conveyed by the massive piers with raised bands and the keystones of the arcade. Entrances are marked by a decorated triangular pediment on the Lebuh Pantai front and two half-moon pediments on the Lebuh Union elevation.

The arched and barred window of the Old China Café, an occupant of ABN AMRO House.

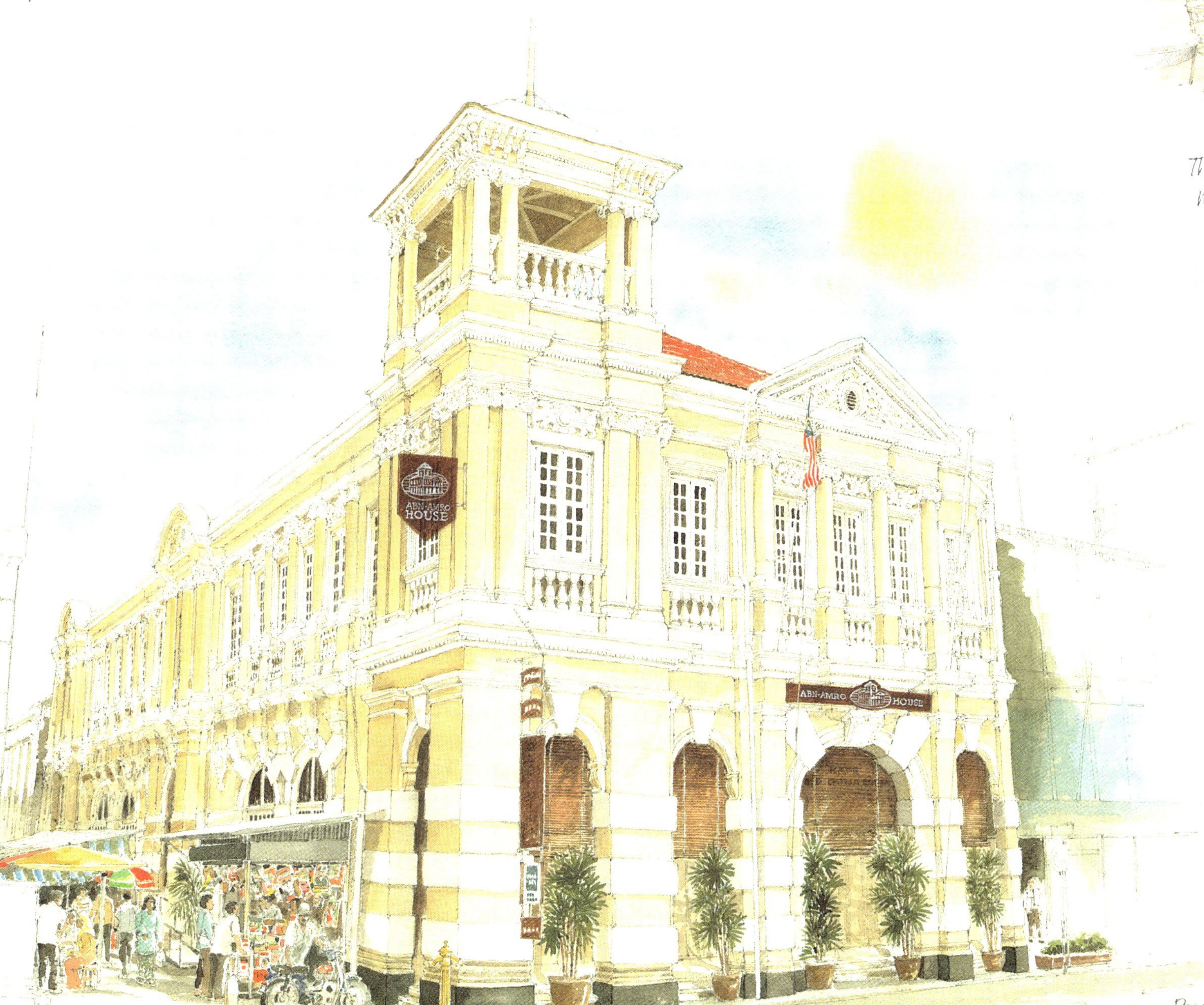

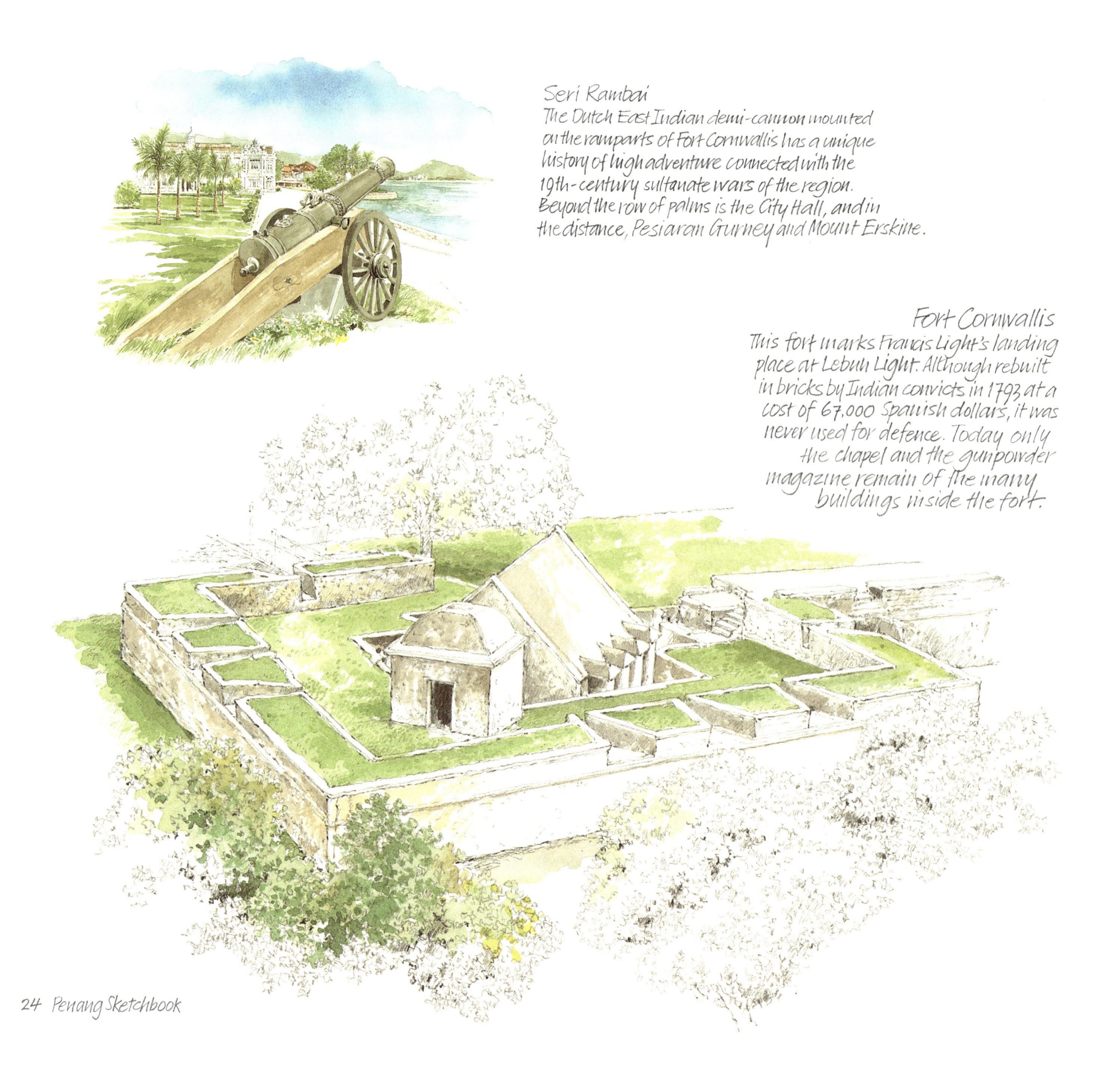

Seri Rambai
The Dutch East Indian demi-cannon mounted on the ramparts of Fort Cornwallis has a unique history of high adventure connected with the 19th-century sultanate wars of the region. Beyond the row of palms is the City Hall, and in the distance, Pesiaran Gurney and Mount Erskine.

Fort Cornwallis
This fort marks Francis Light's landing place at Lebuh Light. Although rebuilt in bricks by Indian convicts in 1793 at a cost of 67,000 Spanish dollars, it was never used for defence. Today only the chapel and the gunpowder magazine remain of the many buildings inside the fort.

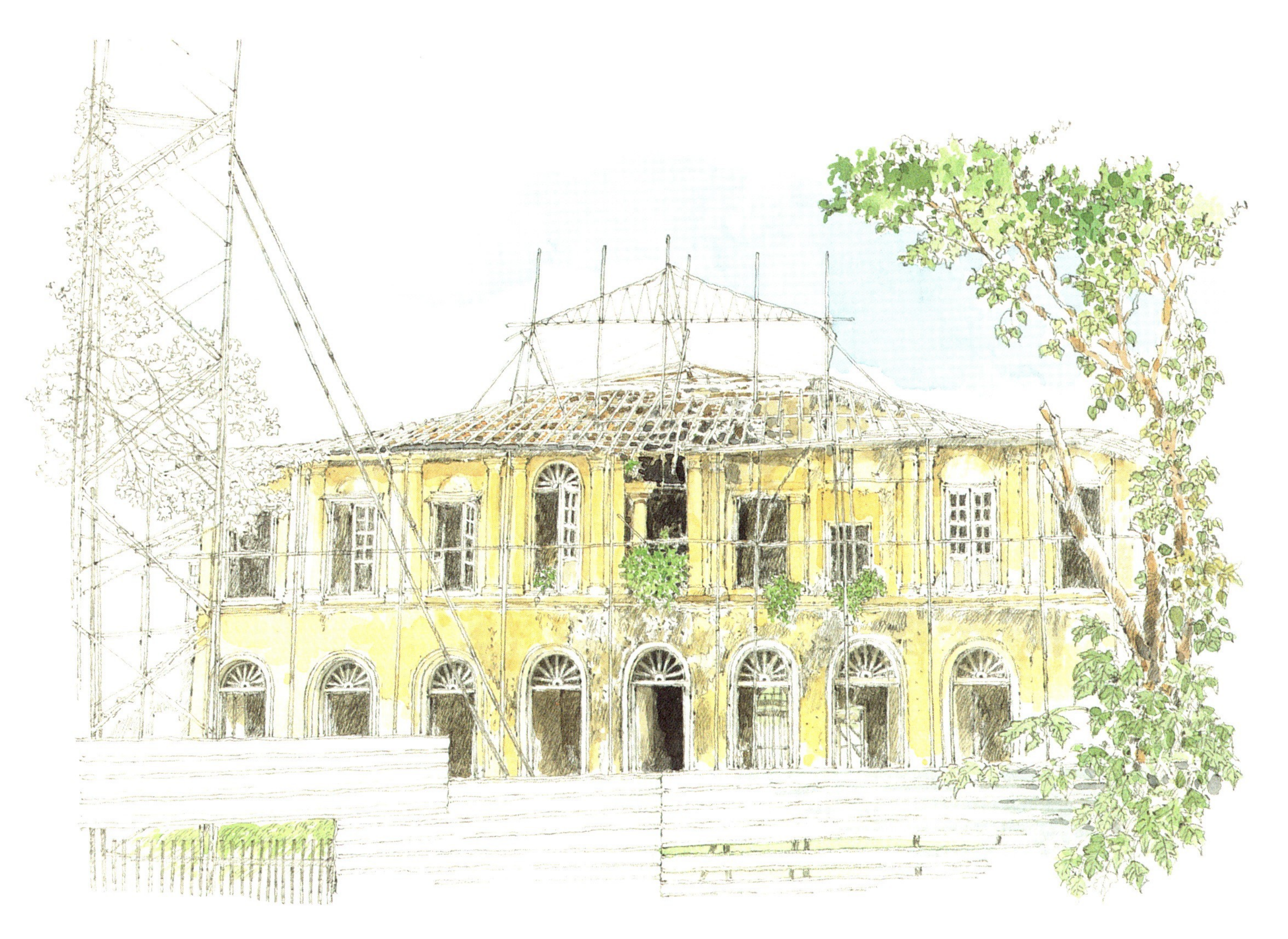

Suffolk House
Penang's first great mansion and the 'purest example of Anglo-Indian architecture outside India' (F. Campbell, Deakin University) is located on Jalan Ayer Itam. It was built by Indian convict labour using Indian bricks and finished in Madrasi chunam, a hard plaster made of a mix of eggshells and lime. Conservation work to stabilise the structure and repair the roof of this historic building has begun.

The paired Tuscan columns, protected by their marble-like chunam plaster, are still in good condition. Elegant Georgian fanlights head doorways.

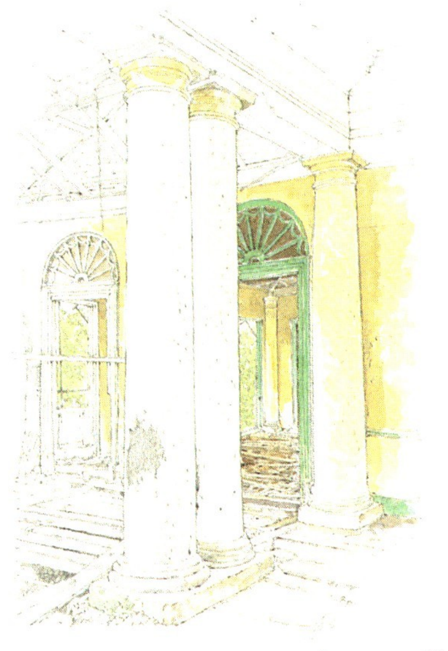

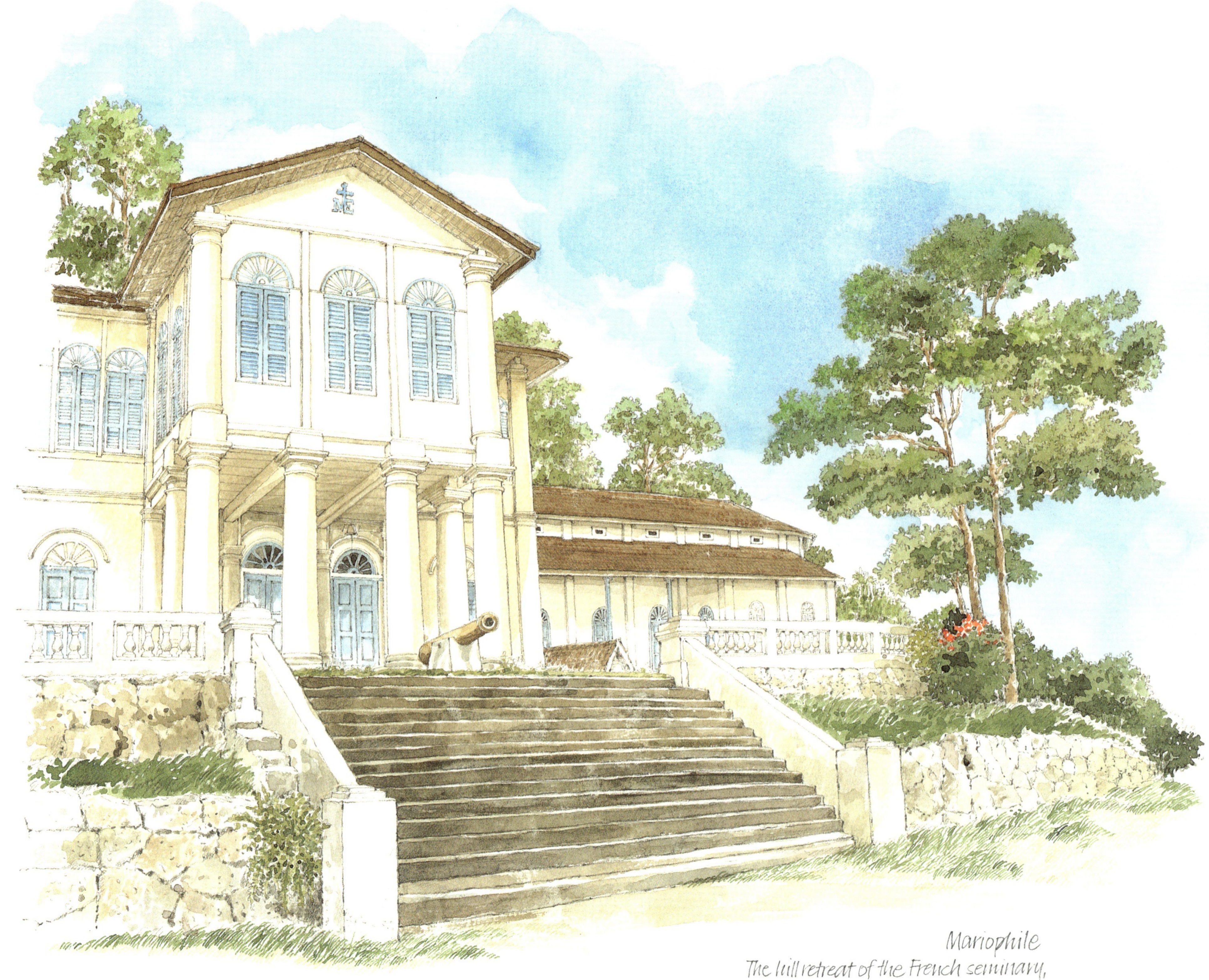

Mariophile

The hill retreat of the French seminary, College-General, on Tanjung Bungah, St. John's Hill, is in a highly original state. The adjoining chapel has the characteristic tall proportion and classical simplicity of the Anglo-Indian style.

State Religious Council
(Majlis Jabatan Agama Islam Negeri)
The grand, white complex in Pesara King Edward and Lebuh Downing faced the sea. It is the only building left of the old government offices which were destroyed by World War II bombs, which explains the unbalanced use of half-round and triangular pediments on the roof entablature.

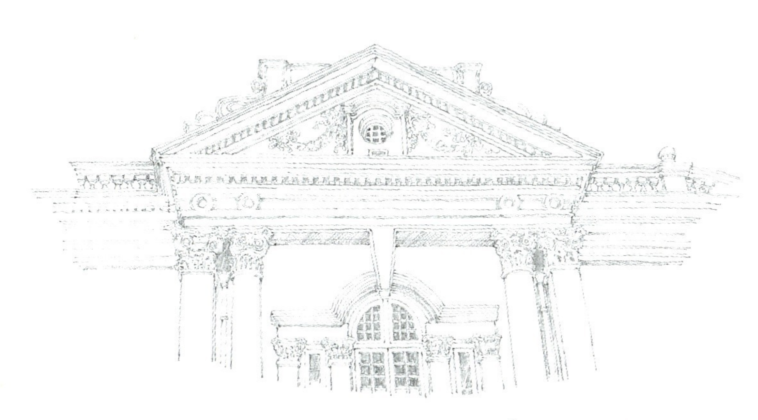

The pediment shows an oculus, grated and framed by swags. Twin Corinthian columns frame a Palladian window punctuated by an obtrusive keystone.

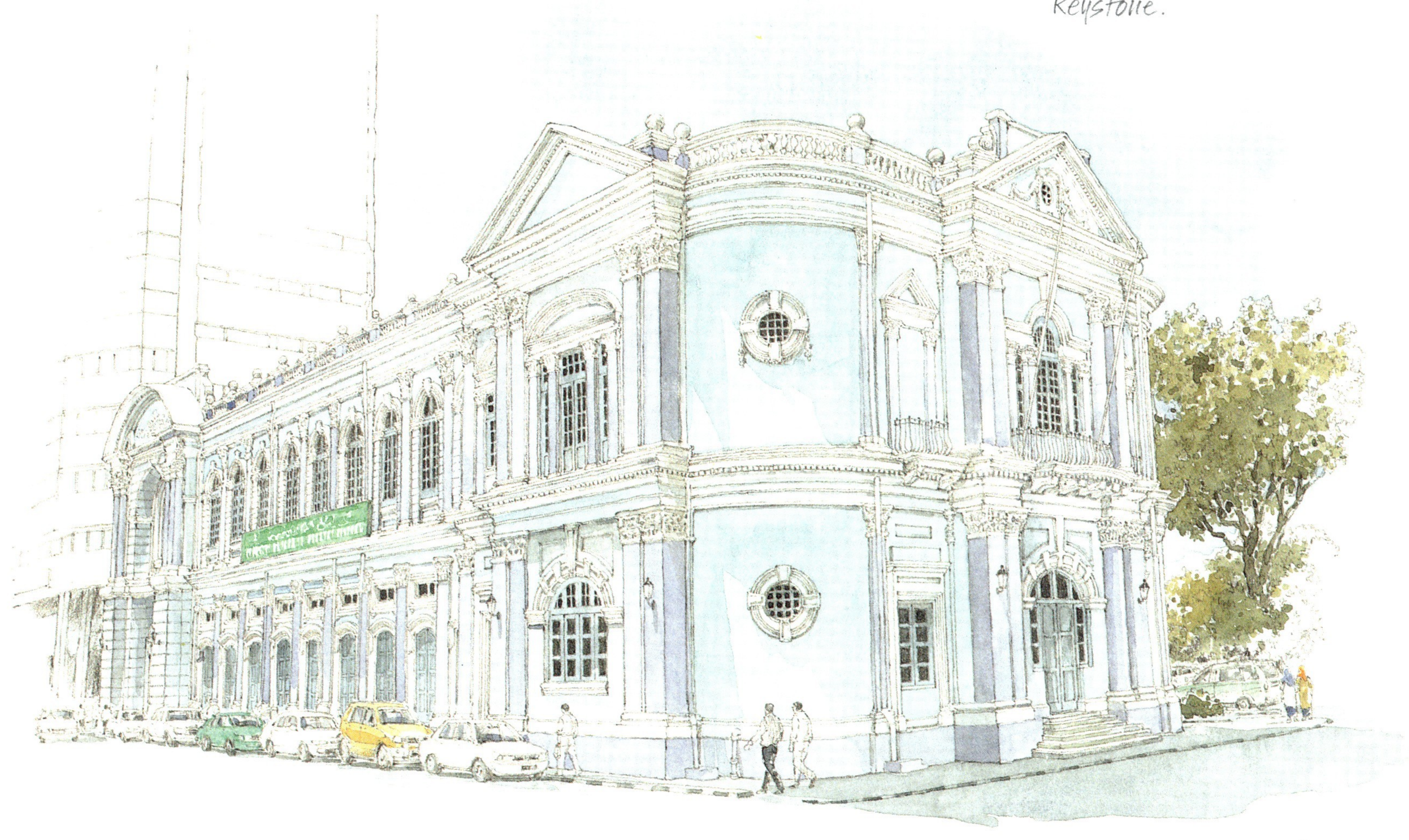

The Southern Indian Connection

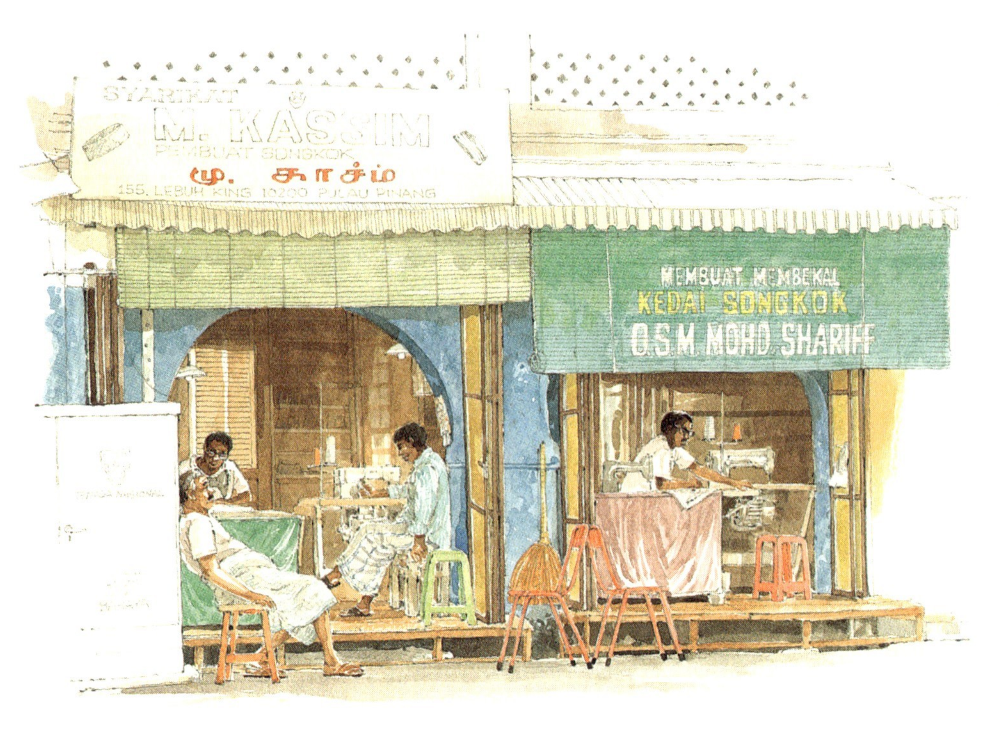

Two arcaded alcoves on the side wall of the Nagore Shrine house makers of the Muslim headwear, the songkok.

The Chulias, Tamil Muslims from southern India, have traded for centuries with Malayan ports and in Sumatra. Long settled in Kedah, they were among the first to follow Light to the new settlement. Lebuh Chulia (then Chulia Street) formed the southern boundary of the early settlement in Light's first street plan. The early urban and business elites of Penang's multi-ethnic community, they built mosques and vernacular schools. Their descendants, offspring of Chulia traders and Malay women, were Jawi Peranakans, who, in turn, were integrated into the modern community of the Penang Malays. Some of their 19th-century Indo-Malay houses survive along Jalan Transfer and its side streets.

After 1789 Penang became a penal station for India. Convict labour from Bengal was used to construct the first roads, bridges and public buildings. They continued to build Penang's government buildings for the next hundred years.

The Chettiars, a clan from Tamil Nadu, were moneylenders and traders. Although they intermarried with the Malays, they strictly maintained their Hindu religion. They lived in *chettinar*, Chettiar enclaves around their temples dedicated to the Hindu deity Murugan.

Penang's largest group of Tamil Muslims comes from one weaving village in southern India, Kadaiyanallur. Following the Industrial Revolution in England that started cotton manufacture, unemployment forced large numbers of men to emigrate to Penang in the late 19th century; the women followed in the 20th century. They married only among themselves.

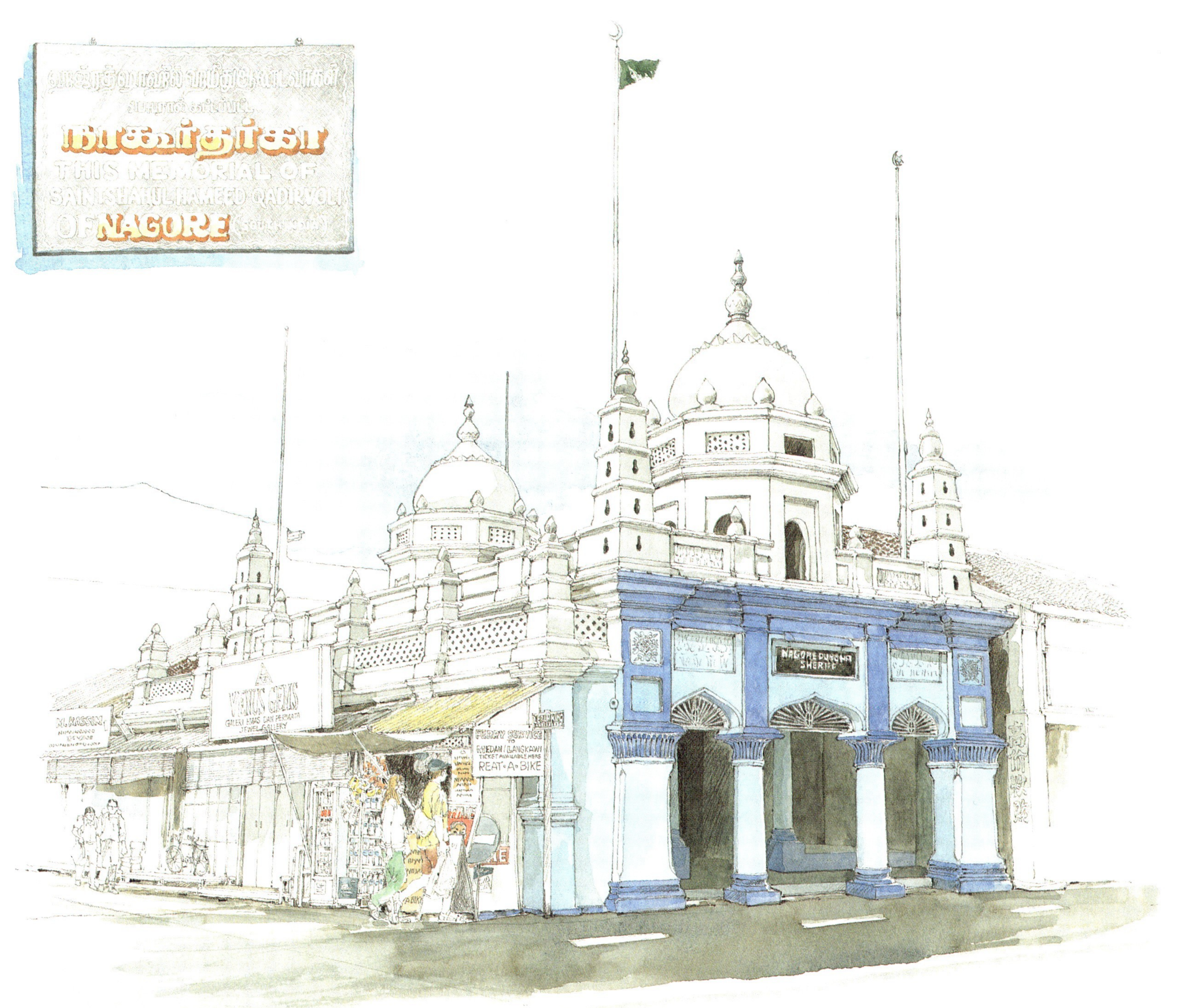

Nagore Shrine

The shrine is the earliest extant Indian Muslim shrine, and stands in its original form at the junction of Lebuh Chulia and Lebuh King. It venerates a 13th-century saint as the signboard (inset) at the entrance to the arcade clearly announces. The domes on top of octagonal towers and the low roof parapet wall with corner minarets show designs typical of Tamil Nadu in southern India.

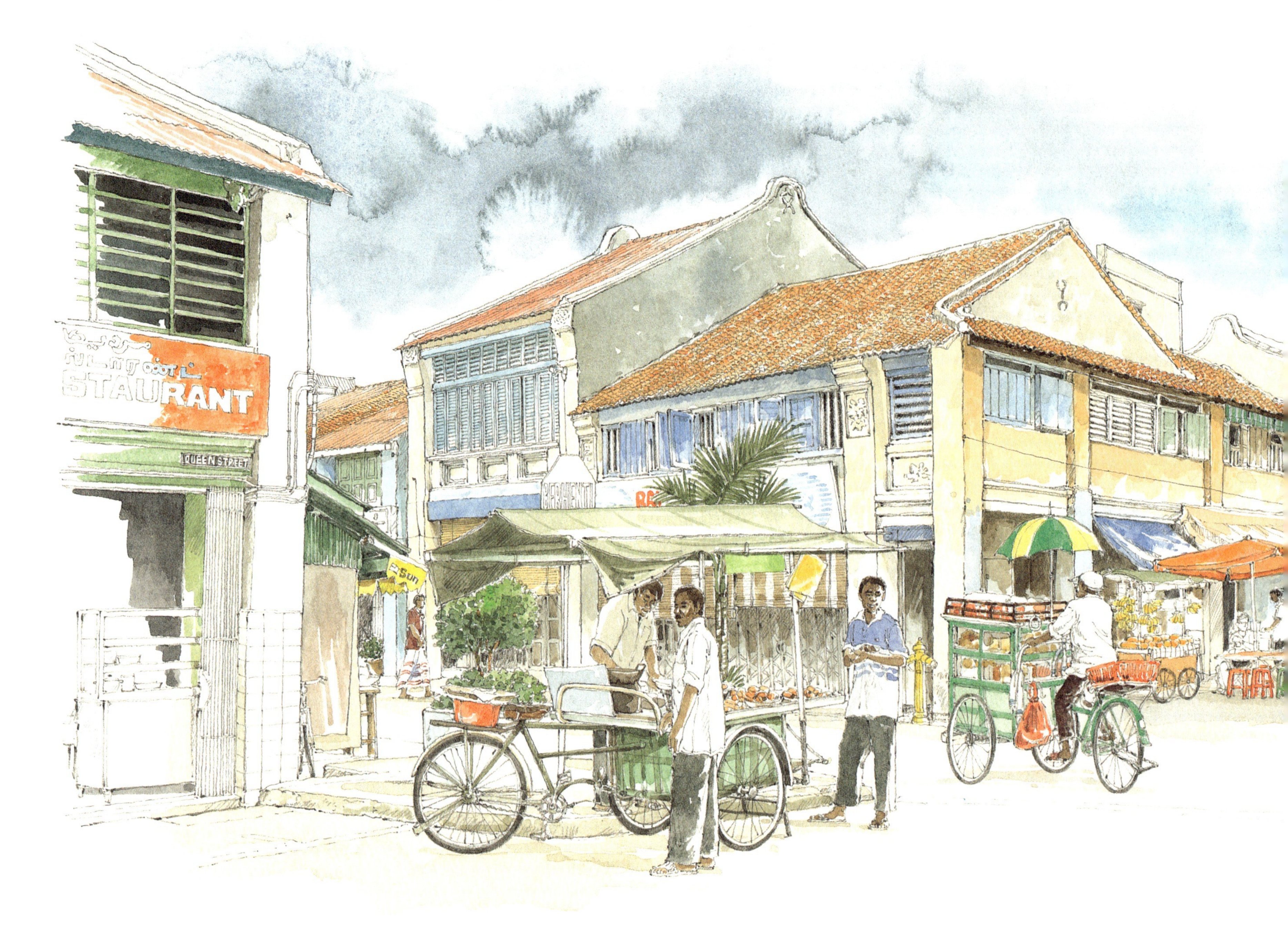

Lebuh Queen

Lebuh Queen was part of the original grid of streets laid out by Francis Light. Also known as Little India, it is the area where Southern Indian Muslim temples are located, and where Indian moneychangers and Chettiar moneylenders ply their trade. Street stalls selling snacks and rotiman (breadman) mobile vendors are features of inner-city life. Some early 19th-century brick shophouses belonging to Chinese settlers can still be seen: squat, sturdy, undecorated and unjustly neglected.

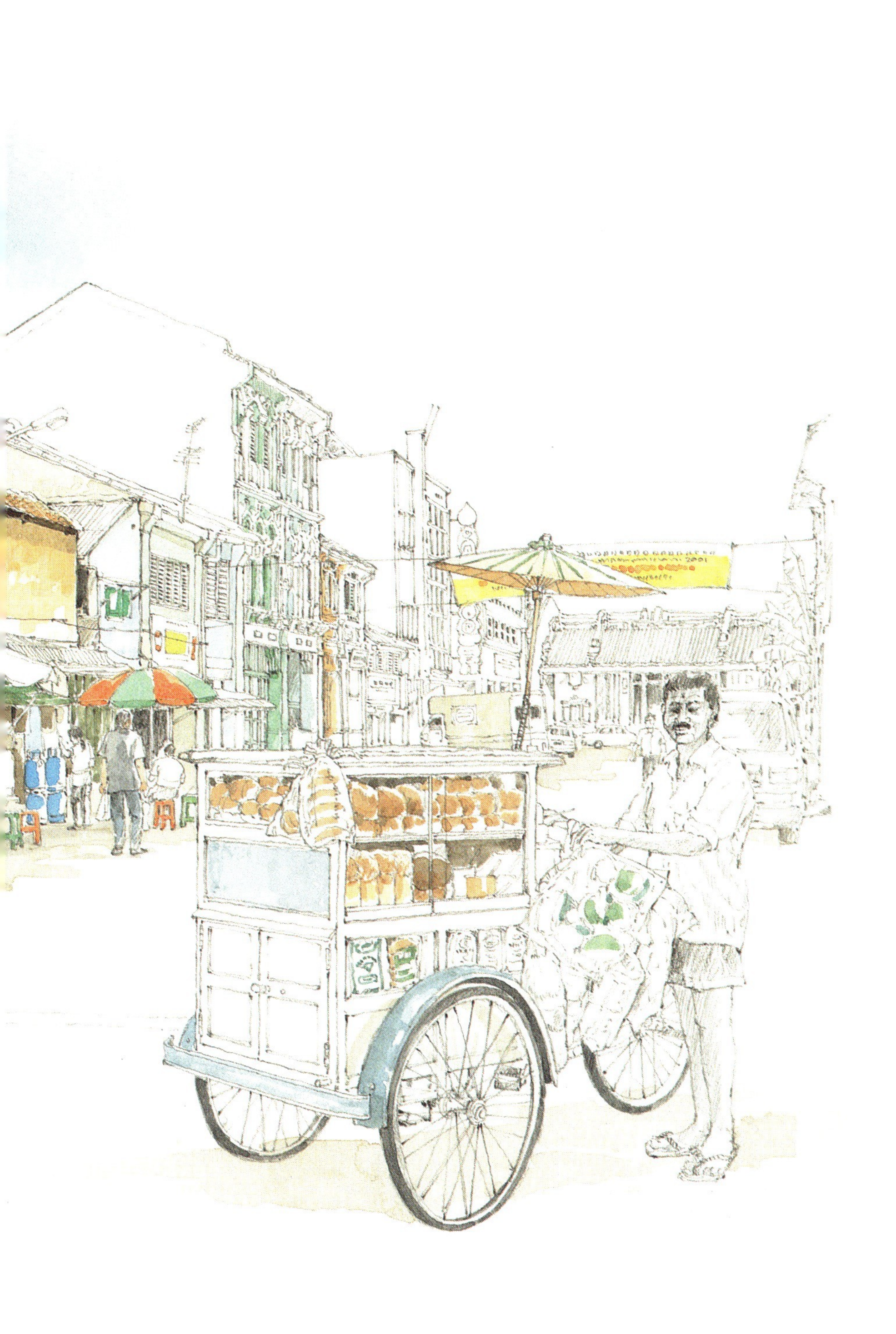

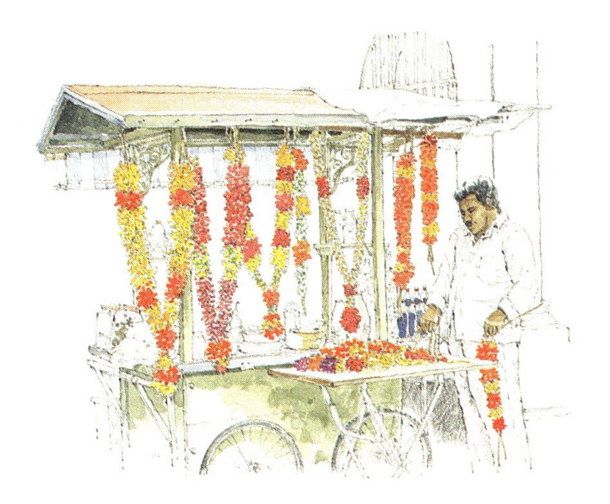

An Indian flower seller threads blooms into a garland at his mobile stall by the Mahamariamman Temple. Indians garland their gods as well as humans they wish to honour.

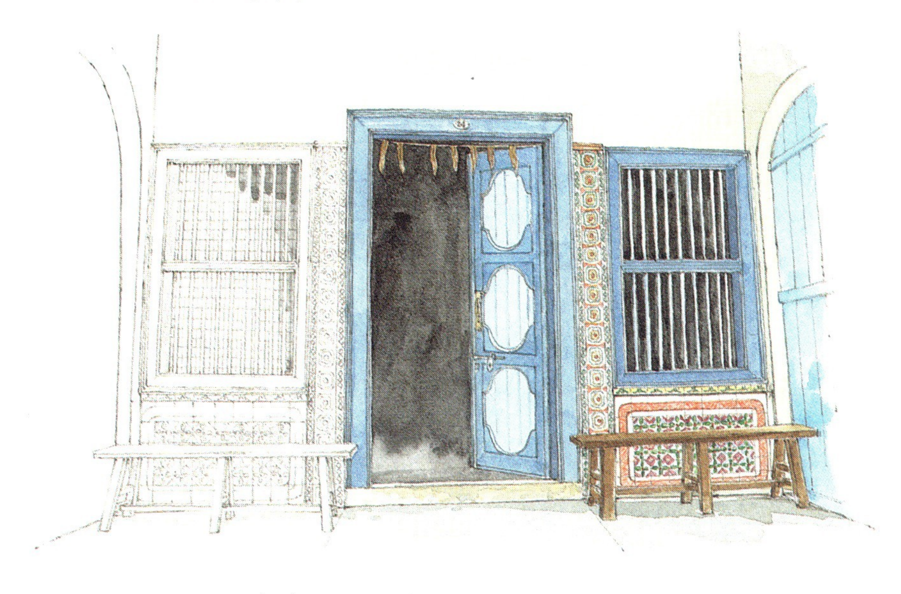

Nagara Viduthi (City Lodge)
No. 24 Lebuh China was formerly a Chinese townhouse. It was established in 1937 by the Chettiars to house immigrants freshly arrived from India. The distinctly Indian doors are matched by decorative dado wall tiles.

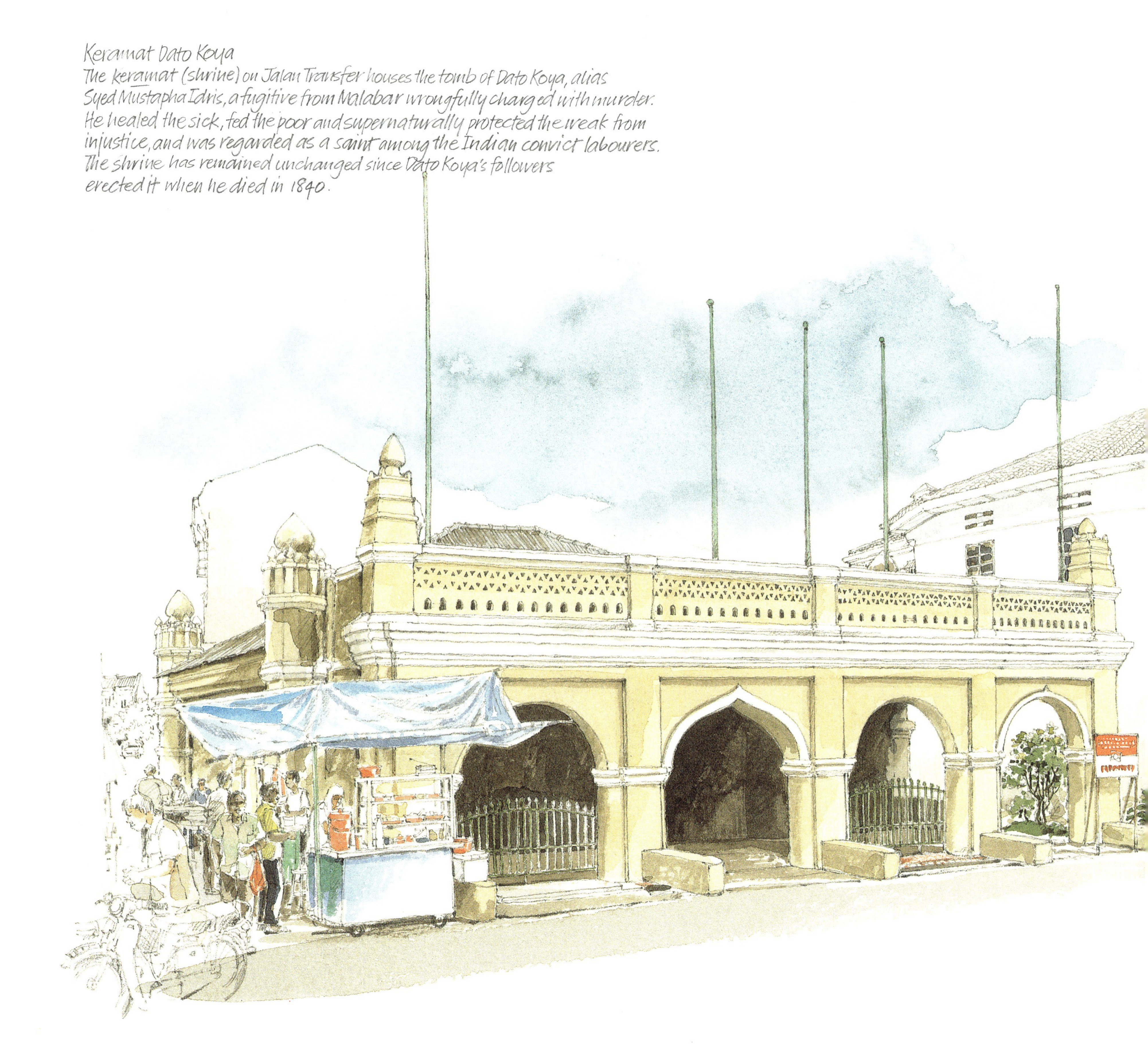

Keramat Dato Koya
The keramat (shrine) on Jalan Transfer houses the tomb of Dato Koya, alias Syed Mustapha Idris, a fugitive from Malabar wrongfully charged with murder. He healed the sick, fed the poor and supernaturally protected the weak from injustice, and was regarded as a saint among the Indian convict labourers. The shrine has remained unchanged since Dato Koya's followers erected it when he died in 1840.

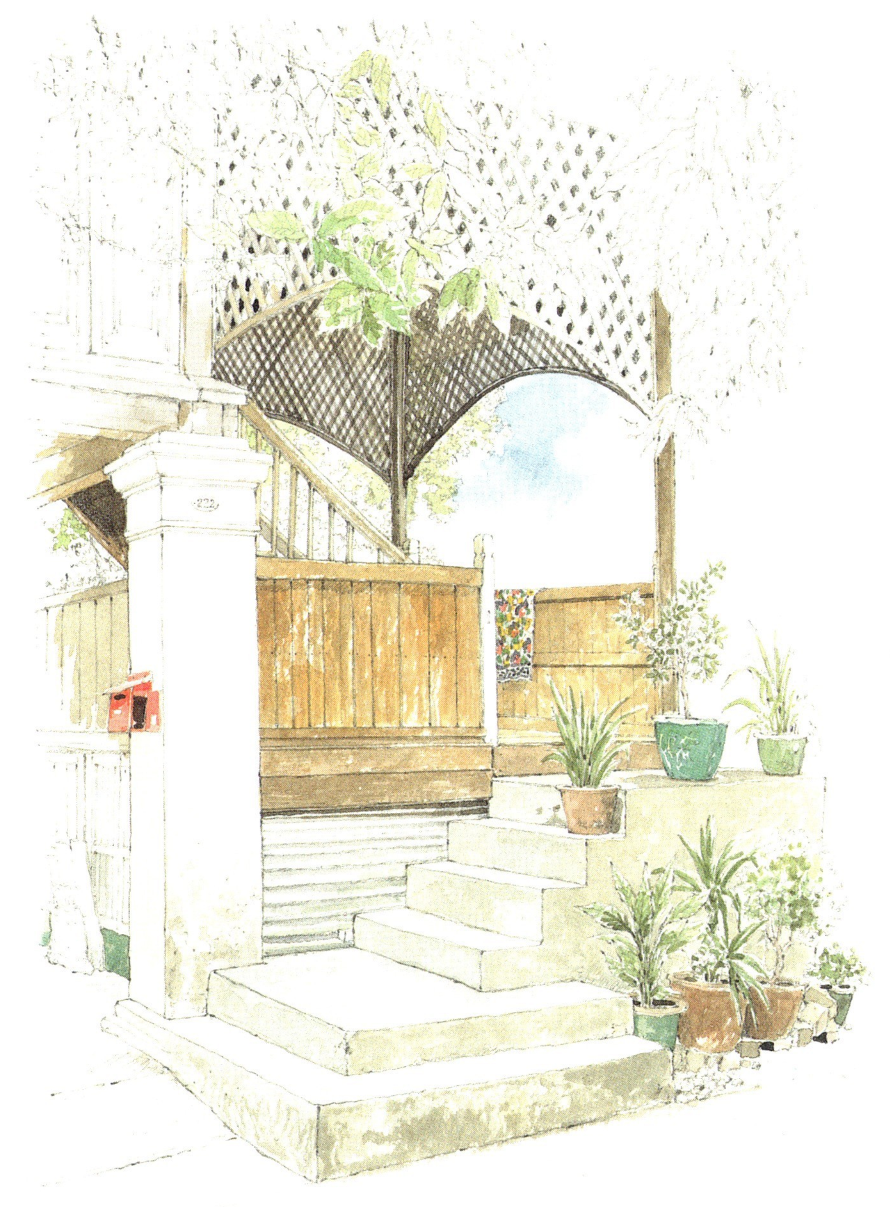

No. 222 Jalan Transfer is a fine example of an Indo-Malay house of the Jawi Peranakans. A short flight of brick masonry steps leads up to the anjong (covered entrance porch), the place where male visitors are met and entertained.

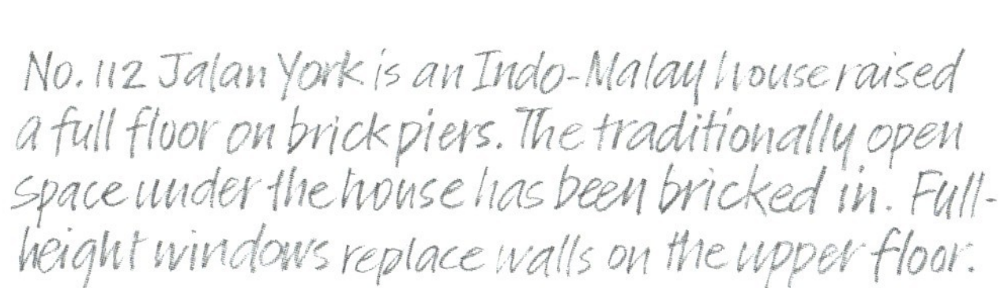

No. 112 Jalan York is an Indo-Malay house raised a full floor on brick piers. The traditionally open space under the house has been bricked in. Full-height windows replace walls on the upper floor.

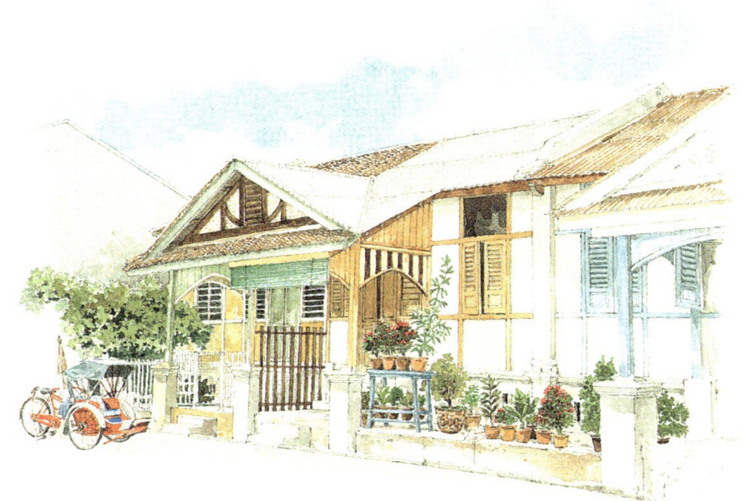

The single-storey terrace houses on Nos. 57-9 Lebuh Melaka are a variant form of Indo-Malay architecture. Usually built by the state, they provide low-cost urban housing. Light wooden fencing, chick (blinds) and potted plants help to personalise the units.

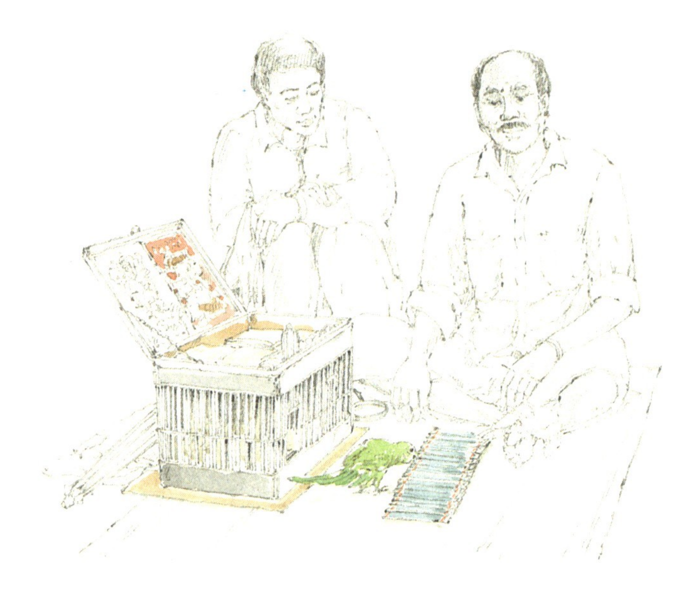

The Indian fortune-teller's trained parakeet picks out a fortune stick from which the fortune-teller divines the hopeful customer's future.

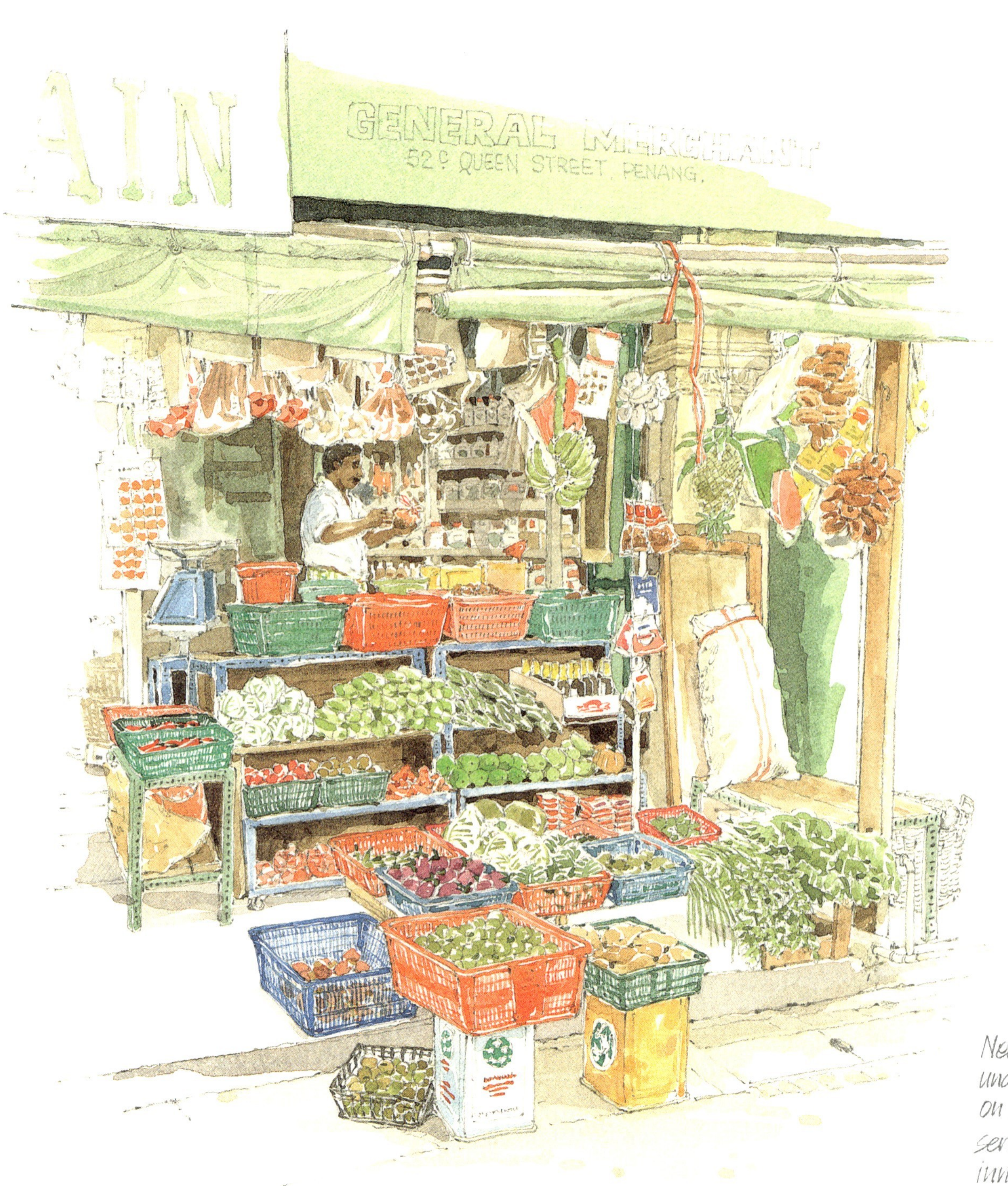

Neat tiers of fresh produce are displayed under a sign reading 'General Merchant' on Lebuh Queen. Small businesses like this serve as neighbourhood corner stores in the inner city. This one stocks special items needed for Muslim cooking.

An Indian *kueh* (cake) vendor conducts business from a portable stall. He is parked in front of shophouses decorated with beautiful plaster details— a frieze of rosettes on the beam face, cornices and below the windows, and panels of swags and ribbons.

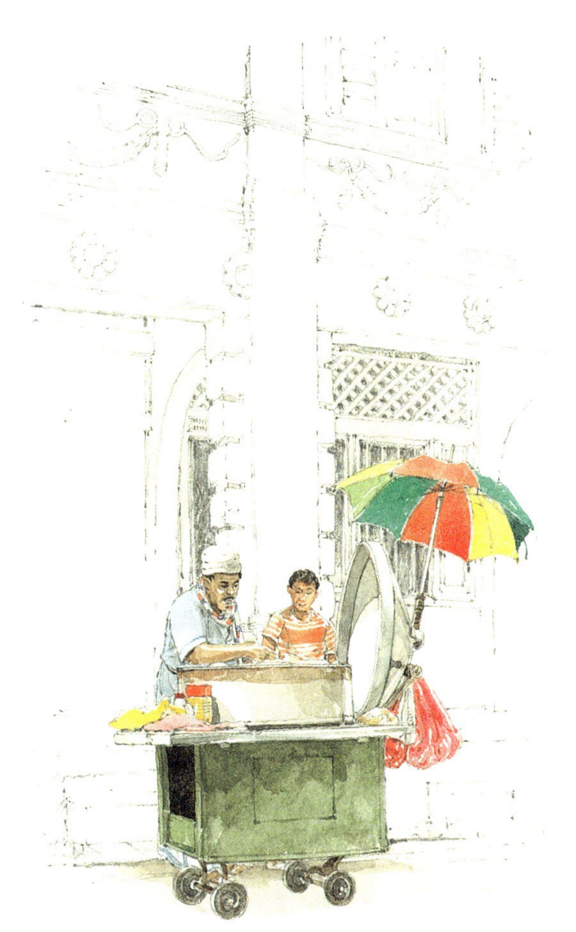

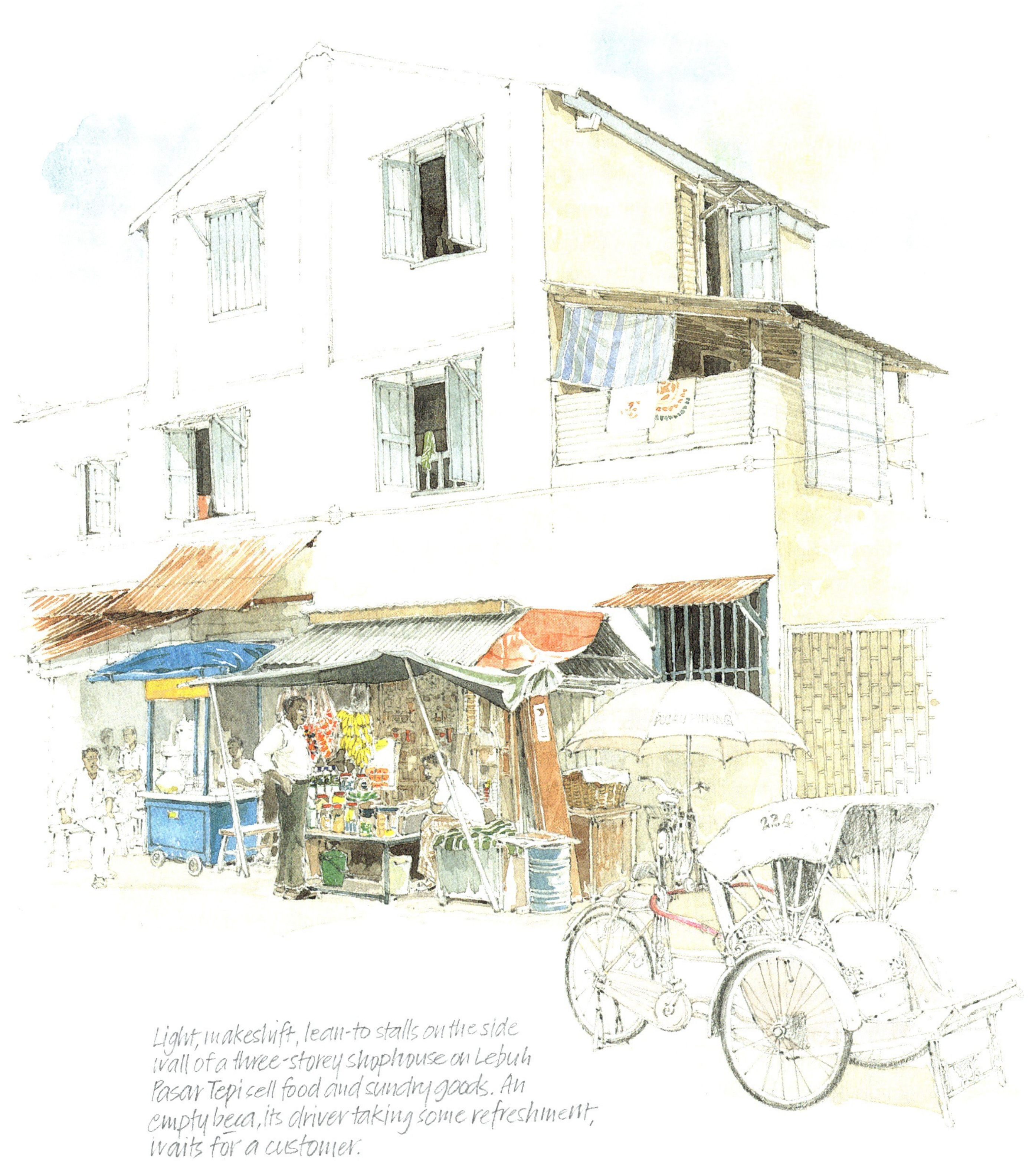

Light, makeshift, lean-to stalls on the side wall of a three-storey shophouse on Lebuh Pasar Tepi sell food and sundry goods. An empty beca, its driver taking some refreshment, waits for a customer.

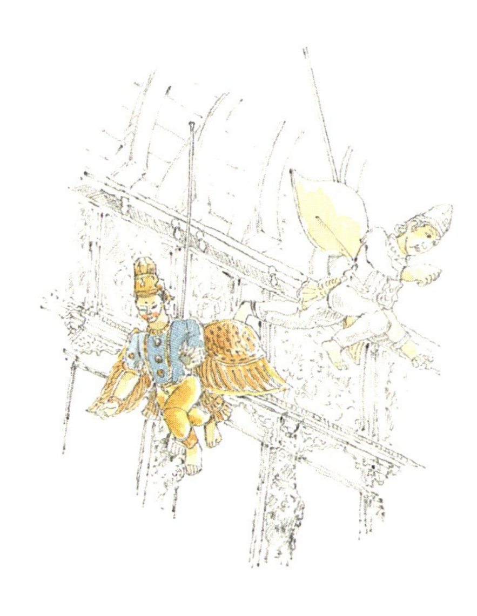

Two angel-like, winged figures are suspended from the ceiling of the temple.

The main aisle of the Nattukkottai Chettiar Temple leads to the garbagraham (sanctum). Open courts on both sides flood the interior with sunlight, creating a chequered pattern of light and shade. Rows of carved, teak columns with capitals support a frieze of paintings above which span finely wrought trusses.

Nattukkottai Chettiar Temple
The unassuming façade along Jalan Waterfall belies the highly original temple inside. Built for a Hindu deity, the young Lord Murugan, the temple is laid out in a traditional southern Indian chokkatan (chequered) plan. Behind its long, whitewashed wall is the chettinar (Chettiar quarters).

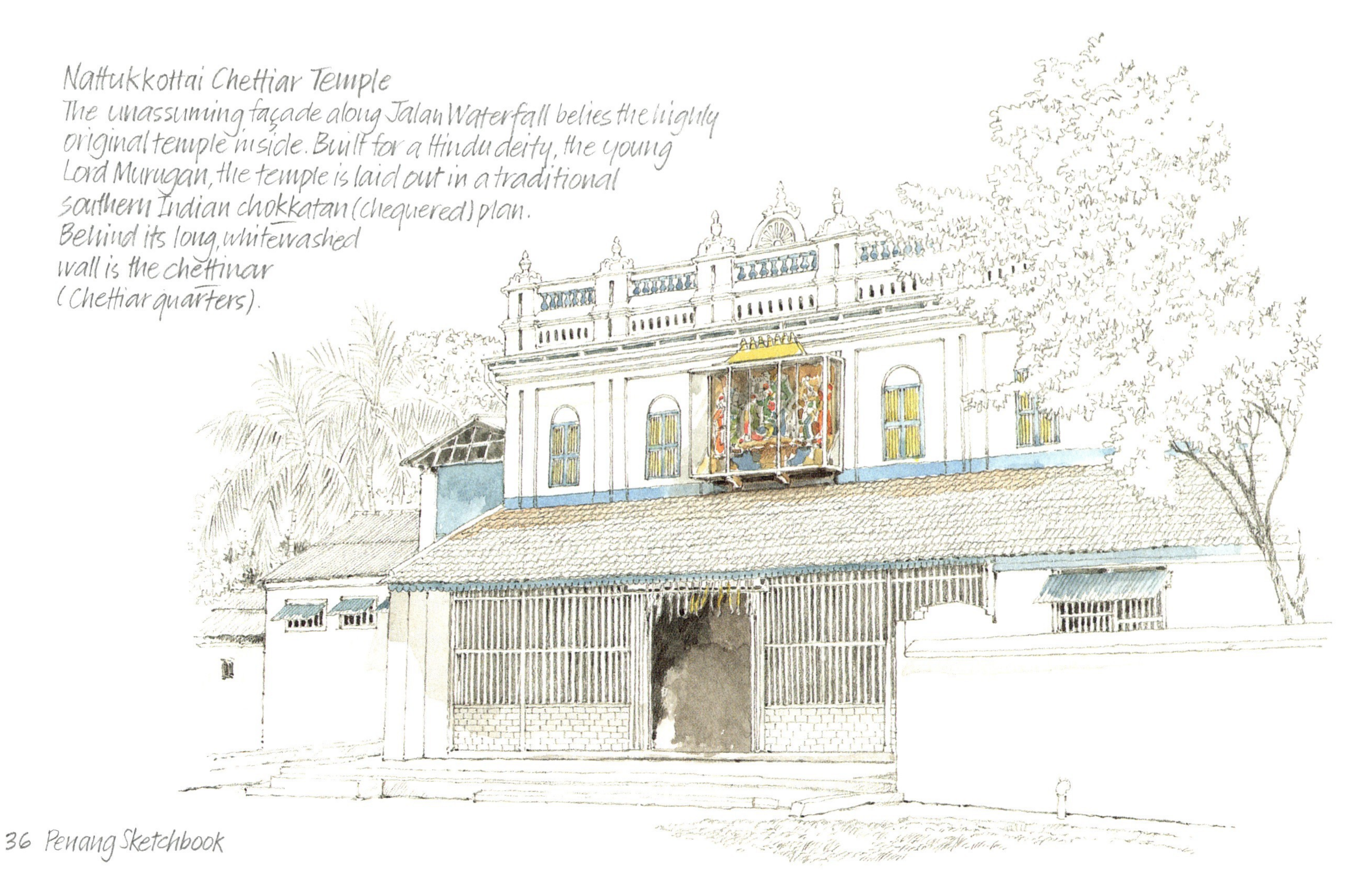

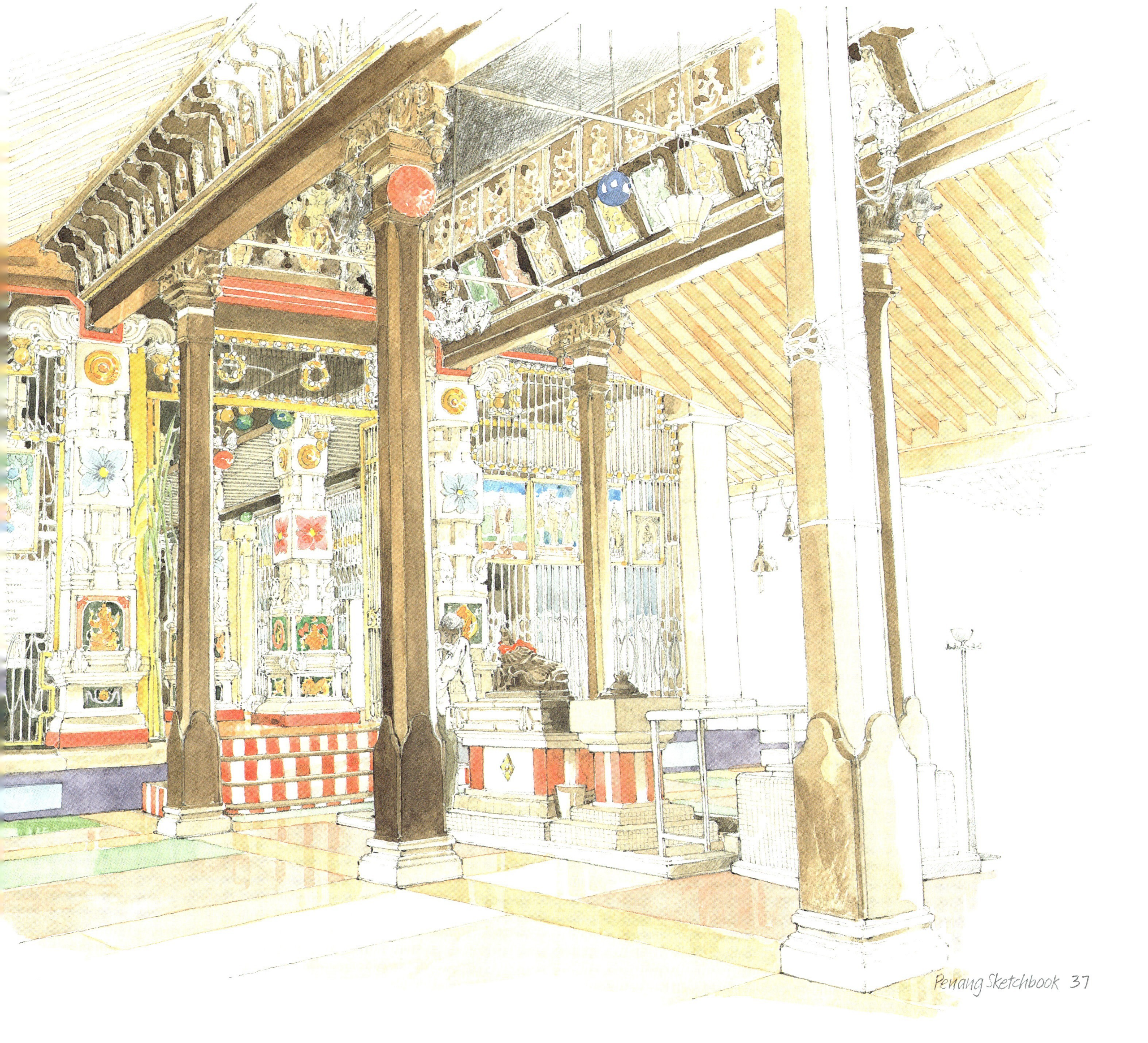

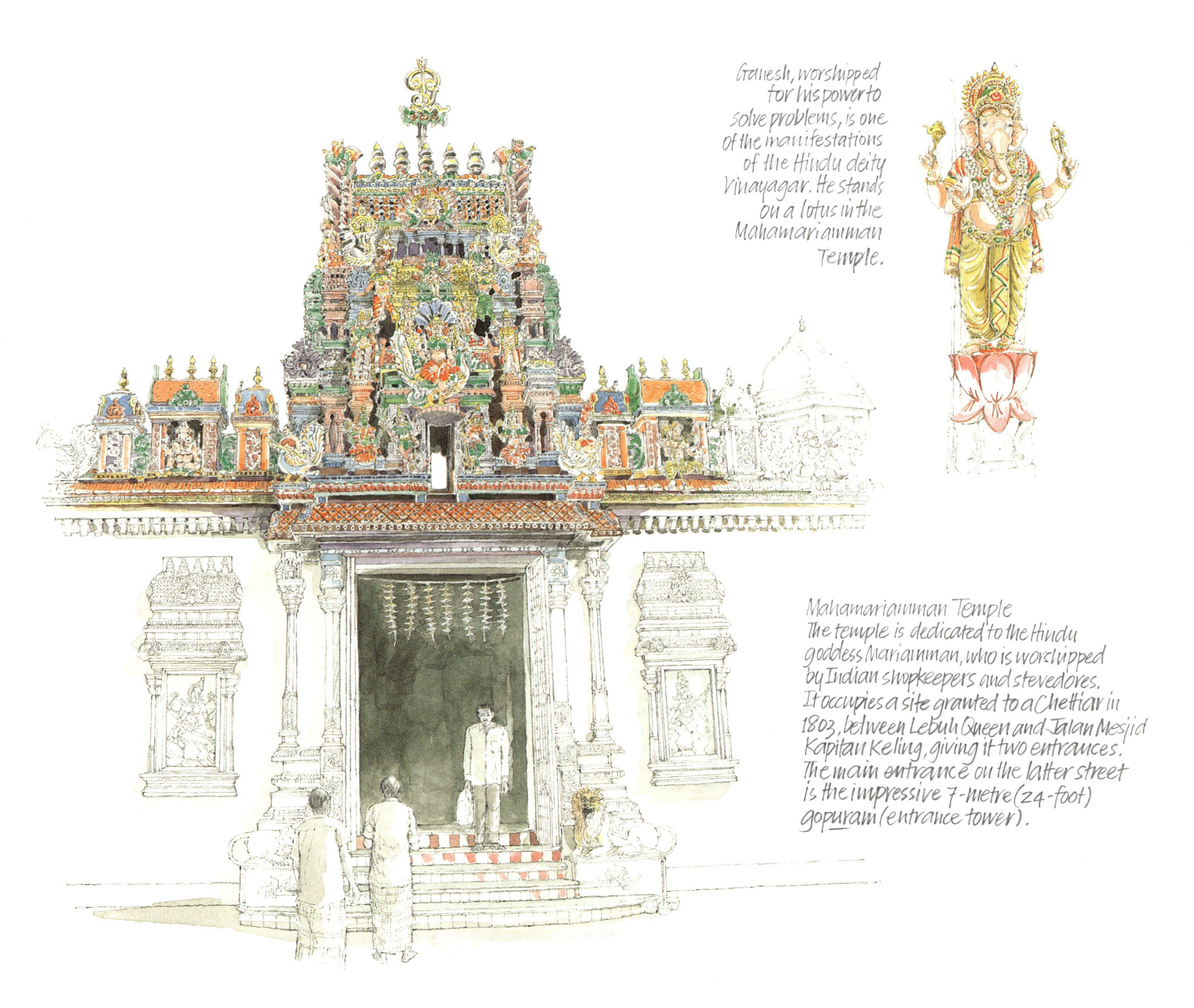

Ganesh, worshipped for his power to solve problems, is one of the manifestations of the Hindu deity Vinayagar. He stands on a lotus in the Mahamariamman Temple.

Mahamariamman Temple
The temple is dedicated to the Hindu goddess Mariamman, who is worshipped by Indian shopkeepers and stevedores. It occupies a site granted to a Chettiar in 1803, between Lebuh Queen and Jalan Mesjid Kapitan Keling, giving it two entrances. The main entrance on the latter street is the impressive 7-metre (24-foot) gopuram (entrance tower).

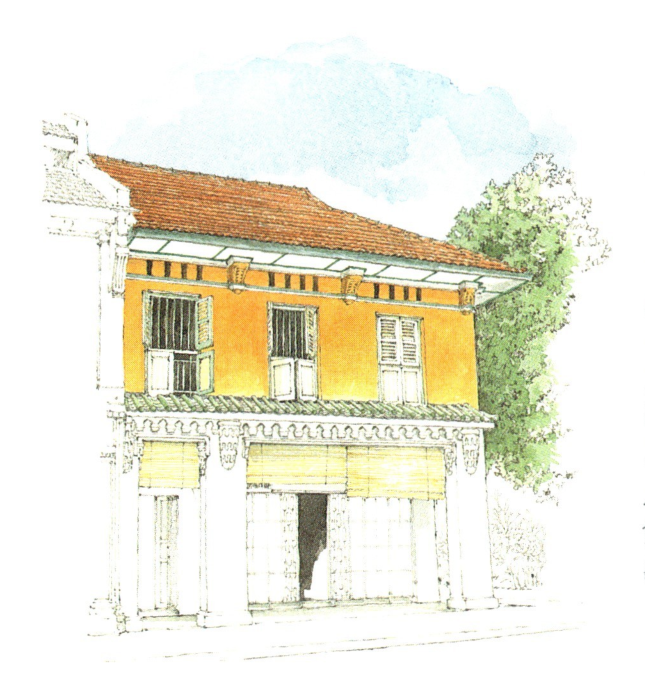

The street elevation of the Kapitan Kling Mosque madrasah (religious school) on Lorong Seck Chuan is modified with utilitarian shophouse doors and windows replacing the horseshoe arcades of the side elevation (right). The fringe roof and eaves of the main design are retained.

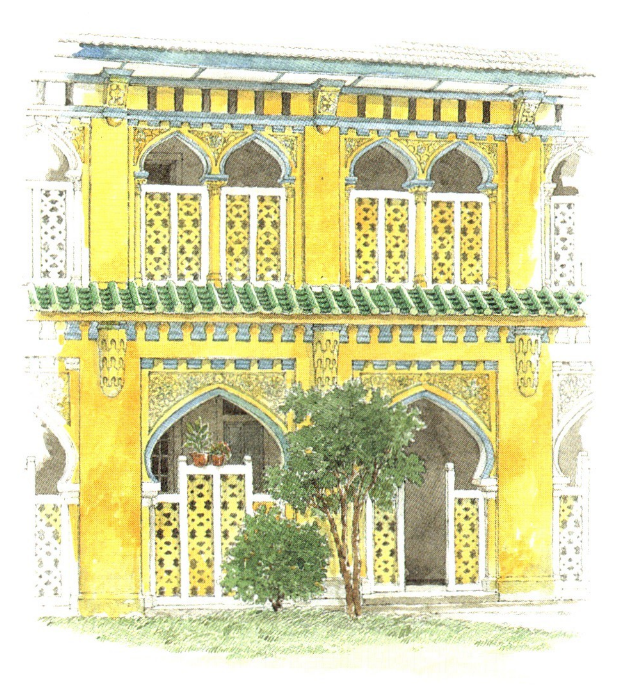

The Kapitan Kling Mosque madrasah is part of the 1916 extension. Paired horseshoe arches are screened with patterned grilles. A shallow fringe roof of green tiles shades the lower arcade while decorated brackets and rows of dentils give additional accents.

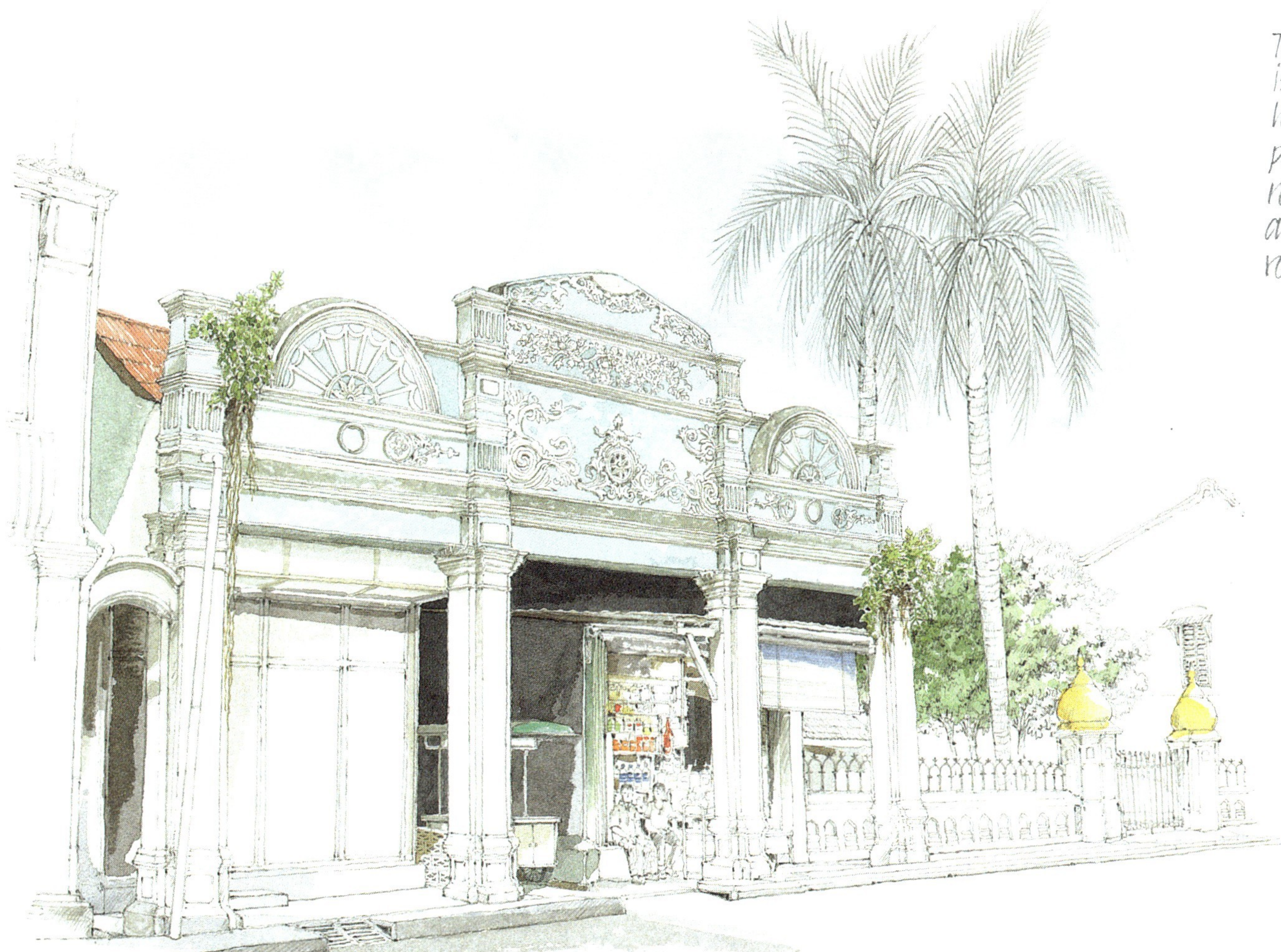

Noordin Family Tomb
The tombs of Mohamed Merican Noordin, a prominent Chulia fleet owner, his mother and family members are located on Lebuh Chulia and are surrounded by an arcade. The three-bay façade is an early 20th-century addition.

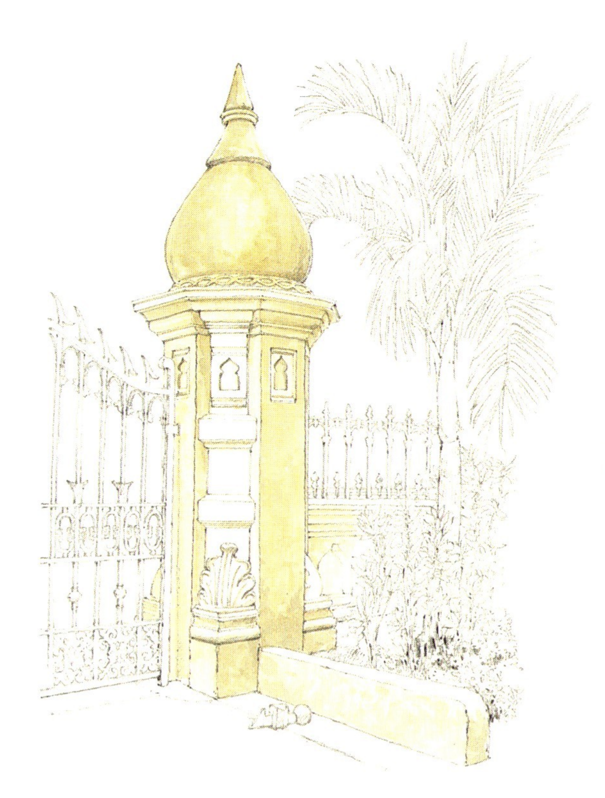

The gateposts are part of the 1916 extension that saw the addition of wrought iron fencing and fence posts topped with onion domes (page 41). Small insets of horseshoe arches run along the perimeter wall. At the base of each gatepost is a beautiful acanthus leaf.

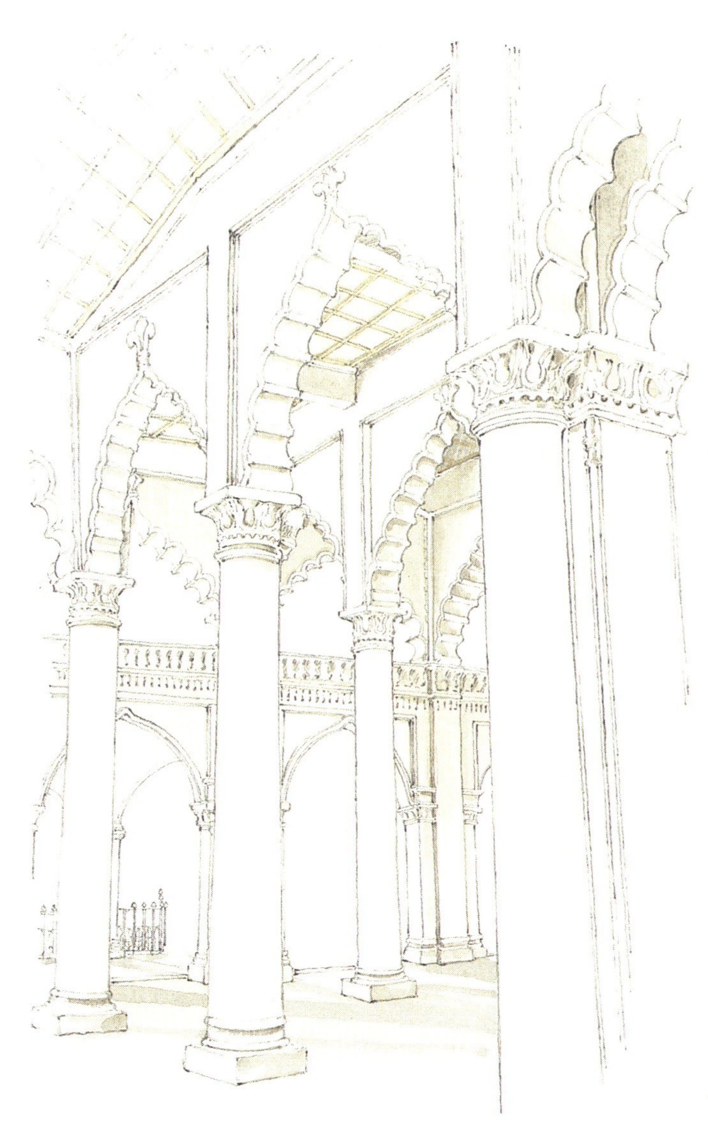

The original red colour of the decorative Islamic pattern formed by twining vines is revealed after recent conservation cleaning.

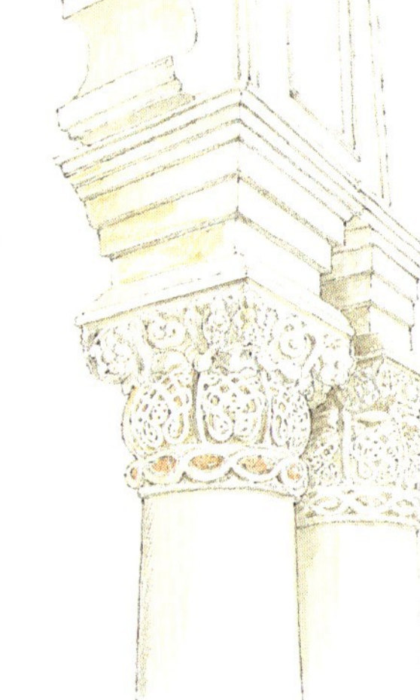

Moorish multi-foil arches from the 1893 to 1916 period form the colonnade around the prayer hall.

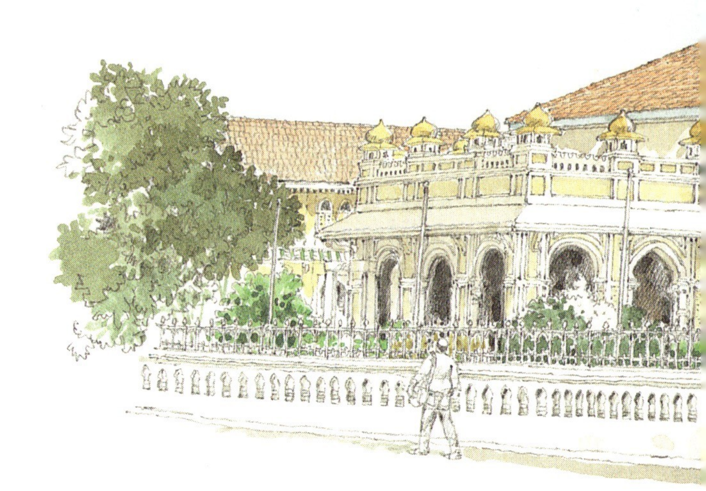

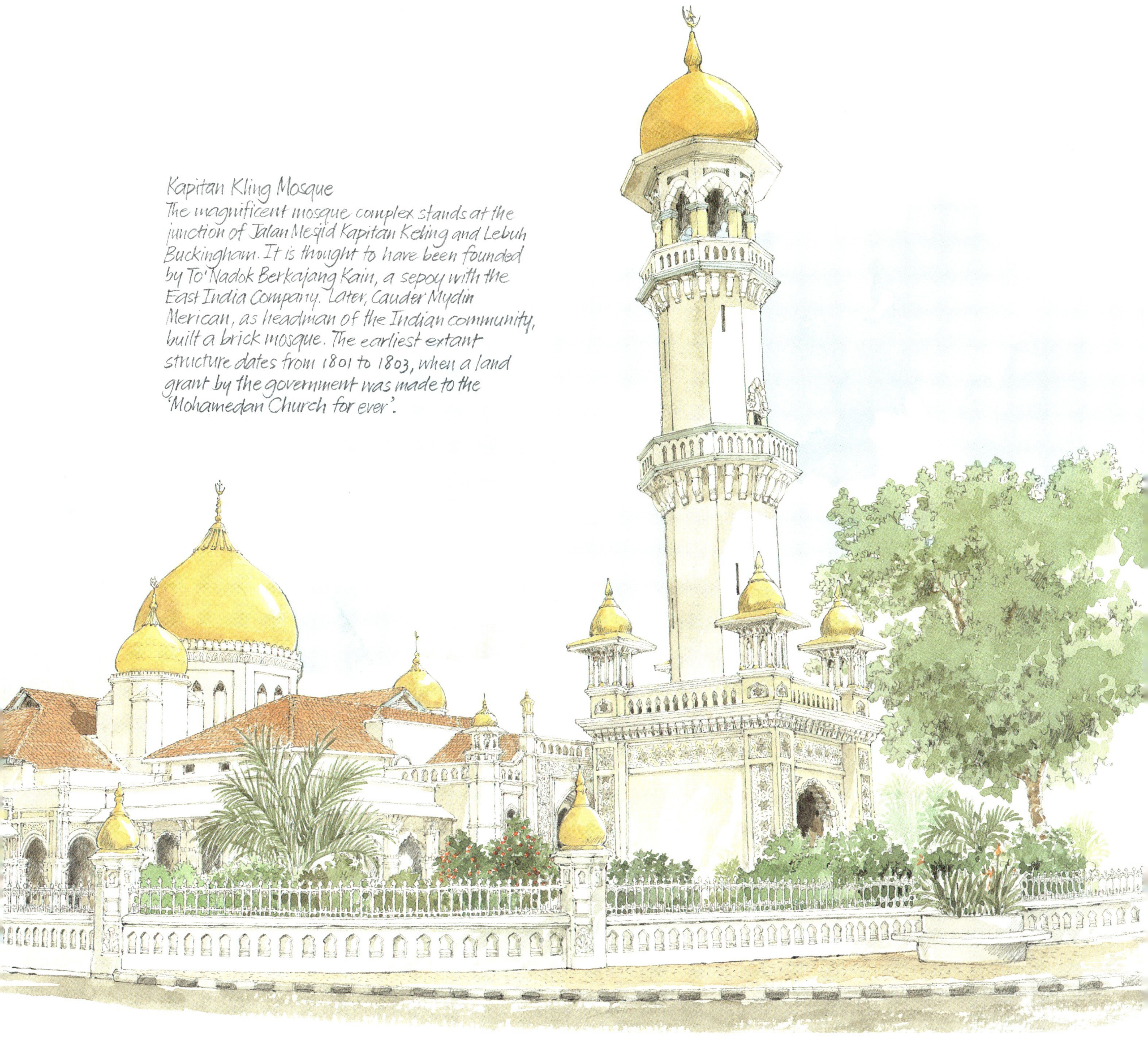
Kapitan Kling Mosque
The magnificent mosque complex stands at the junction of Jalan Mesjid Kapitan Keling and Lebuh Buckingham. It is thought to have been founded by To' Nadok Berkajang Kain, a sepoy with the East India Company. Later, Cauder Mydin Merican, as headman of the Indian community, built a brick mosque. The earliest extant structure dates from 1801 to 1803, when a land grant by the government was made to the 'Mohamedan Church for ever'.

The Chinese Legacy

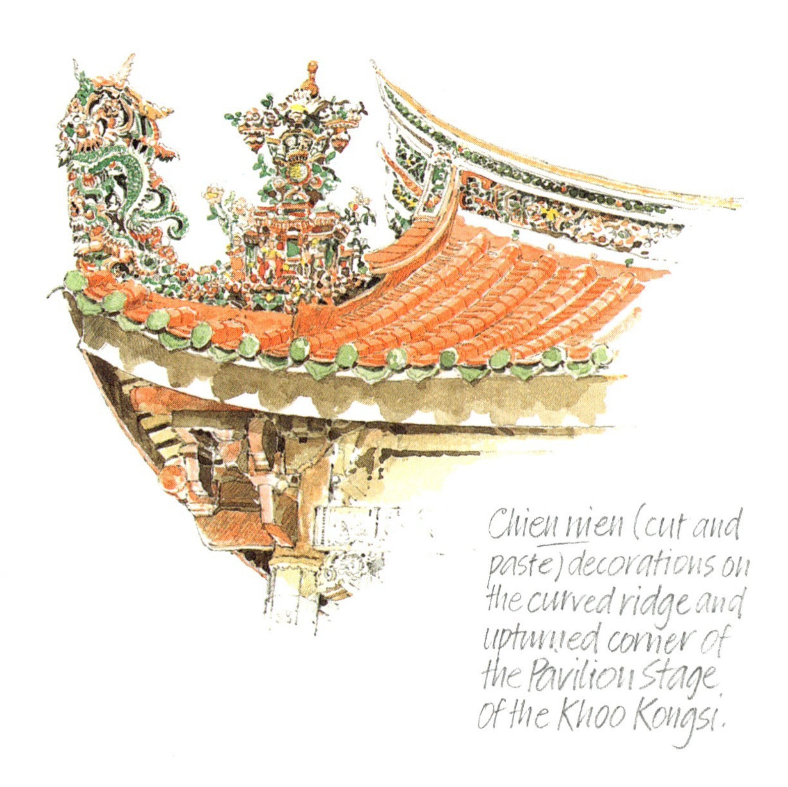

Chien mien (cut and paste) decorations on the curved ridge and upturned corner of the Pavilion Stage of the Khoo Kongsi.

The Chinese were an established community in the Melaka Sultanate in the early 15th century. A hardworking people, they were '... spread all over the Malay Countries and exercise[d] almost all the handicraft professions and carr[ied] on most of the retail trade' (Clodd, page 55). They were among the first to take advantage of new outlets for trade in Penang, and Captain Kydd reported to the Bengal government in 1787 that the shops started by the Chulias were principally kept by the Chinese.

Like their Chettiar and Chulia counterparts, they married local women as Chinese women were not allowed to emigrate until after 1894, a policy of successive Chinese dynasties to ensure the return of male emigrants or at least the repatriation of money earned in the Nanyang (South Seas). The offspring of the intermarriages, the Straits-born Chinese, came to be known as Peranakans or Babas (men) and Nonyas (women). They spoke Malay, the lingua franca of the Malay Archipelago, and adopted Malay custom in dress and cuisine. As successful urban elites they were more open and receptive to European influences. It was their taste for the finest things from both East and West that primarily created the Straits Eclectic style.

The mid-19th century opening up of tin mines in Perak and Selangor brought fresh waves of Chinese coolies. Penang, as the entrepôt for the world's tin market, attracted new immigrants. Later waves of *sinkeh* (new guests) led to the establishment of *kongsi* (clan associations) organised along the same surnames as the villages in China. Penang has the largest number of and the richest *kongsi* buildings in the country.

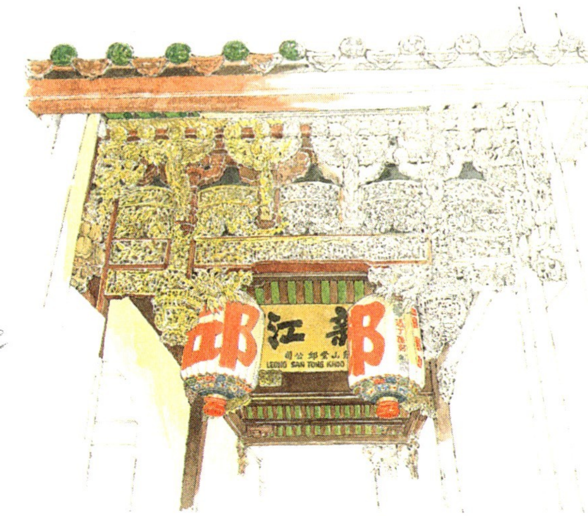

The formal entrance to the temple on Lebuh Pantai, like all entrances to Penang clan complexes, is in a narrow lane for better defence, a legacy of the 19th-century triad wars.

Khoo Kongsi

The Khoo Kongsi at Medan Cannon has retained it's historic setting. It stands in a medan (square) surrounded by the terrace houses of clan members, the association office and the Pavilion Stage. The temple, a masterpiece of late Ching Dynasty Minnan architecture, is raised up a whole floor and has a transitional porch building, a feature of Anglo-Indian-Malay buildings in the British Settlement.

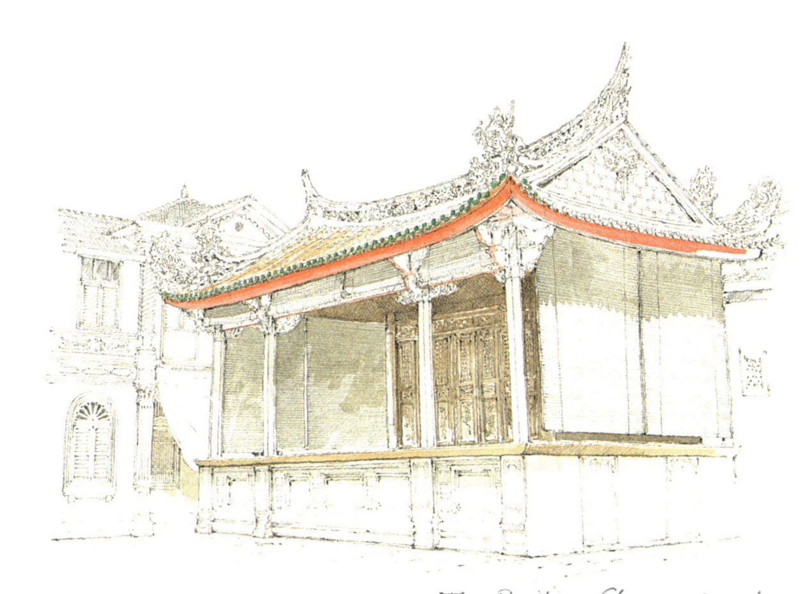

The Pavilion Stage stands on a granite podium. Chinese operas are staged here in the seventh lunar month during the Festival of the Hungry Ghosts.

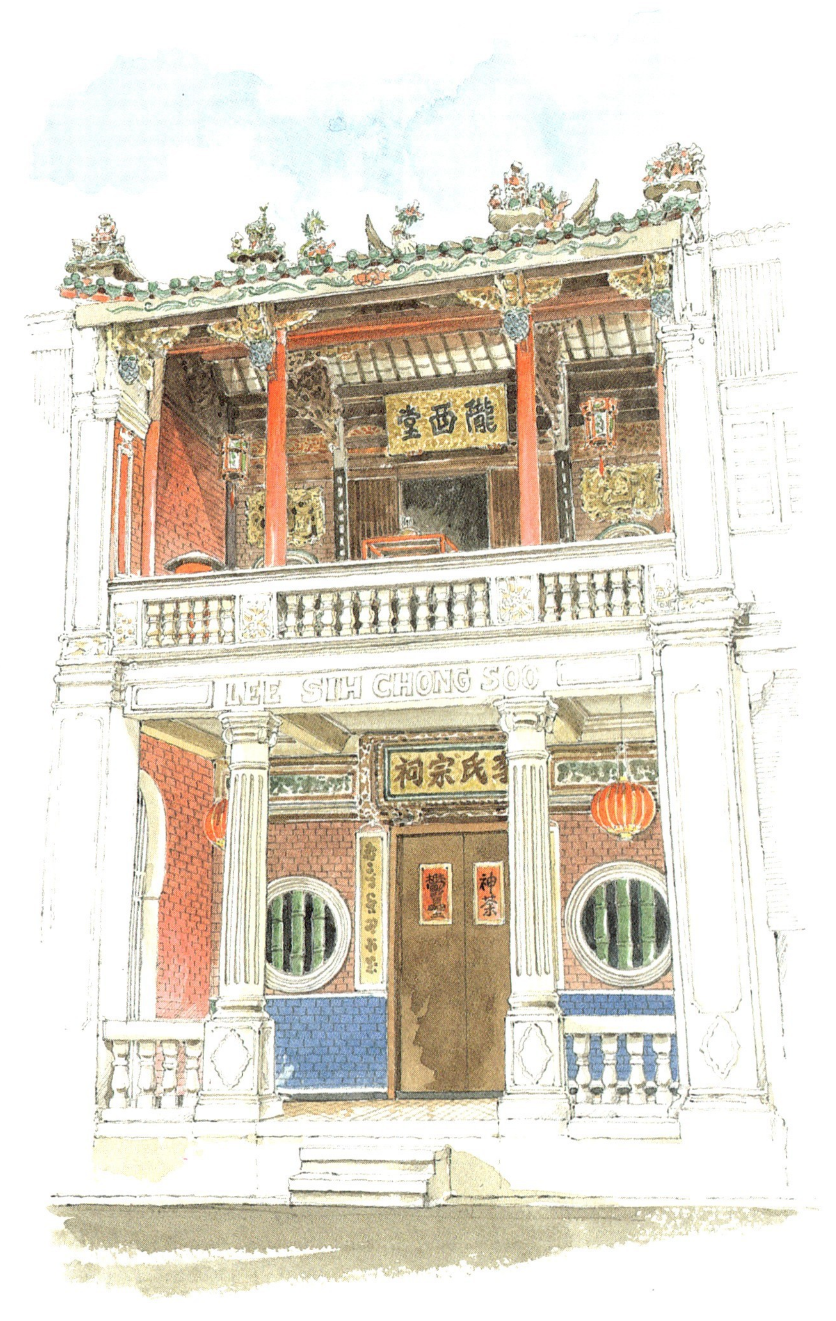

Lee Sih Chong Soo
The Lee surname clan association, housed in three shophouses on Lebuh King, was renovated in the 1920s in the Straits Eclectic style. It features a pair of tall Ionic Order columns carrying a balcony with vase-shaped balustrades. The upper floor is in the traditional Chinese temple style while the central door and round windows are in the townhouse temple style.

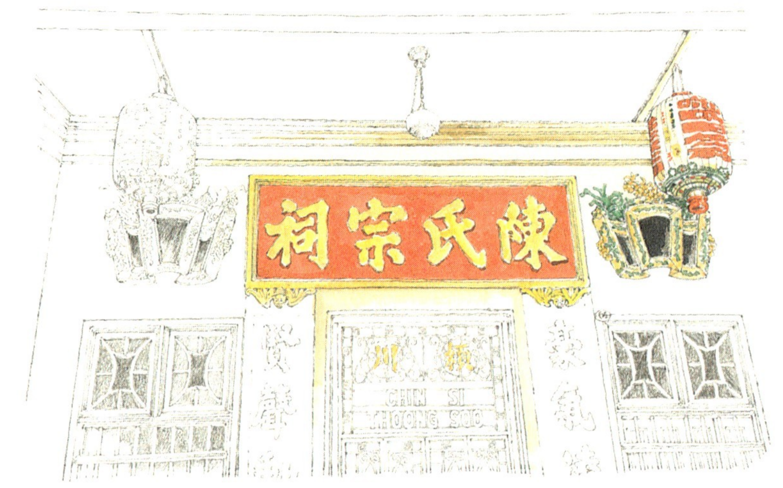

Chin Si Thong Soo
The clan temple on Lebuh King has a plaque with four Chinese characters above the high central door, identifying it as the Chin surname clan association.

The balcony railings of the Cheah Kongsi are done in the Straits Eclectic style. A pomegranate decorates the floor cornice line.

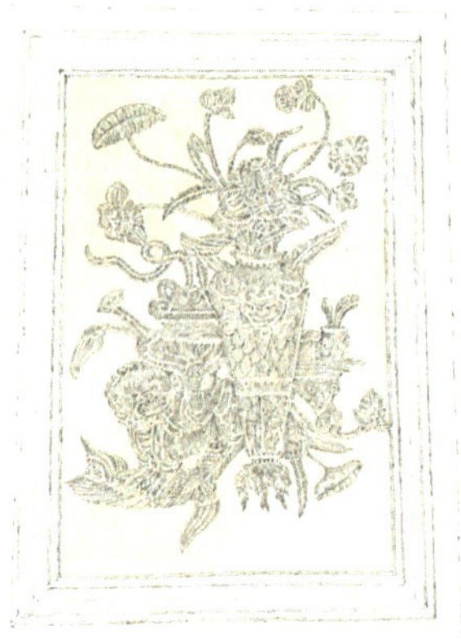

The granite panel in bas-relief from the Cheah Kongsi depicts flowers in a vase and a small crouching lion.

Cheah Kongsi

The entrance gateway to the Cheah Kongsi on Lebuh Armenian leads into a typically narrow lane. Facing bricks and granite blocks carry a plaque with four Chinese characters. The curved ridge with swallowtail ends is decorated with chien nien mosaic and surmounted by a pair of sinuous blue dragons.

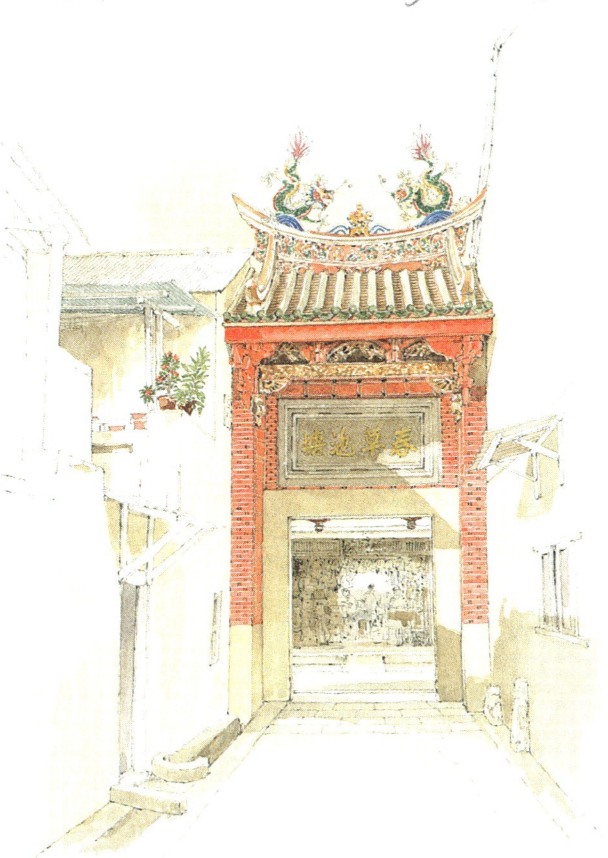

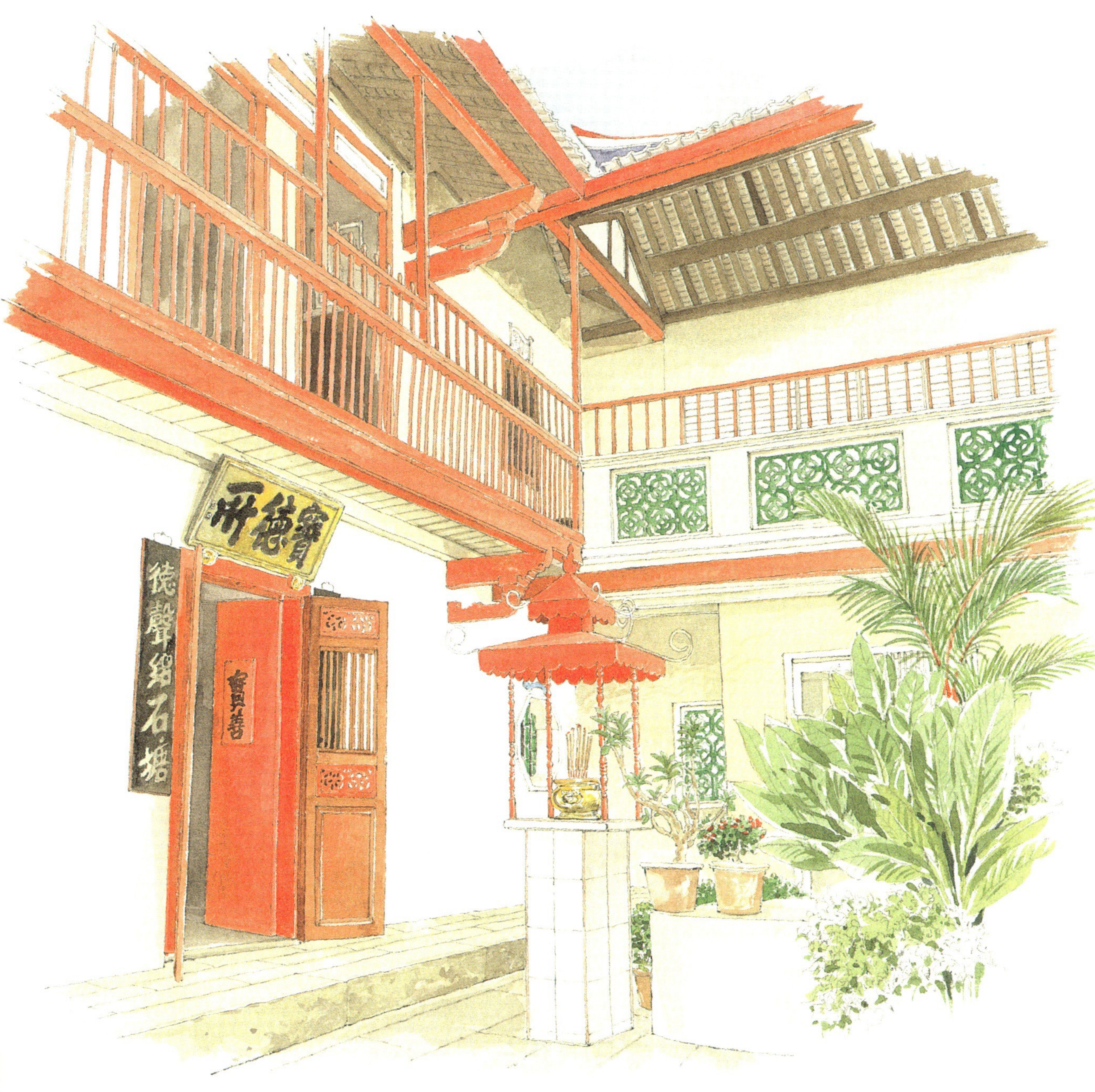

Roofed galleries on the upper floor overlook the internal courtyard. The roof timber structure is clearly exposed to show the tou kung (brackets) and the underside of the clay roof tiles, typical features of traditional Chinese architecture. The joss sticks of the devotees, sheltered by a miniature pavilion, burn up fully, thus ensuring that the prayers reach the gods.

Lo Pan Hang (Carpenters' Guild)
The temple has a relatively plain façade that belies its historical significance as the 'mother temple' of all Chinese building guilds in the country. It is dedicated to Lo Pan, patron deity of all building artisans.

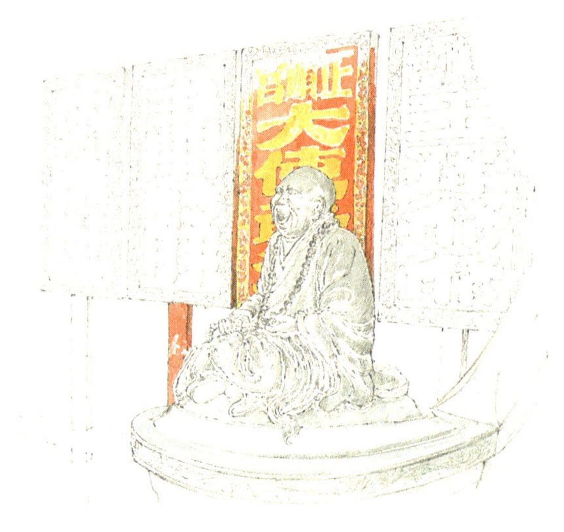

Laughing Buddha, seated atop the handrail end of the stone stairs in the Khoo Kongsi, is laughing because he is sitting on money symbolised by a copper coin in the crevice of the handrail.

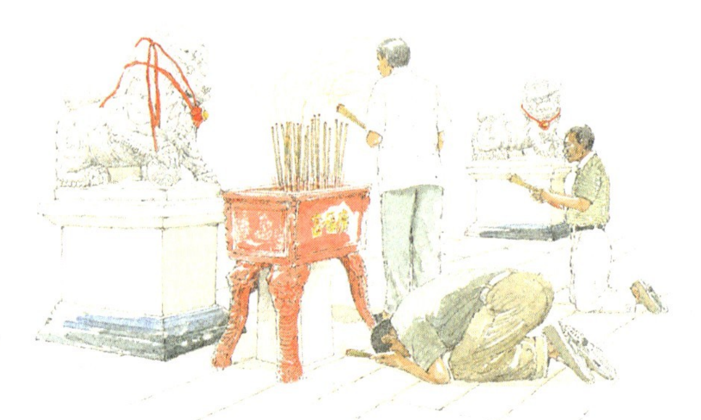

Devotees in three different postures of prayer at the Kwan Yin Temple place lit joss sticks in a holder before a festooned stone lion.

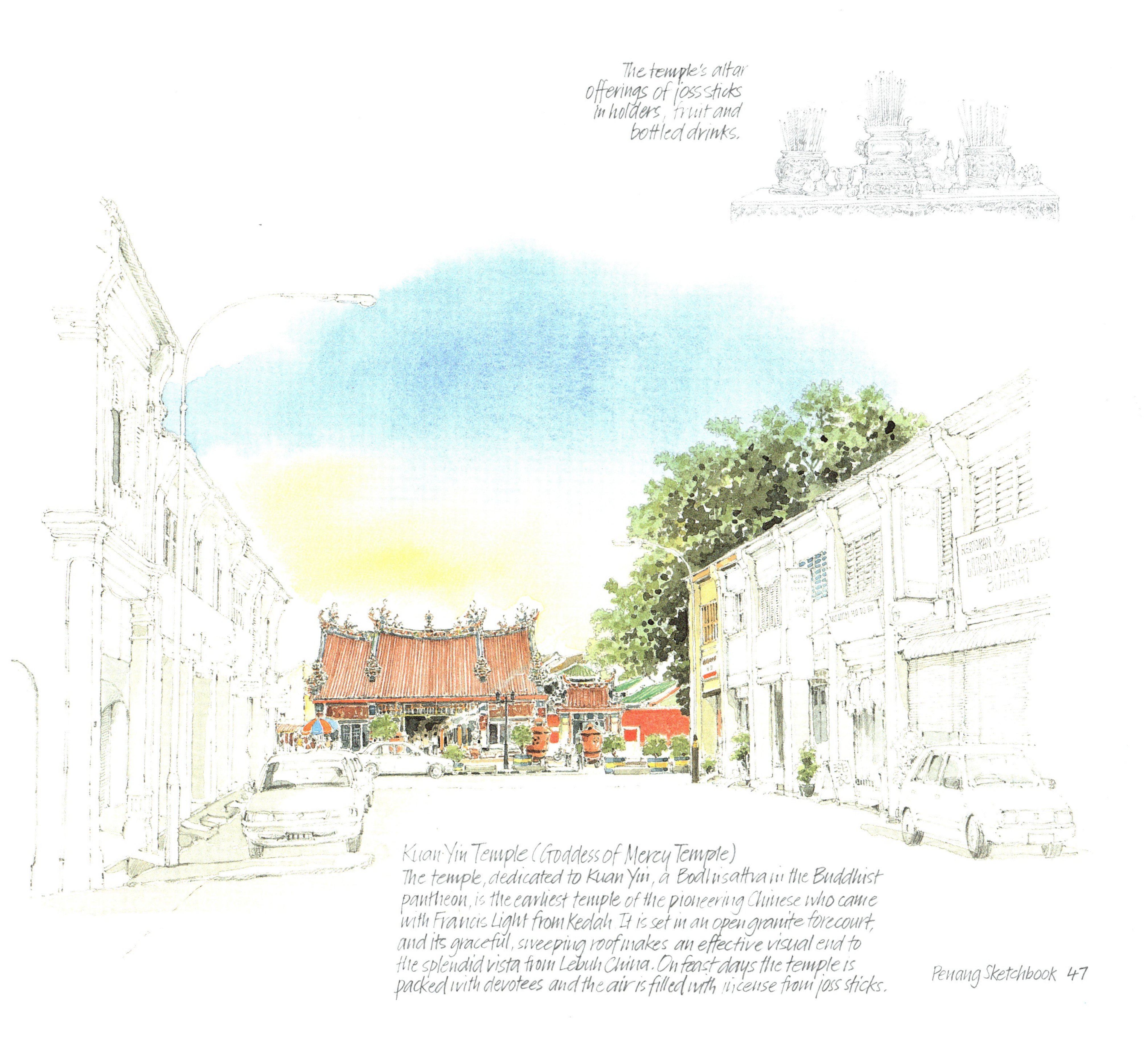

The temple's altar offerings of joss sticks in holders, fruit and bottled drinks.

Kuan Yin Temple (Goddess of Mercy Temple)
The temple, dedicated to Kuan Yin, a Bodhisattva in the Buddhist pantheon, is the earliest temple of the pioneering Chinese who came with Francis Light from Kedah. It is set in an open granite forecourt, and its graceful, sweeping roof makes an effective visual end to the splendid vista from Lebuh China. On feast days the temple is packed with devotees and the air is filled with incense from joss sticks.

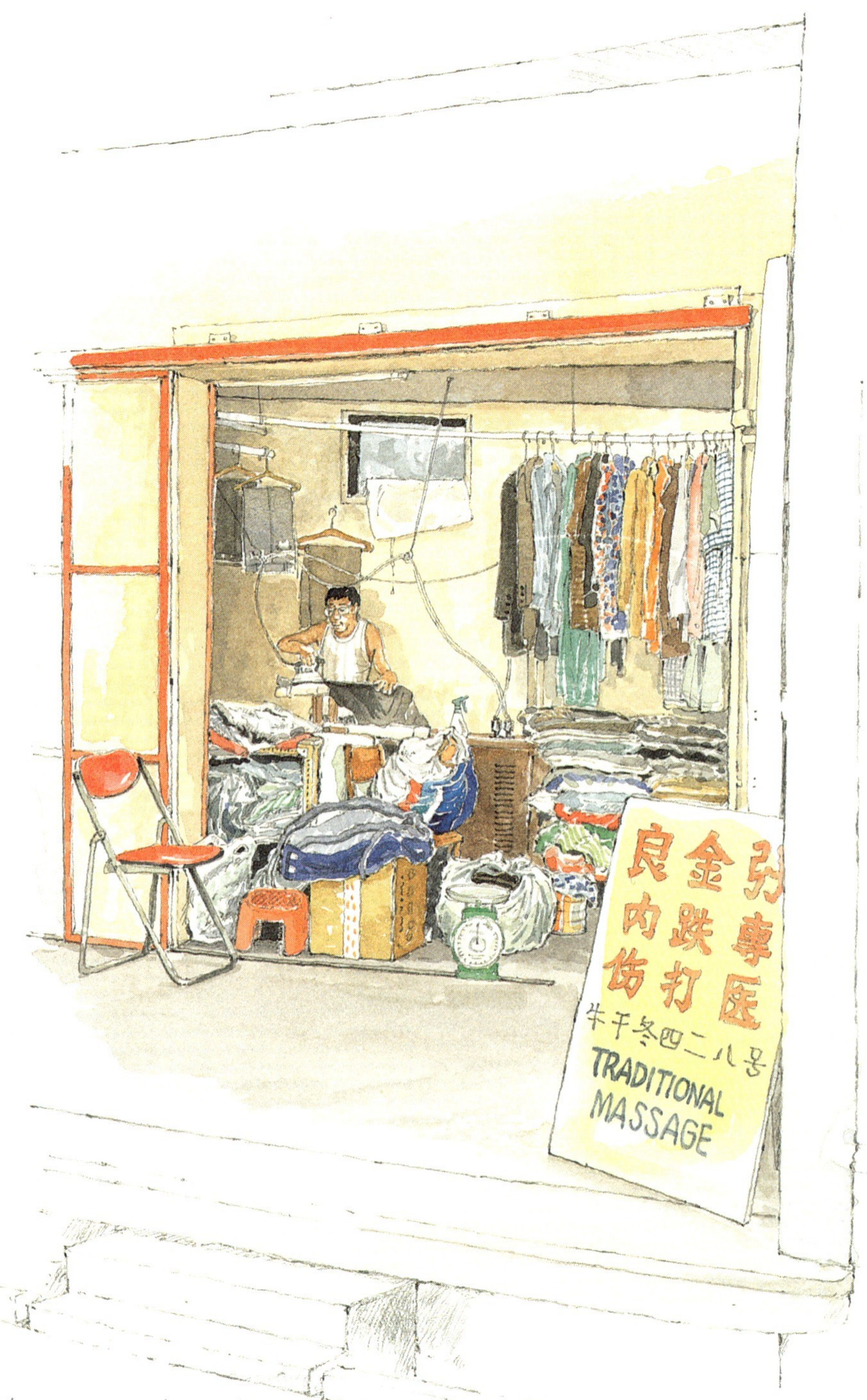

A laundry man irons clothes in a hole-in-the-wall shop in a five-foot way on Lebuh Leith, although the signboard advertises 'Traditional Massage'. Small trades like this are quickly disappearing with the effective repeal of the Rent Control Act on 1 January 2000.

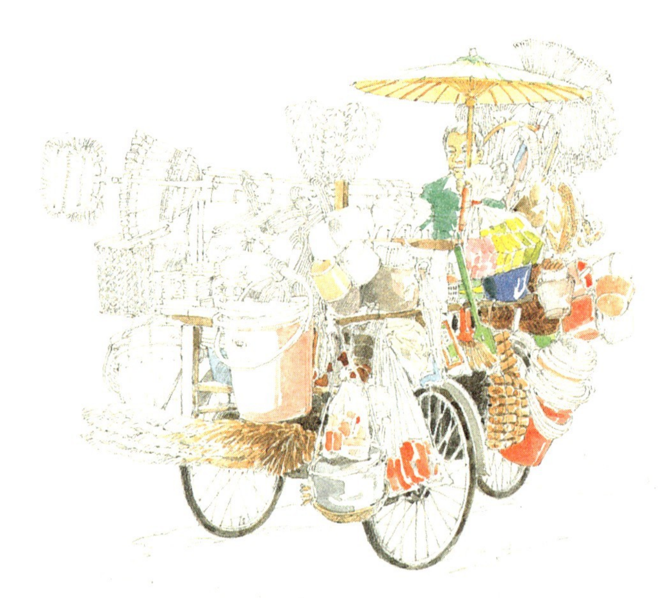

Loaded with all manner of cleaning implements, the roving broom seller rides through the streets, hawking his wares and saving his customers from making a trip to the shops or the supermarket.

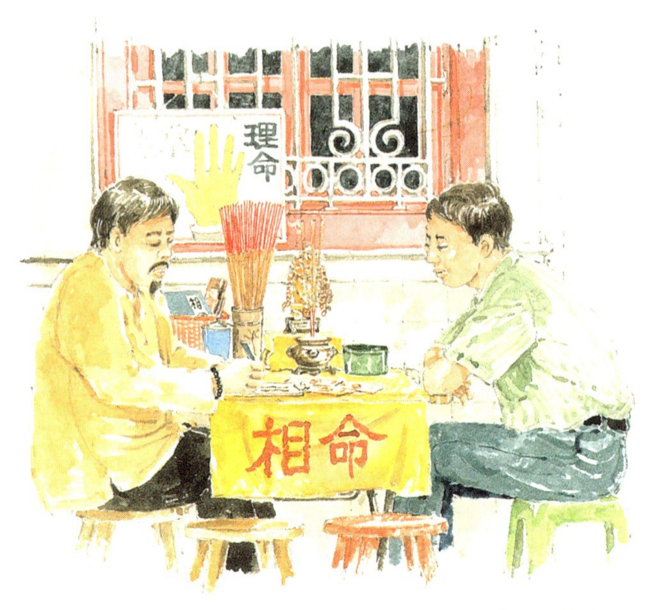

Two Chinese characters, seong meng (scrutinise life), on the tablecloth advertise this five-foot way fortune-teller's trade. The only paraphernalia he needs are a portable table, stools and a believing customer looking for answers to life.

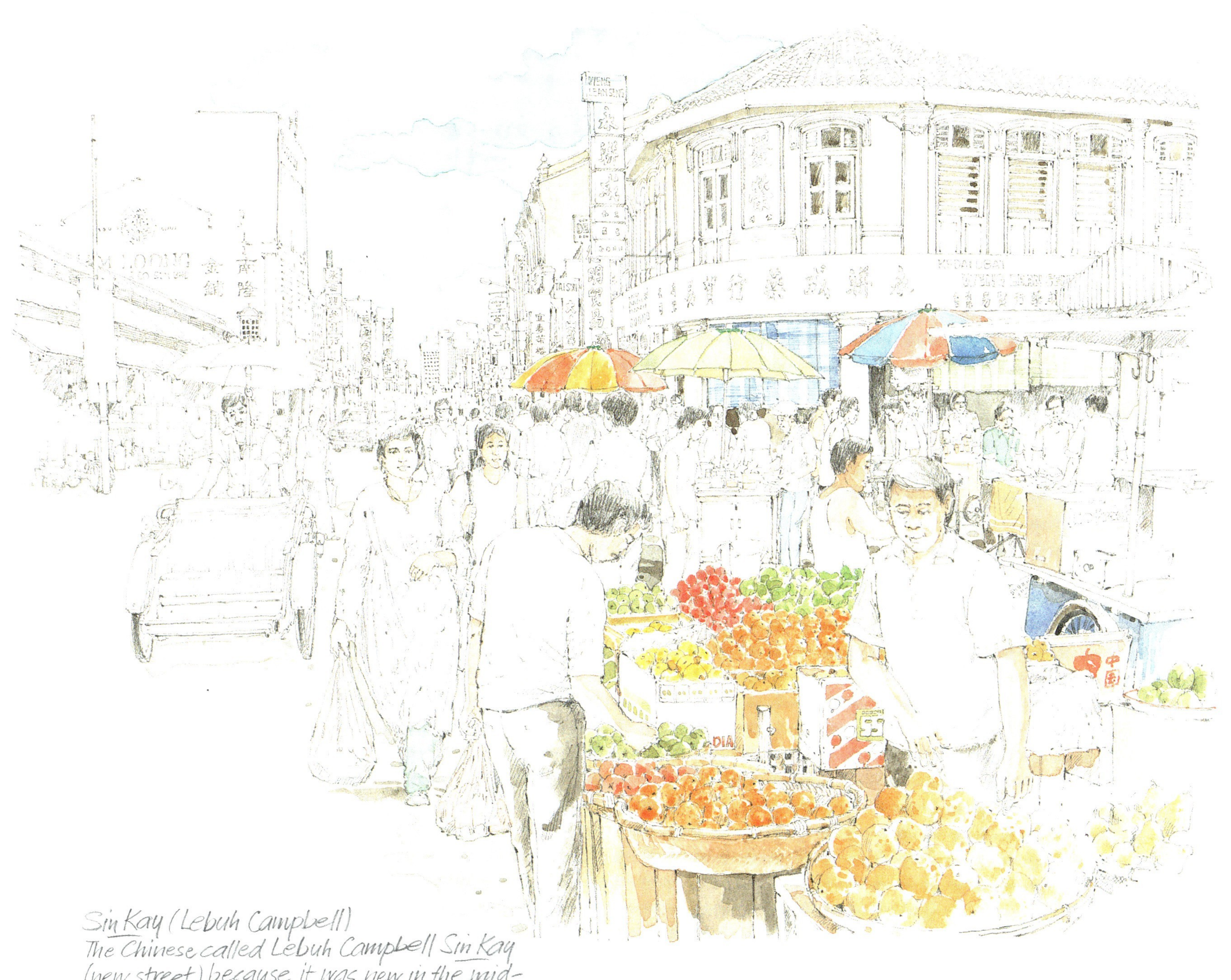

Sin Kay (Lebuh Campbell)
The Chinese called Lebuh Campbell Sin Kay (new street) because it was new in the mid-19th century, and sounded like 'fresh chicken', a pun on the young prostitutes who worked in the pleasure dens along the street.

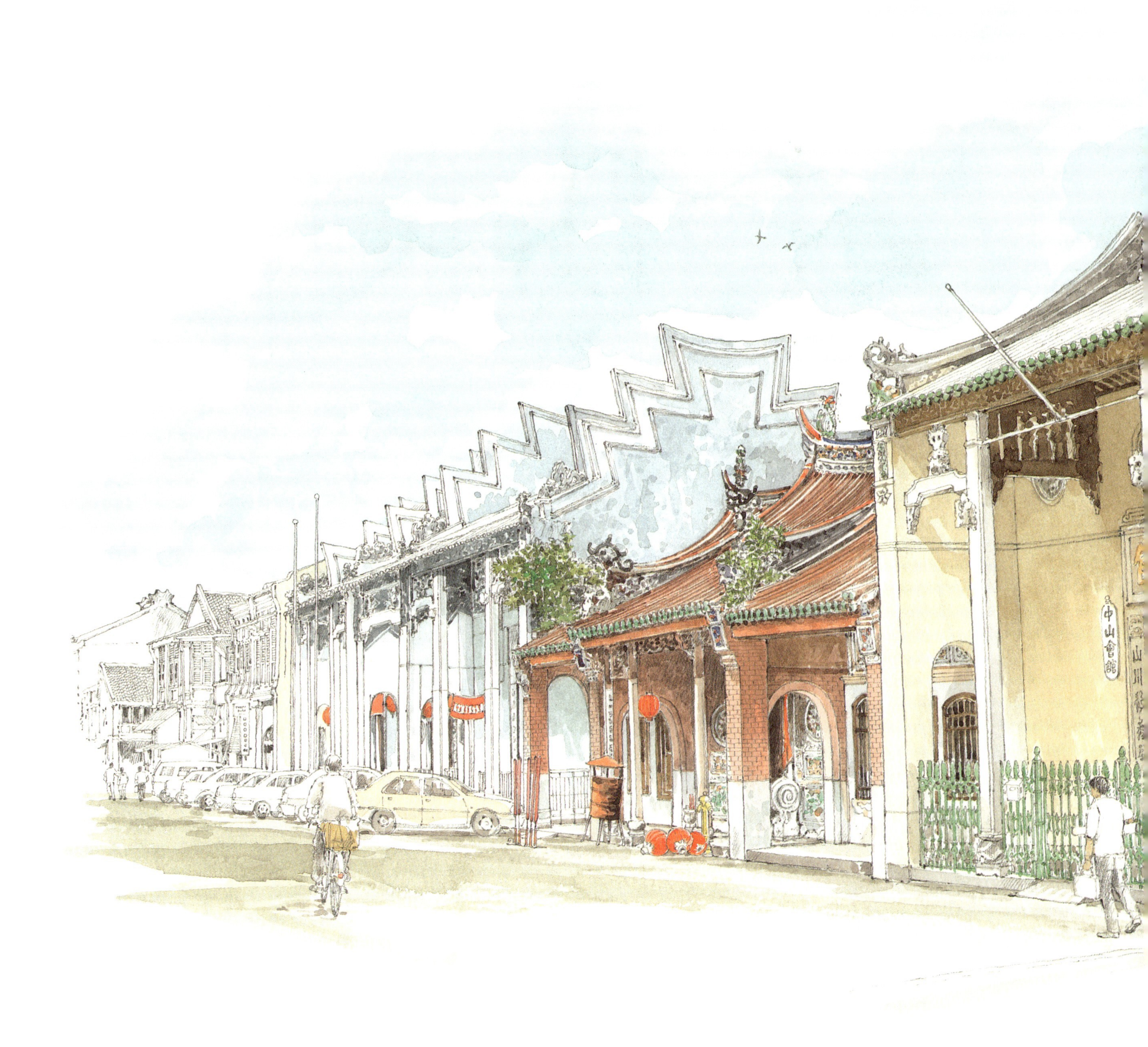
中山會館

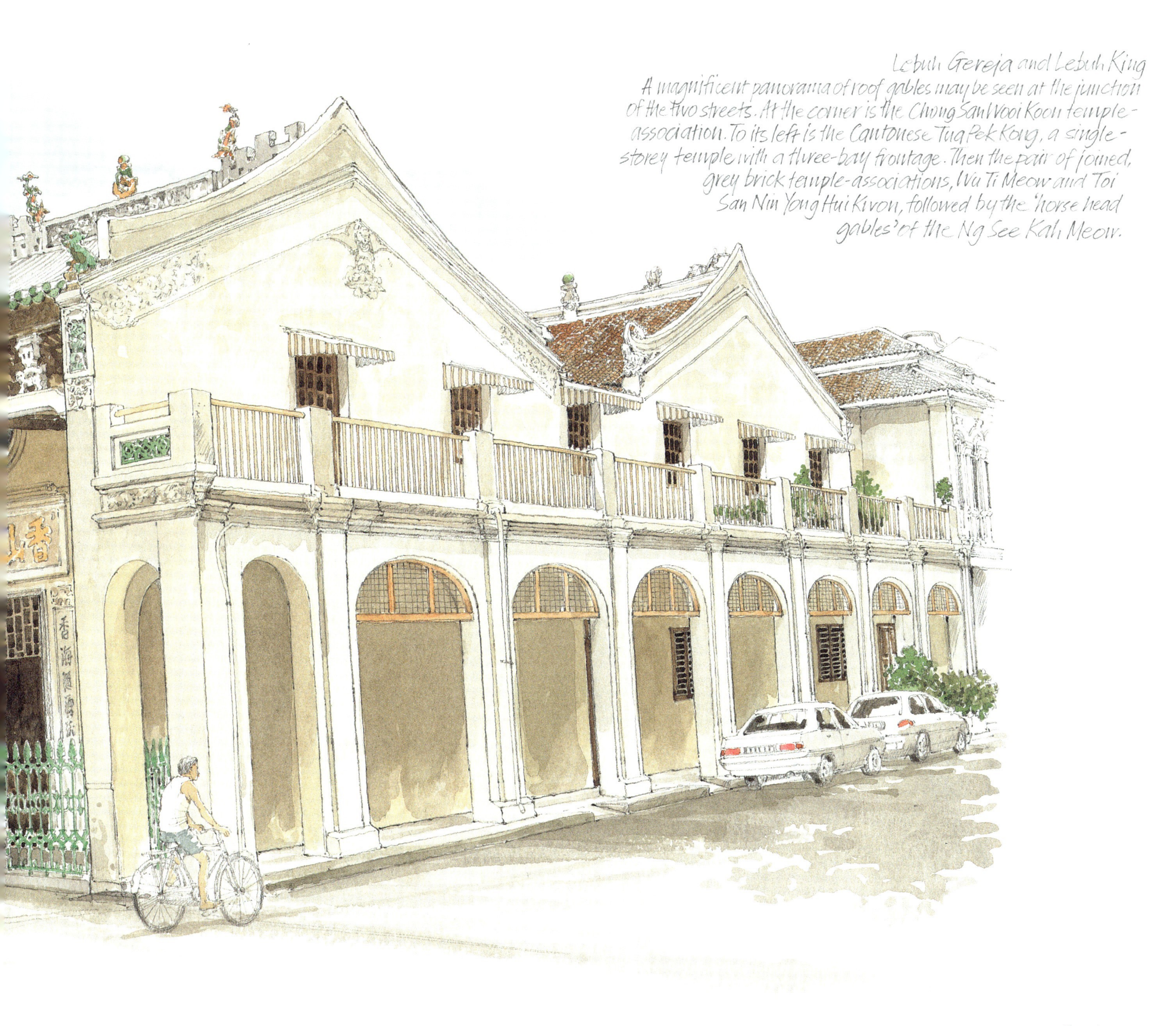

Lebuh Gereja and Lebuh King
A magnificent panorama of roof gables may be seen at the junction of the two streets. At the corner is the Chong San Wooi Koon temple-association. To its left is the Cantonese Tua Pek Kong, a single-storey temple with a three-bay frontage. Then the pair of joined, grey brick temple-associations, Wu Ti Meow and Toi San Nin Yong Hui Kwon, followed by the 'horse head gables' of the Ng See Kah Meow.

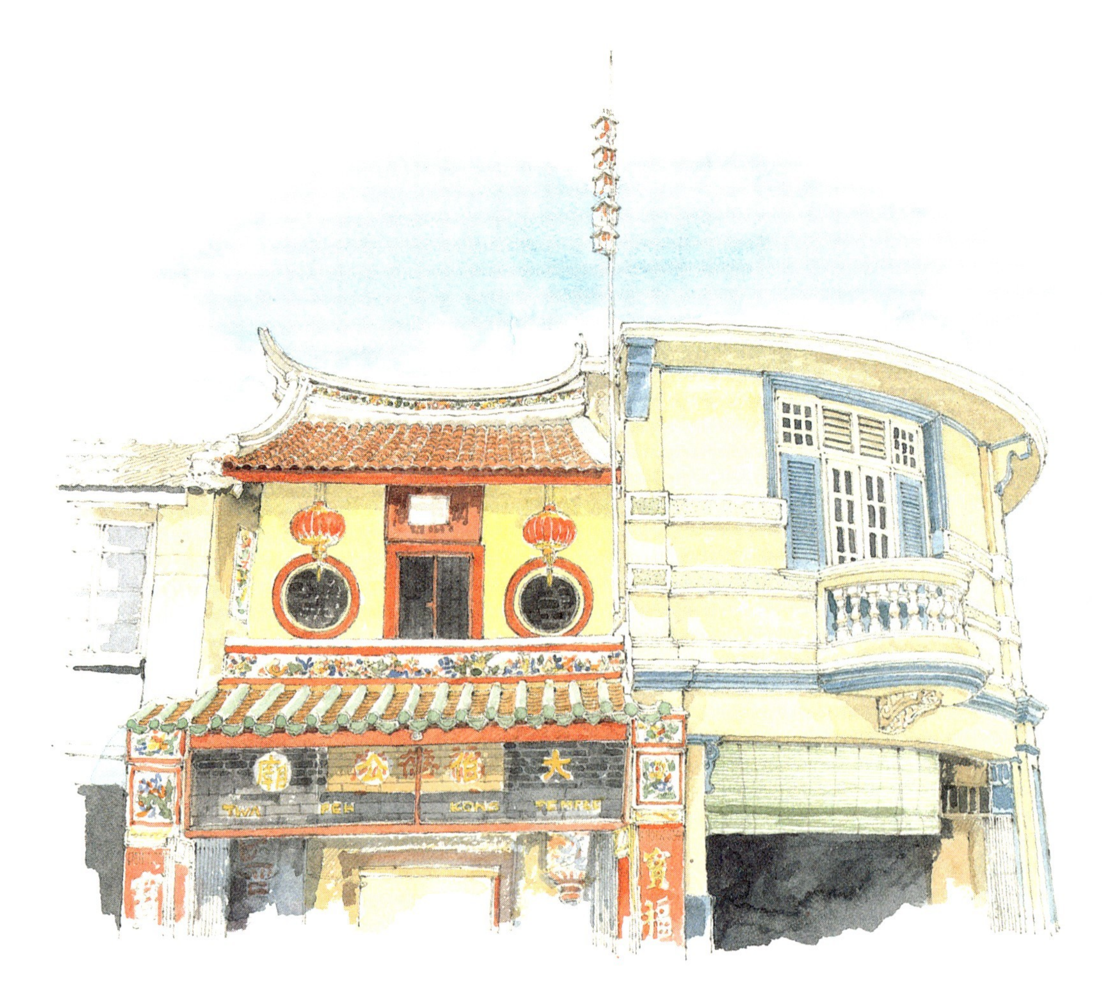

A narrow entrance at Lebuh Armenian leads to the carefully hidden Hokkien Tua Pek Kong Temple. The temple has a typical shophouse-temple frontage with a green-tiled fringe roof and a first-storey balcony. The roof ridge ends in long swallowtails. The Straits Eclectic style coffee shop that adjoins it follows the street's curve right up to its roofline, resulting in a complete contrast in style from the temple.

No. 120 Lebuh Armenian was the Penang base of Dr Sun Yat Sen, the founder of Modern China. The late 19th-century townhouse is owned by Khoo Salmah Nasution, author of Streets of George Town Penang, who restored it. The interior courtyard is sun-lit and filled with plants and period furniture.

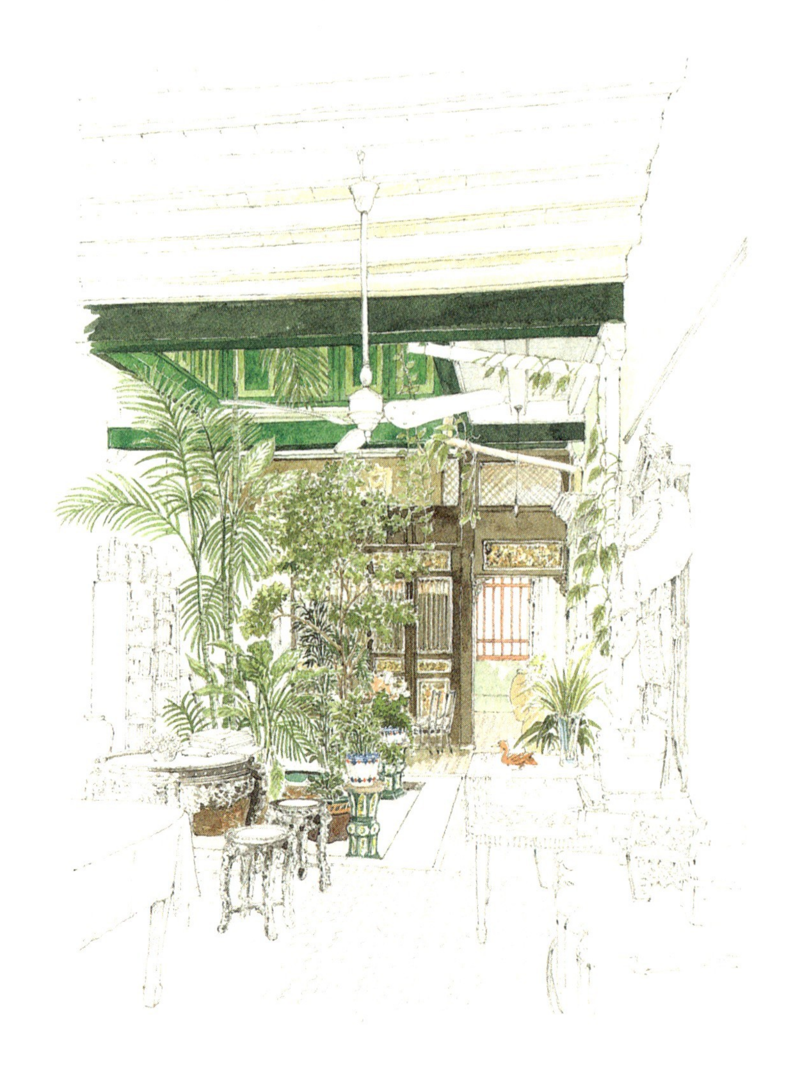

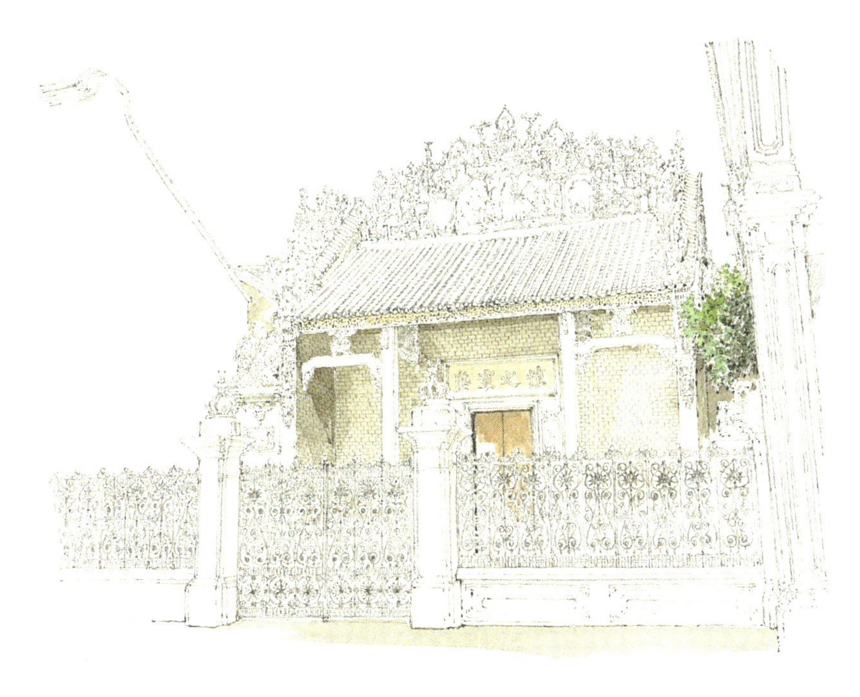

Chung Keng Kwee Temple
The temple was named after the leader of the Hakka Hai San secret society which fought in the Larut tin wars in Perak. It was built after 1893 at the site of a former Chinese school on Lebuh Gereja as an ancestral hall and family school.

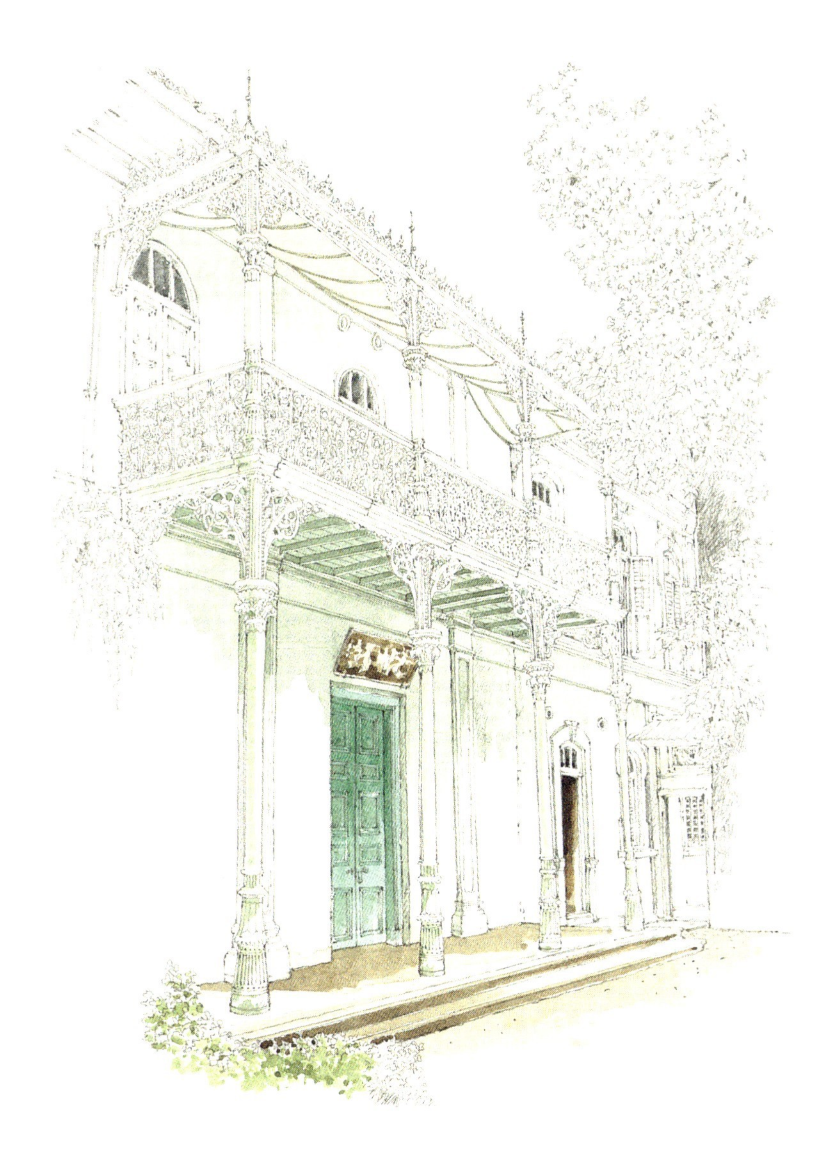

On the mansion's side, a roofed balcony supported by slender columns overlooks a courtyard kept private by railings and gateposts similar to those of the Chung Keng Kwee Temple.

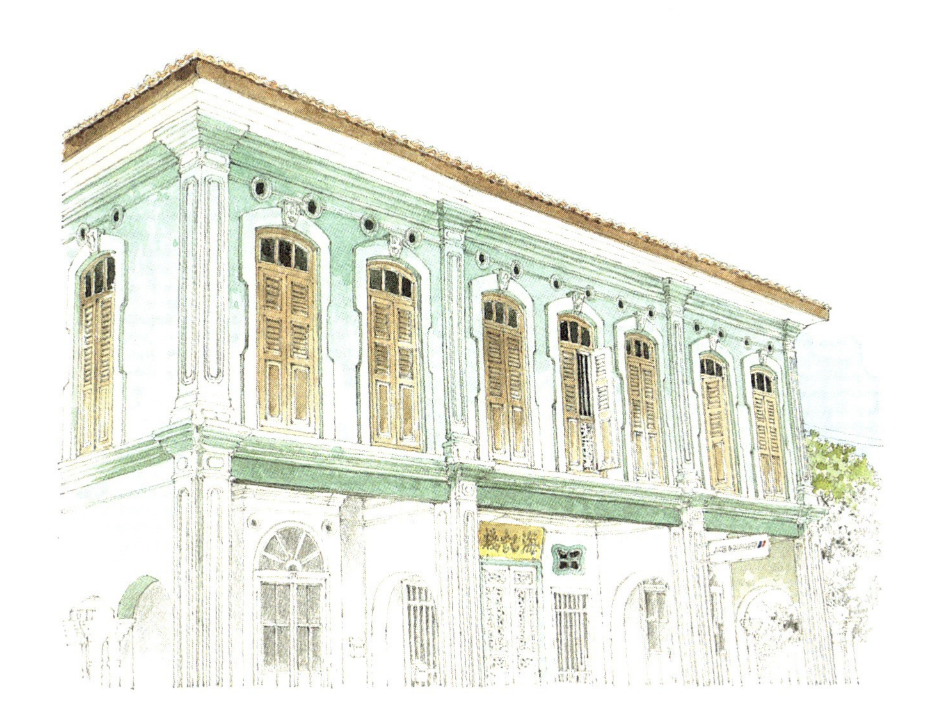

Hai Kee Chan Office-residence
The three-townhouse frontage of the Straits Eclectic style mansion consists of two-and-three-window bays and a five-foot way.

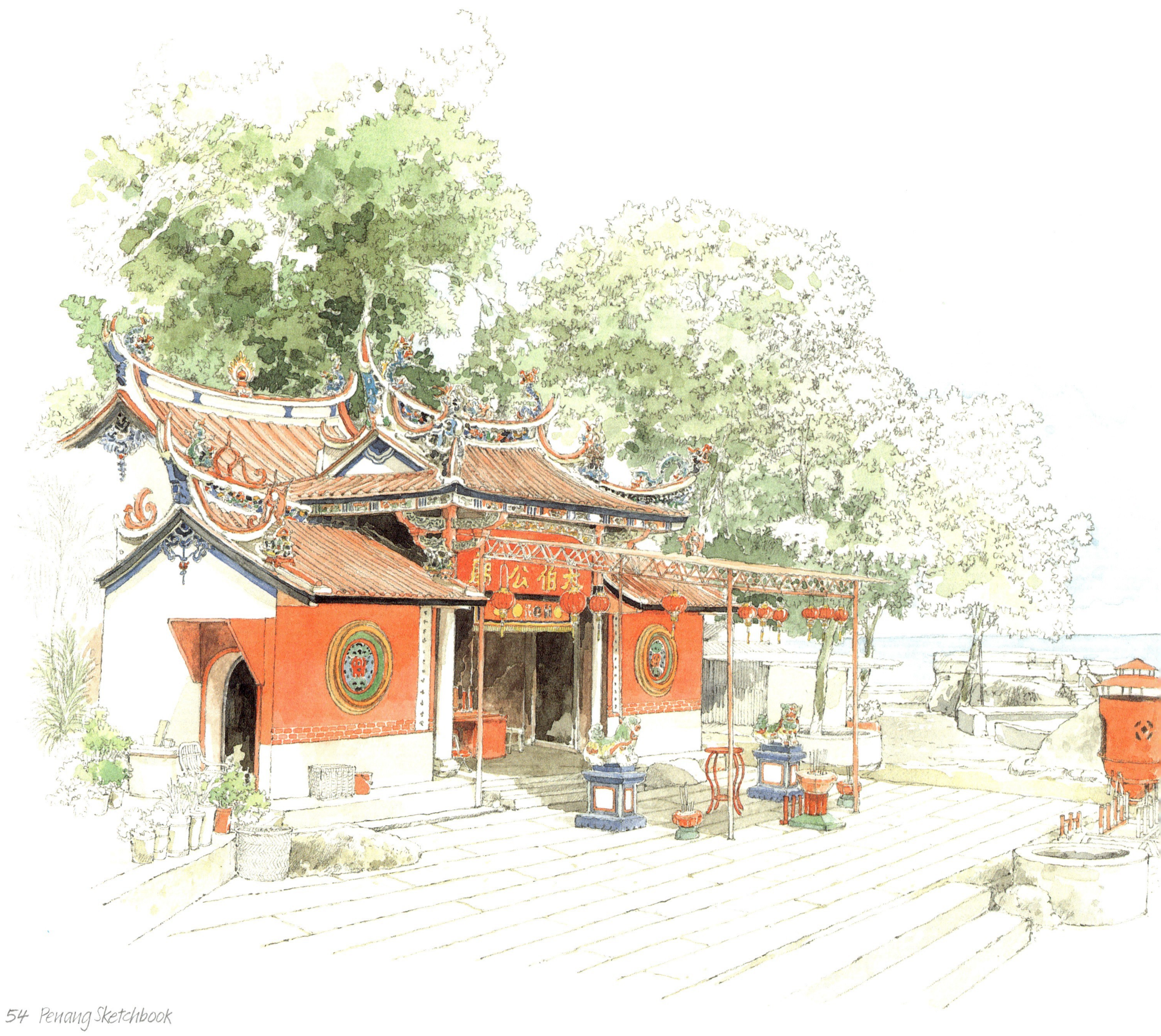

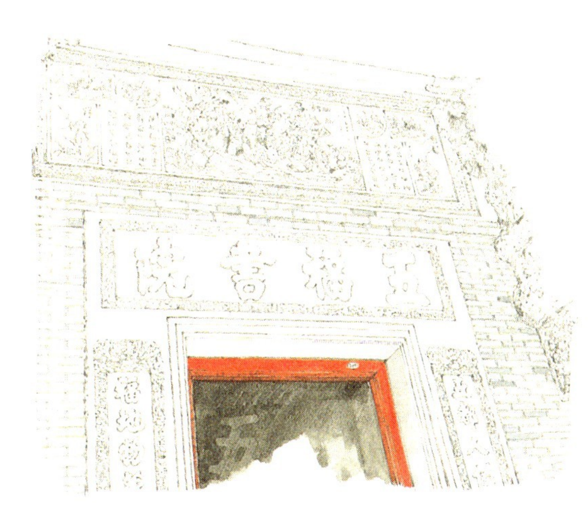

Ng Fook Tong (Five Luck Villa) is announced in gold Chinese characters over the doorway formed by three massive granite blocks. This was the early Chinese school displaced by the Chung Keng Kwee Temple (page 53).

Framed by tall granite columns, a clerk sits at his office desk beside the entrance. The raised threshold requires a person to look down on entering, a traditional device to make the visitor bow in respect to the main altar, which usually faces the door.

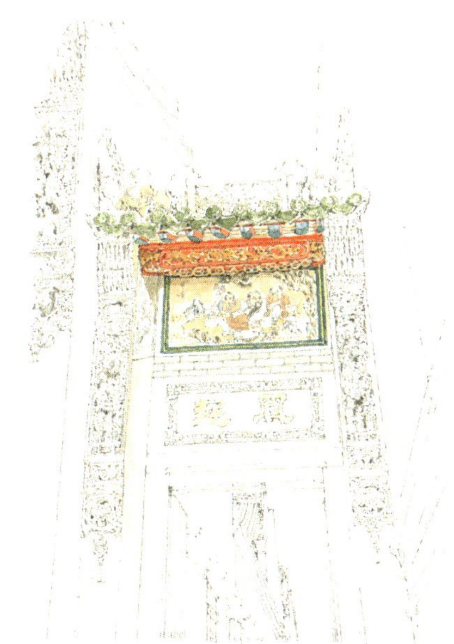

A decorated side entrance opens onto a narrow alleyway leading to private houses. A fringe roof shades a mural and side panels of finely carved figures.

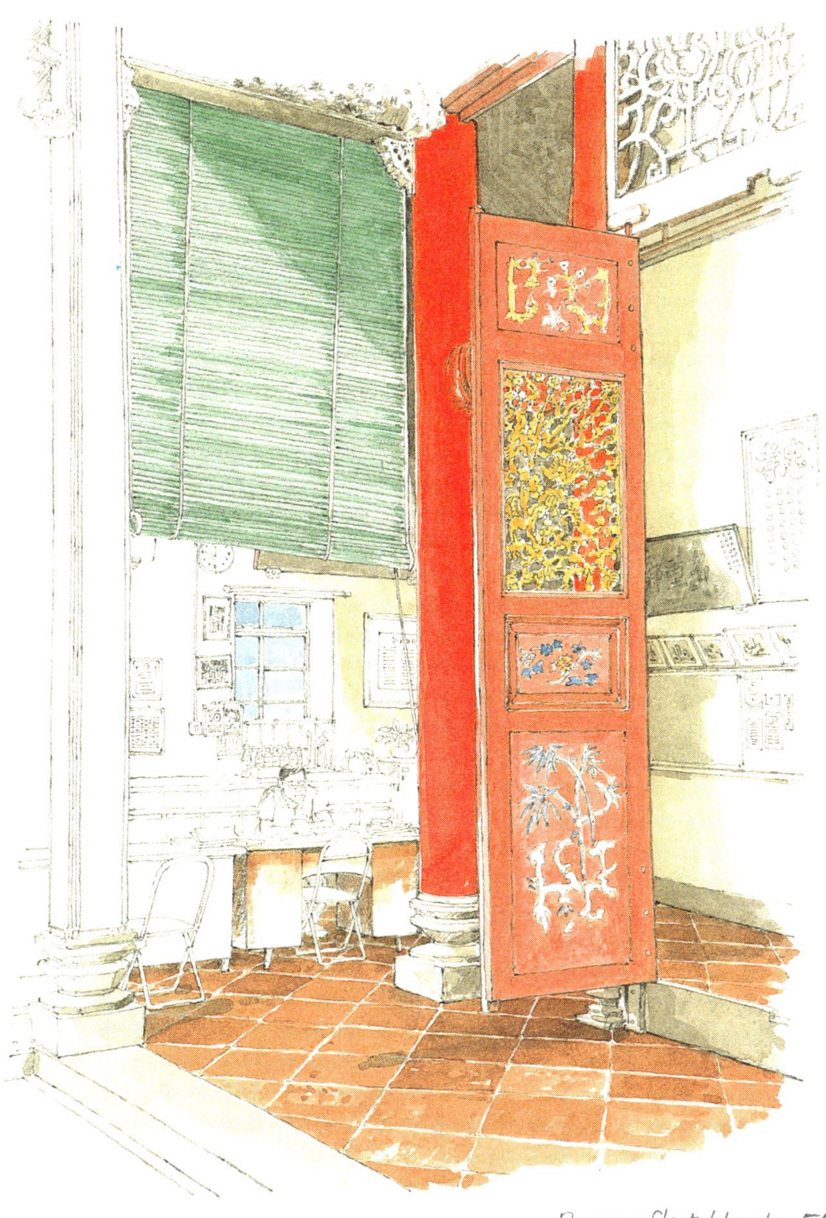

Tua Pek Kong Temple
The 'mother temple' of Penang's three Tua Pek Kong Temples at Tanjung Tokong (Cape of the Temple) is located behind a Chinese fishing village at the cape named after it. The temple's main prayer hall has a higher roof. Side halls are lower with round windows set in the middle of red painted walls.

The Sumatran Link

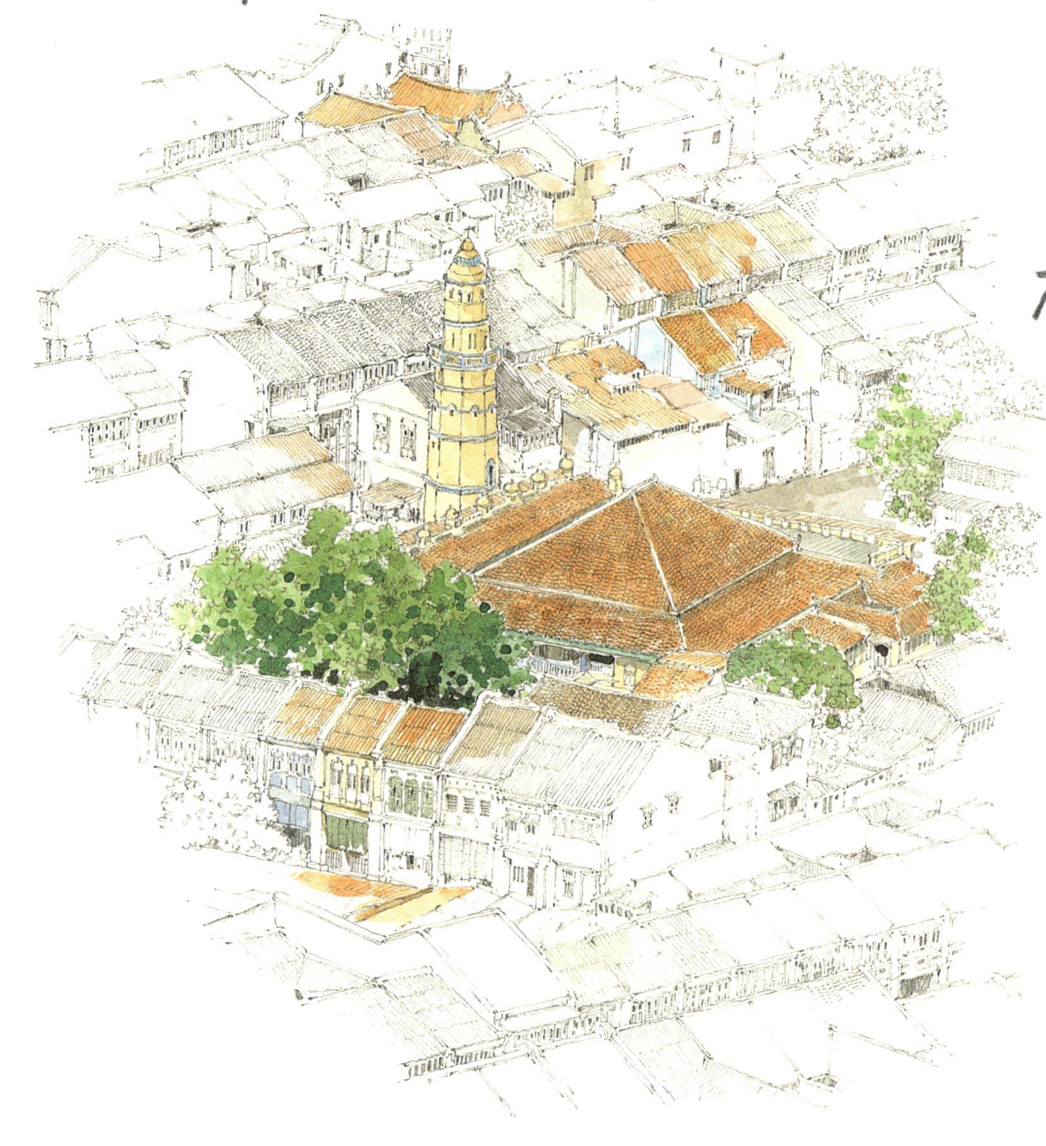

Mesjid Lebuh Acheh (Acheen Street Mosque)
An aerial view shows the 1808 mosque with its octagonal minaret and out-buildings surrounded by two-storey terrace houses in the old Malay Town of the early settlement. The entrance verandah is an early 20th-century extension.

Acheh in northern Sumatra was Penang's earliest trading partner. It was the alternative centre of the spice trade after Melaka came under Dutch rule in 1641 and also the centre of Arab and Indian Muslim trade from the 11th century.

Before the advent of the airplane, steamships known as *kapal haji* transported pilgrims to Jeddah to perform the hajj. The pilgrims gathered in Lebuh Acheh from all over the country and from Sumatra and Thailand to await their ship, and the area was busy with the hajj business—ticket agents, pilgrim hotels, shops and religious press.

The Muslim community, consisting of the Arab, Malay and Achehnese societies, lived in the urban kampong (Malay village) south of George Town, around the Mesjid Lebuh Acheh. The Indo-Malay, half-timber, half-brick bungalows were their earliest urban dwellings.

Tengku Syed Hussain Al-Aidid, an Arab trader and a member of the Achehnese royal house, was a prominent figure in the community. He moved to Penang in 1792, and founded the Mesjid Lebuh Acheh. Gudang Acheh, his godown-cum-office on the waterfront, was a prominent landmark. He was reputed to be the richest man on the island: his brick house was valued at 6,000 Spanish dollars in 1793.

The Basheer clan, another Arab family, arrived in Penang from Acheh around the same time. Generations of Islamic teachers and missionaries came from this family.

Syed Mohamed Alatas was another influential figure. He was an Achehnese-Arab pepper trader and leader of the Bendera Merah (Red Flag) secret society and ally of the Hokkien Khian Teik.

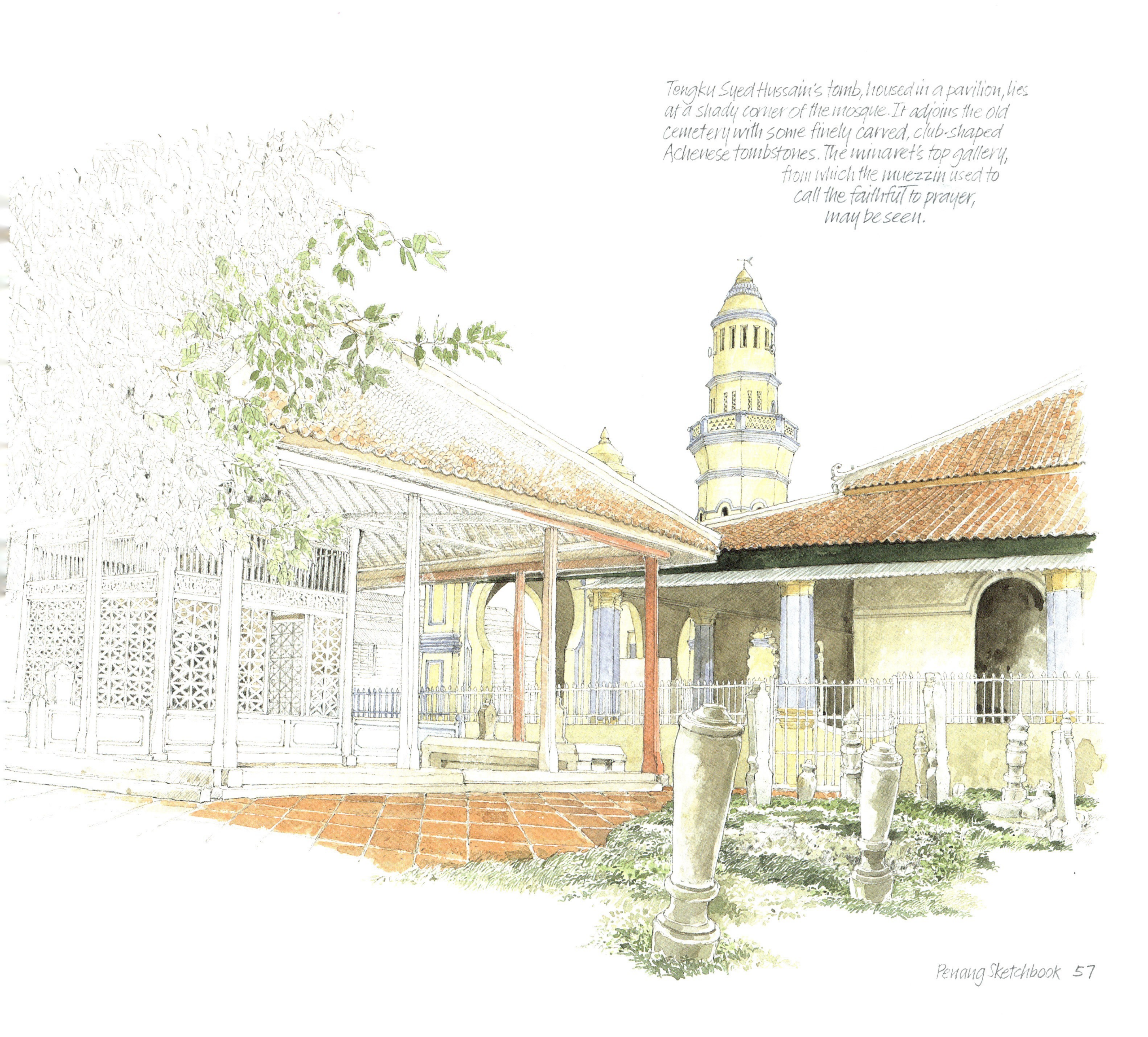

Tengku Syed Hussain's tomb, housed in a pavilion, lies at a shady corner of the mosque. It adjoins the old cemetery with some finely carved, club-shaped Achenese tombstones. The minaret's top gallery, from which the muezzin used to call the faithful to prayer, may be seen.

Gudang Acheh (Achehnese Godown)
This was a former gaol turned into Tengku Syed Hussain's office and spice godown. Its four storeys, still known to Malays as Rumah Tinggi (Tall House), made it Penang's first high-rise building. It was a prominent landmark for spice traders approaching the Gat Lebuh Acheh on the old waterfront. The shopfront is a later addition.

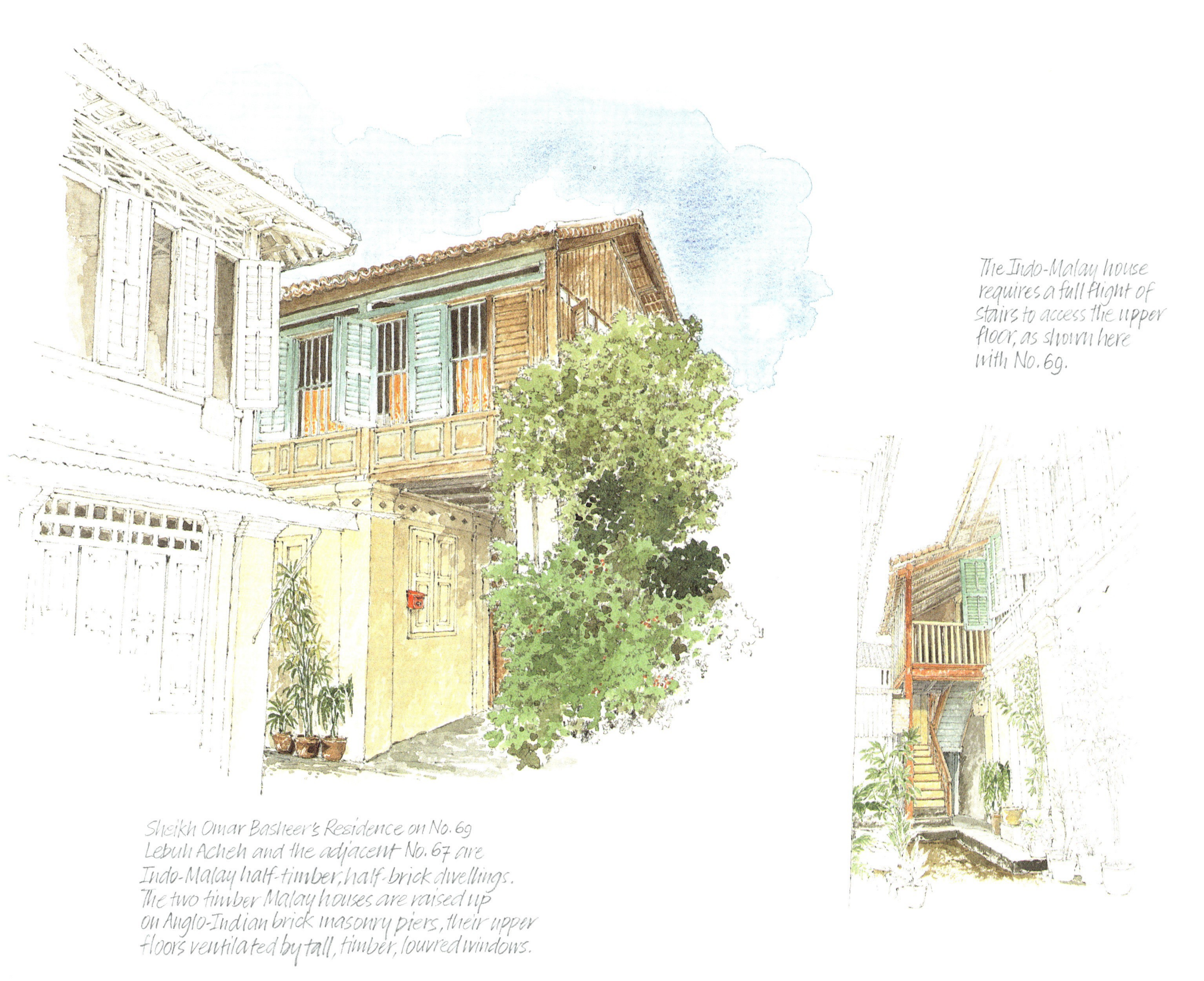

The Indo-Malay house requires a full flight of stairs to access the upper floor, as shown here with No. 69.

Sheikh Omar Basheer's Residence on No. 69 Lebuh Acheh and the adjacent No. 67 are Indo-Malay half-timber, half-brick dwellings. The two timber Malay houses are raised up on Anglo-Indian brick masonry piers, their upper floors ventilated by tall, timber, louvred windows.

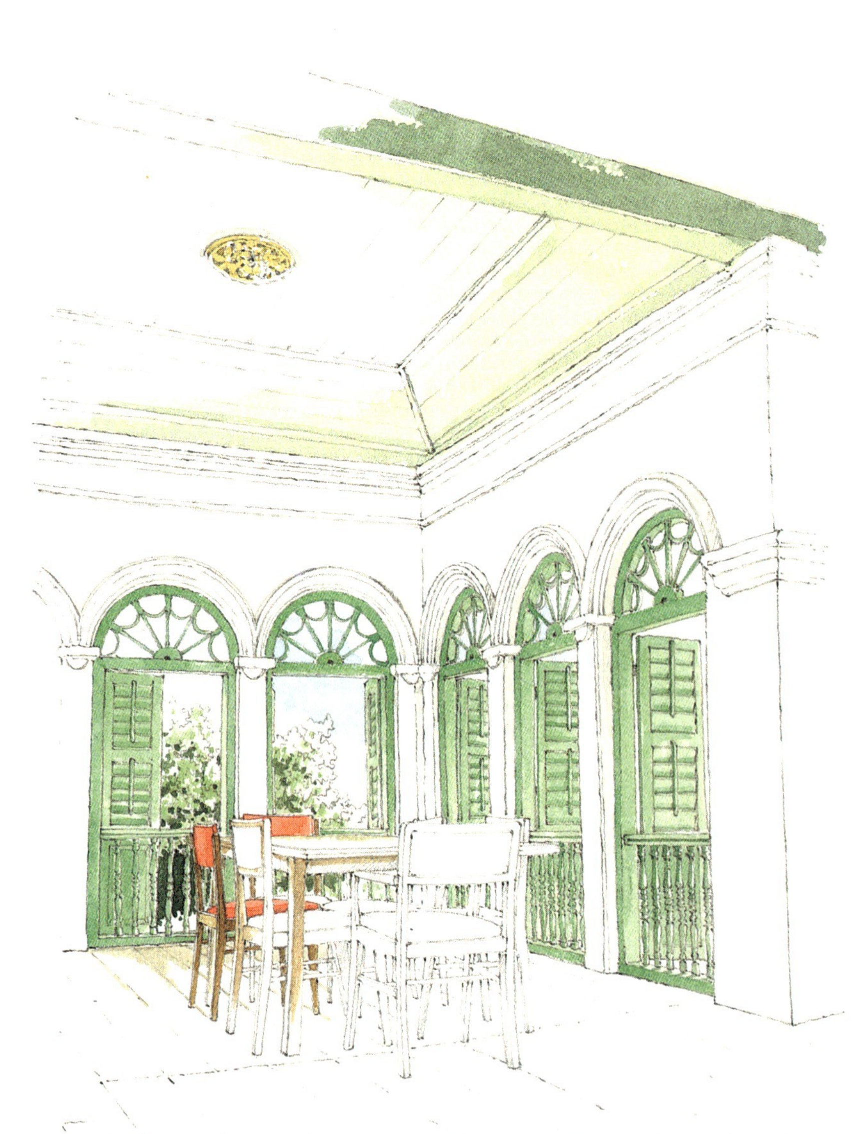

Syed Alatas Mansion's upper hall is well lit and ventilated on three sides by full-height windows. The coved timber ceiling rises above the cornices, and a decorative ceiling rose ventilates the roof space. The mansion has been restored to its original colours of pale indigo, yellow ochre and deep green.

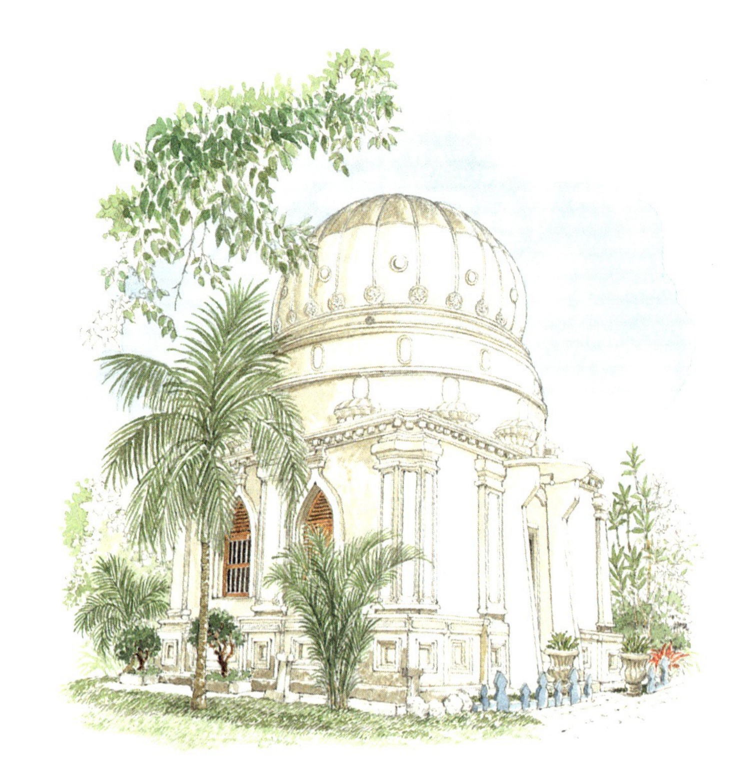

Sheikh Omar Basheer Mausoleum
After Sheikh Omar, teacher and Sufi mystic, died in 1881, his son Zachariah, built this mausoleum on Ayer Itam with the help of labourers from India.

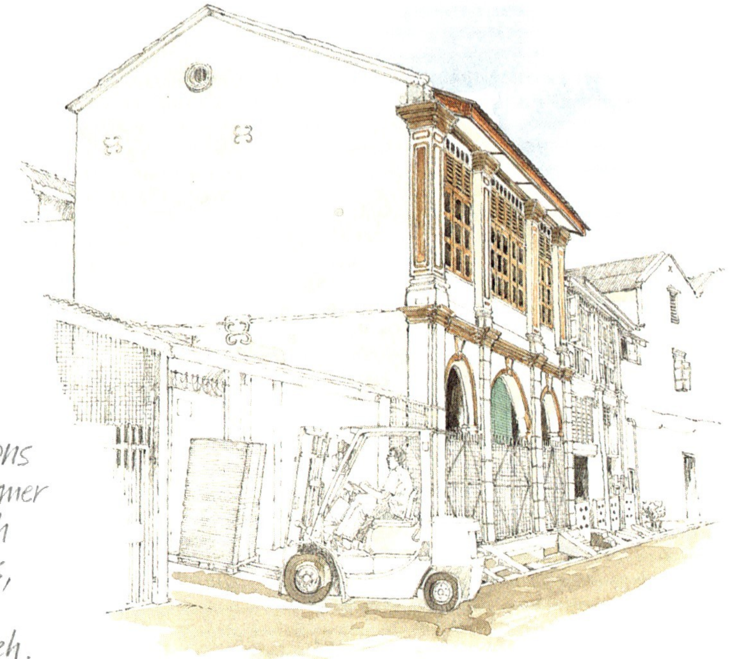

Sheikh Zachariah Basheer & Sons
No. 6 Lorong Lumut housed the former trading company of 'SR Zachariah Basheer & Sons, Commission Agents, Penang'. The premise had two connecting godowns off Lebuh Acheh.

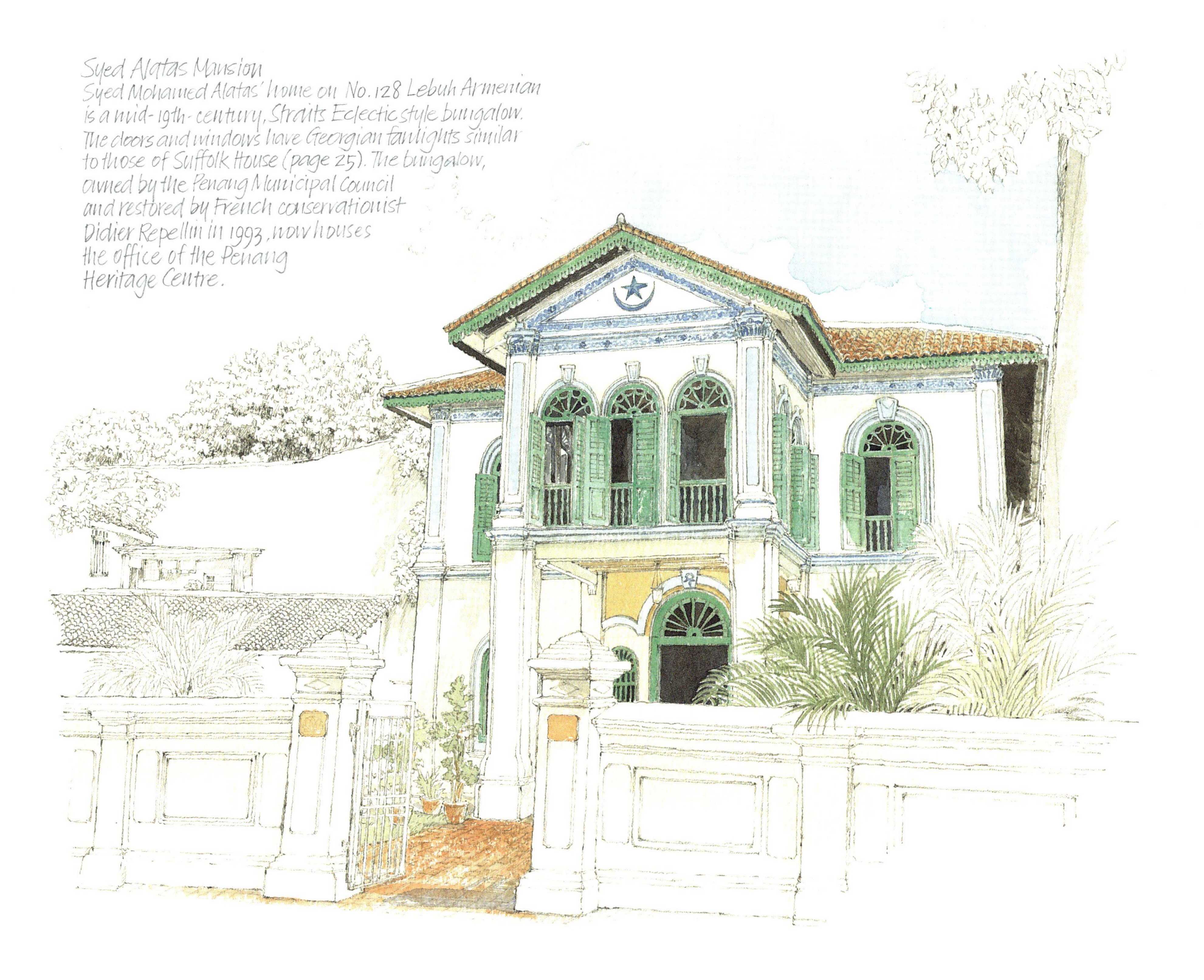

Syed Alatas Mansion
Syed Mohamed Alatas' home on No. 128 Lebuh Armenian is a mid-19th-century, Straits Eclectic style bungalow. The doors and windows have Georgian fanlights similar to those of Suffolk House (page 25). The bungalow, owned by the Penang Municipal Council and restored by French conservationist Didier Repellin in 1993, now houses the office of the Penang Heritage Centre.

The Straits Eclectic Style

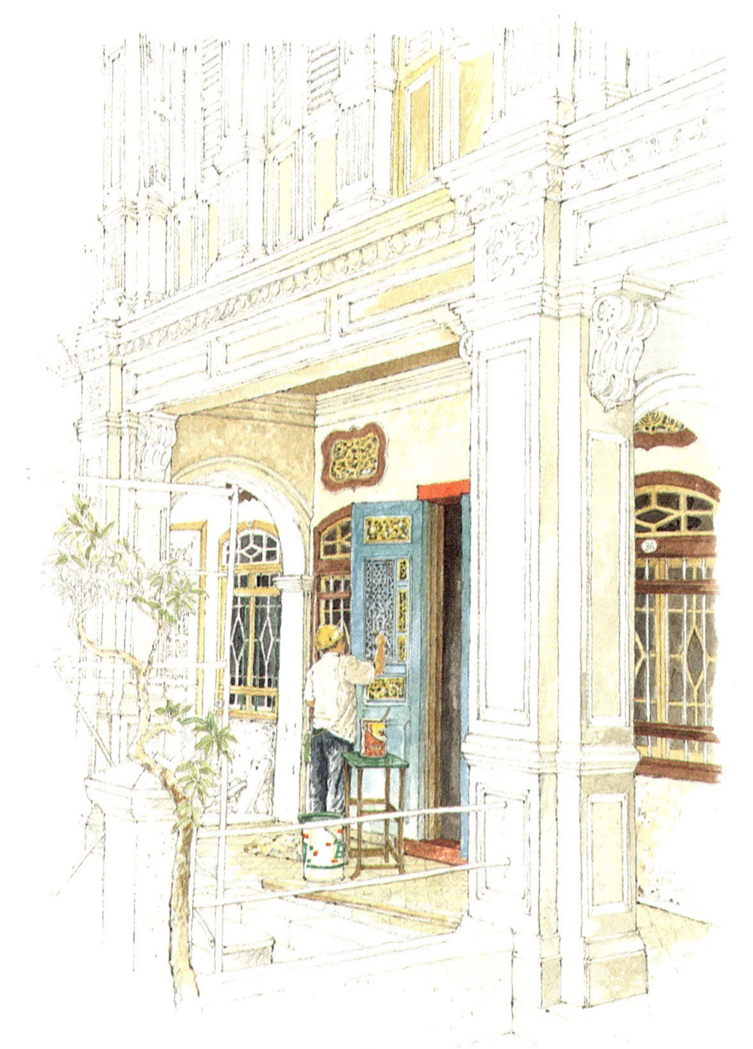

Media House
A painter is touching up the ornately carved front door of No. 36 Jalan Nagore, a townhouse in Sino-Palladian-Malay or Straits Eclectic style. The side windows have Art Deco bars, and above them are intricately carved, shaped ventilators. The house frontage is set behind a forecourt.

Penang was the point at which, socially and architecturally, the Anglo-Indian empire encountered the Chinese civilisation in the Malay world (Khoo, page 18). Light's 'liberal haven' was more than a free trading port: the traders came not only to trade but also to stay, put down roots and build for the future. The first settlers kept to traditional building practices from the lands of their origin while adapting to the wet tropical climate and using available local materials.

As people traded and lived together in Light's compact grid of streets, they learnt and borrowed from one another. Over time their interaction was reflected in the mixed styles of their buildings: the Malay house on timber posts raised on brick pillars became the Anglo-Indian bungalow; Chinese roof tiles replaced *attap* roofs to prevent fires; and the 'jack-roof' married Chinese and Malay building traditions. The high Anglo-Indian godowns or warehouses introduced a new word and a new scale. Southern Indian skill and masonry covered with *chunam* led to the rich plaster details and decorations of Penang's 19th-century buildings. The southern Chinese two-storey shophouses in rows defined the urban core of Penang's inner city. Their subsequent development and that of the townhouse variant reflect the changing architectural styles from the mid-19th century to the present time. The melding of the different strands of the East and the West using both ethnic and classical idioms gave birth to the hybrid Straits Eclectic style.

The style was favoured by the ethnically mixed communities, in particular the Peranakans. Their Straits Eclectic style bungalows and villas are an important part of Penang's rich legacy.

Lebuh Campbell Market
Two long sheds meet at the junction of Lebuh Campbell and Lebuh Carnarvon forming the entrance to the municipal wet market on the old burial ground of the Kapitan Kling Mosque (pages 39–41).

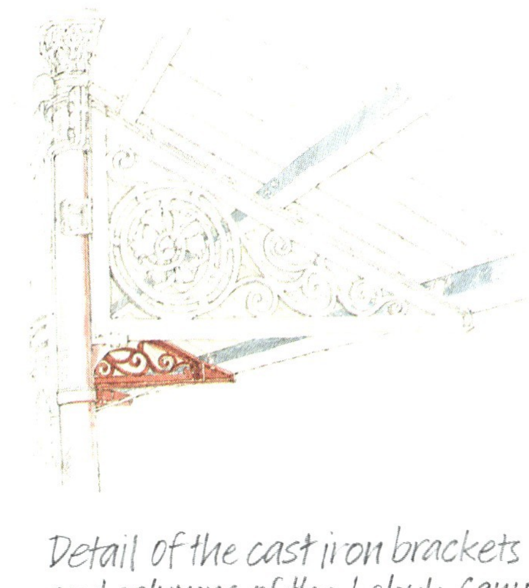

Detail of the cast iron brackets and columns of the Lebuh Campbell Market. The triangular brackets supporting the roof eaves are decorated with twining vines and flowers which add bracing strength to the brackets.

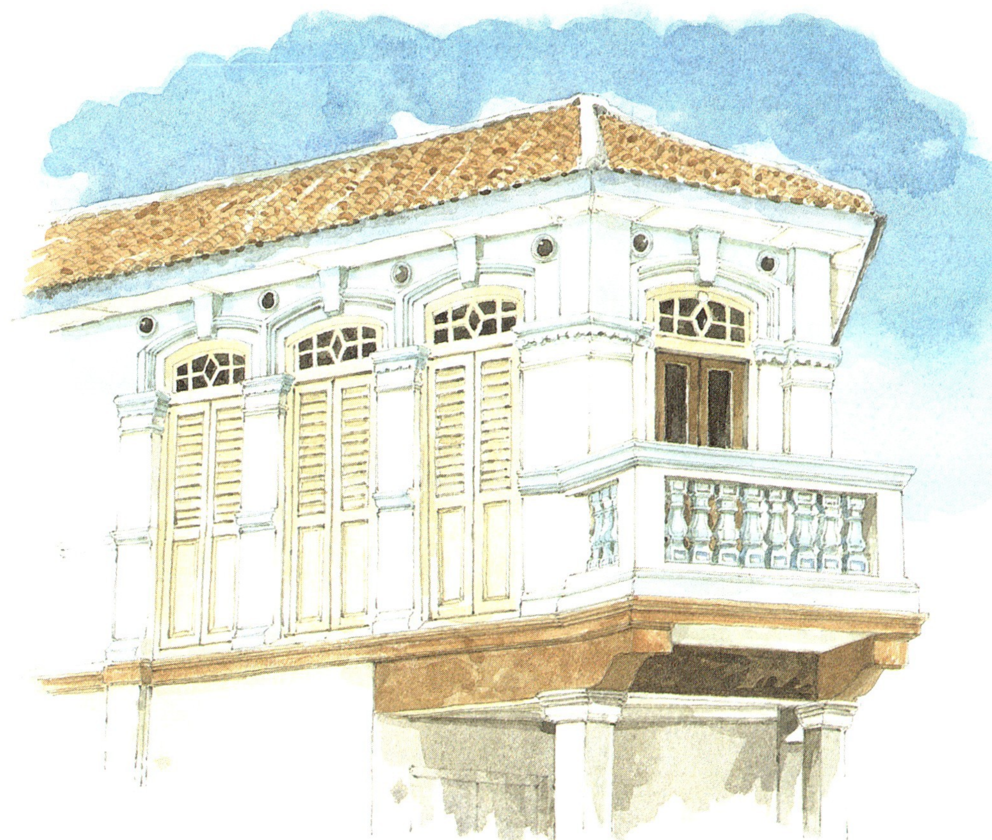

A pair of brackets on columns supports the corner balcony of a shophouse facing the junction of Lebuh Pantai and Gat Lebuh Gereja. The French windows are framed between Tuscan pilasters and have segmental fanlights. Circular vents below the roof eaves help ventilation.

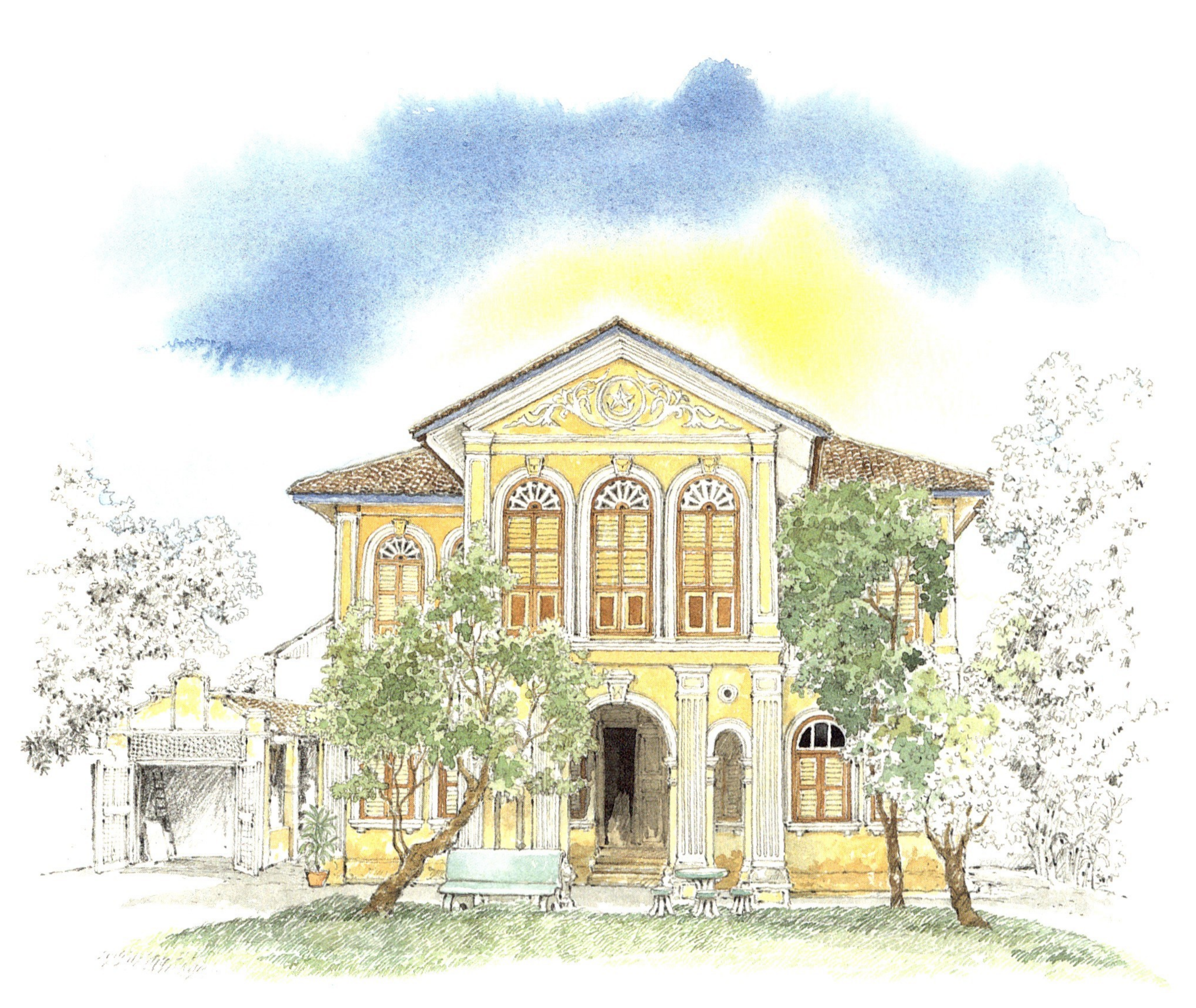

Teh Bunga's House
No. 138 Lorong Hutton is the home of third-generation Indian Muslims, and is one of the houses on the road that is also named 'Muslim Millionaires' Row'. It is a fine example of a Straits Eclectic style bungalow, and is in its original ochre colour.

Lorong Bangkok Terrace Houses
The neatly paired frontages of the terrace houses have private verandahs raised a few steps from the road. The balconies on the upper floors have largely been filled in with glass, louvred windows. Period striped chick are used on both levels for additional shading. Potted plants add to the quiet charm of the street.

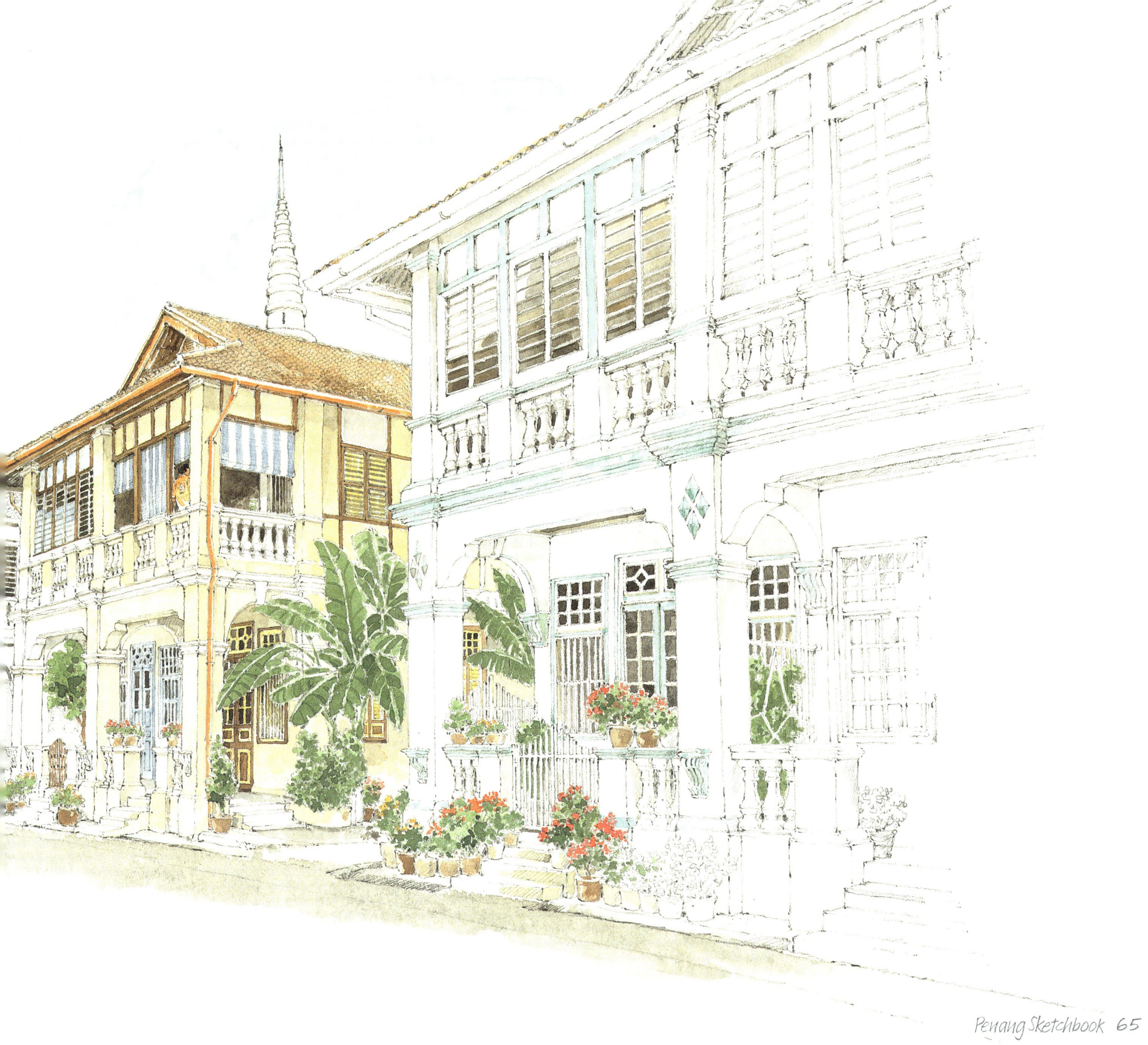

Shih Chung School
Built by Cheah Tek Soon in the 1880s, Penang's first five-storey mansion, No. 11 Jalan Sultan Ahmad Shah, was known as the Chinese Residency. Old photographs show it as a layered landmark in a distinctive mix of Anglo-Chinese style. It was turned into a hotel known as 'Raffles-By-The-Sea' after its famous Singapore namesake before becoming a school.

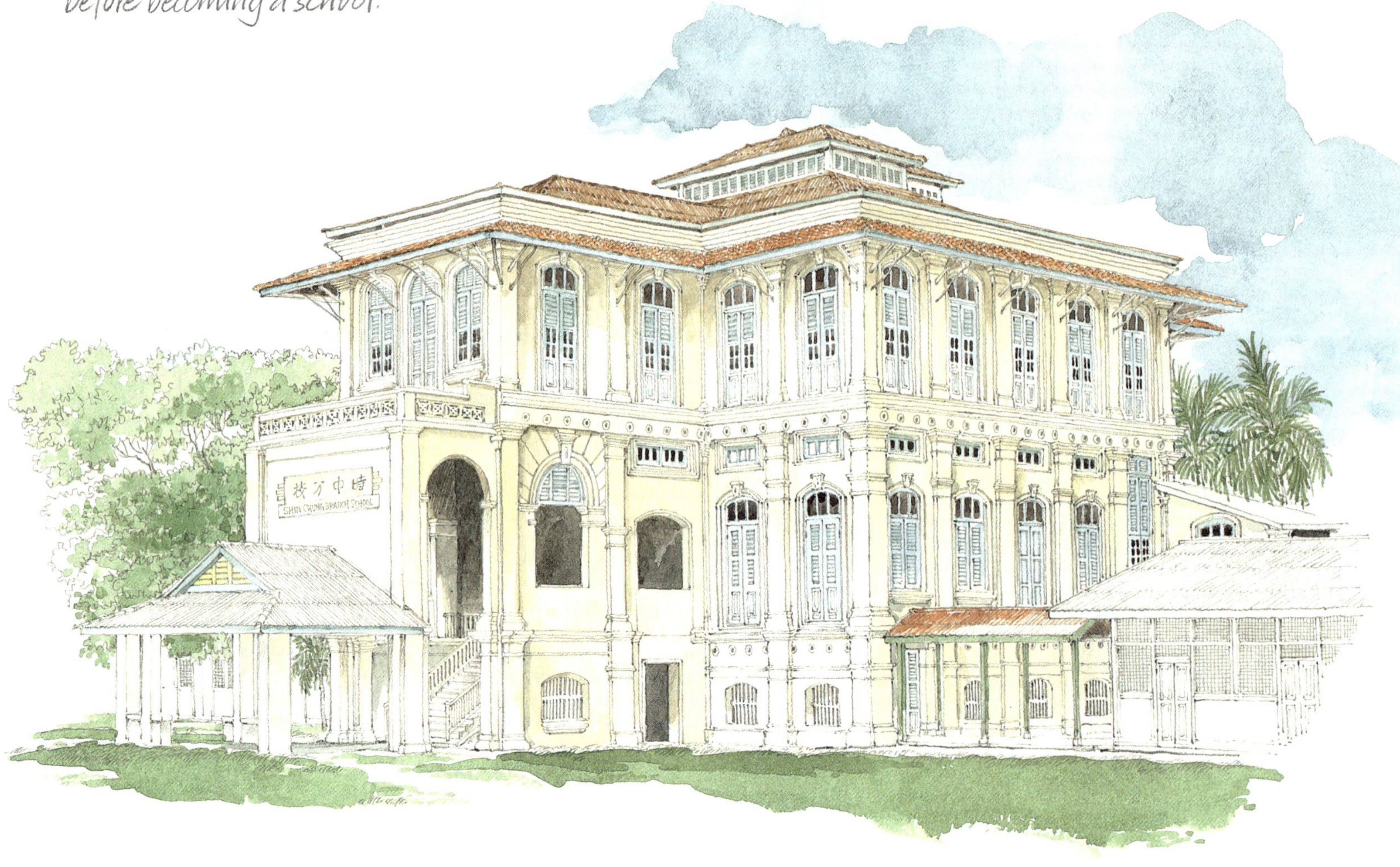

Cathay Hotel

The hotel on No. 15 Lebuh Leith is housed in a converted Straits Eclectic style mansion. The fully paved forecourt has covered up the original circular driveway and lawn. The twin hipped roofs joined by side wings enclose an internal courtyard. The roofs of Cheong Fatt Tze Mansion (pages 72-3) are in the foreground.

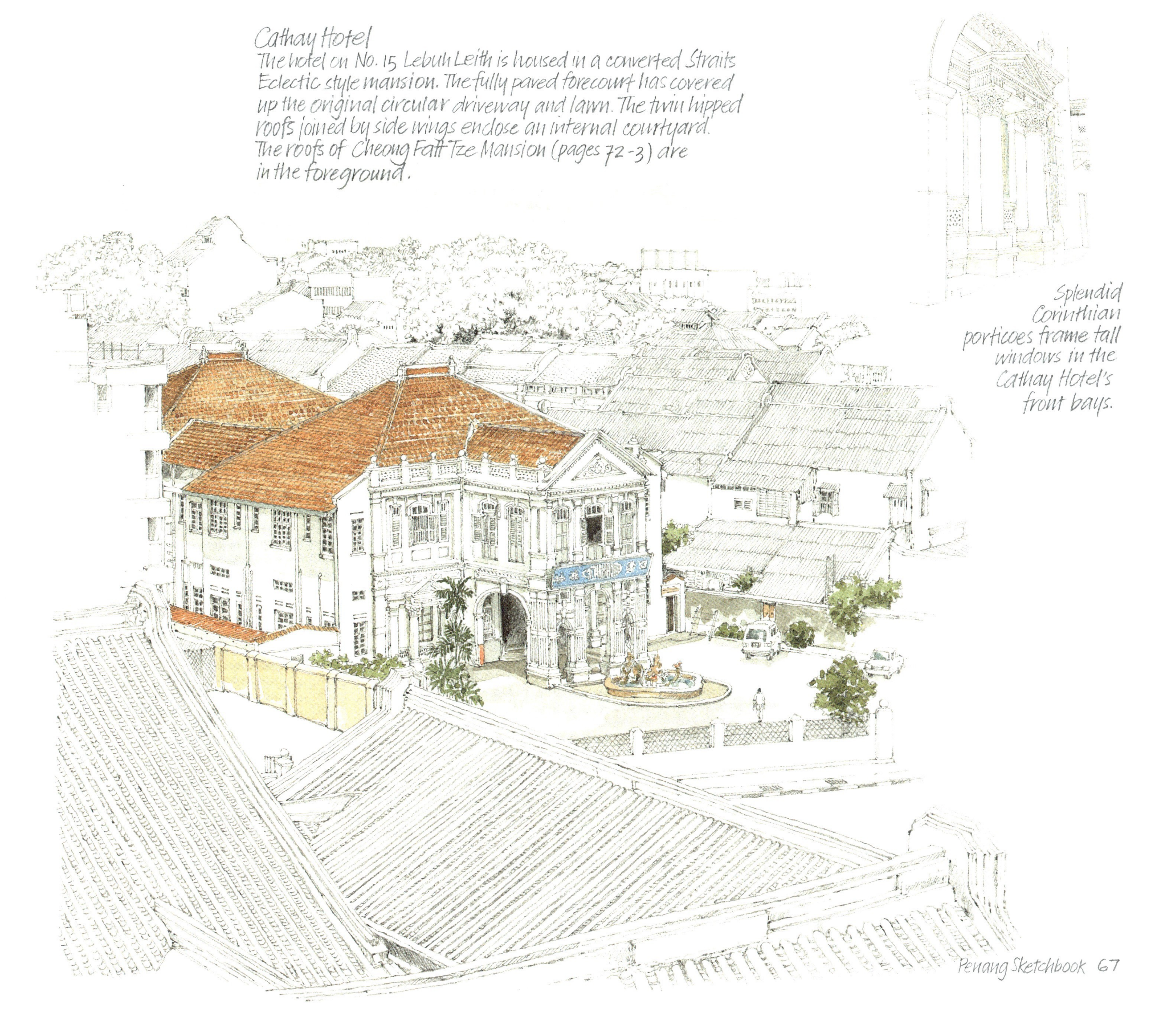

Splendid Corinthian porticoes frame tall windows in the Cathay Hotel's front bays.

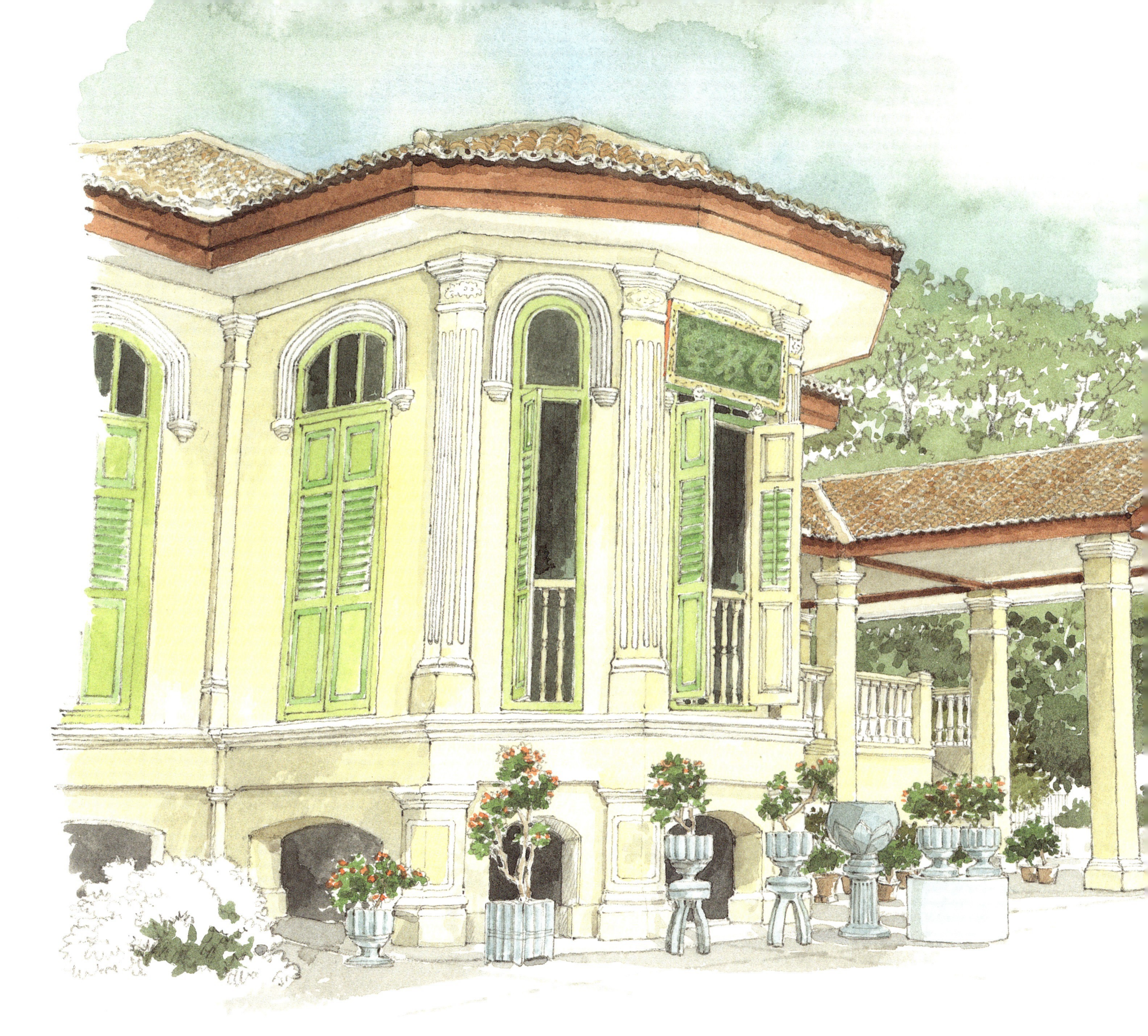

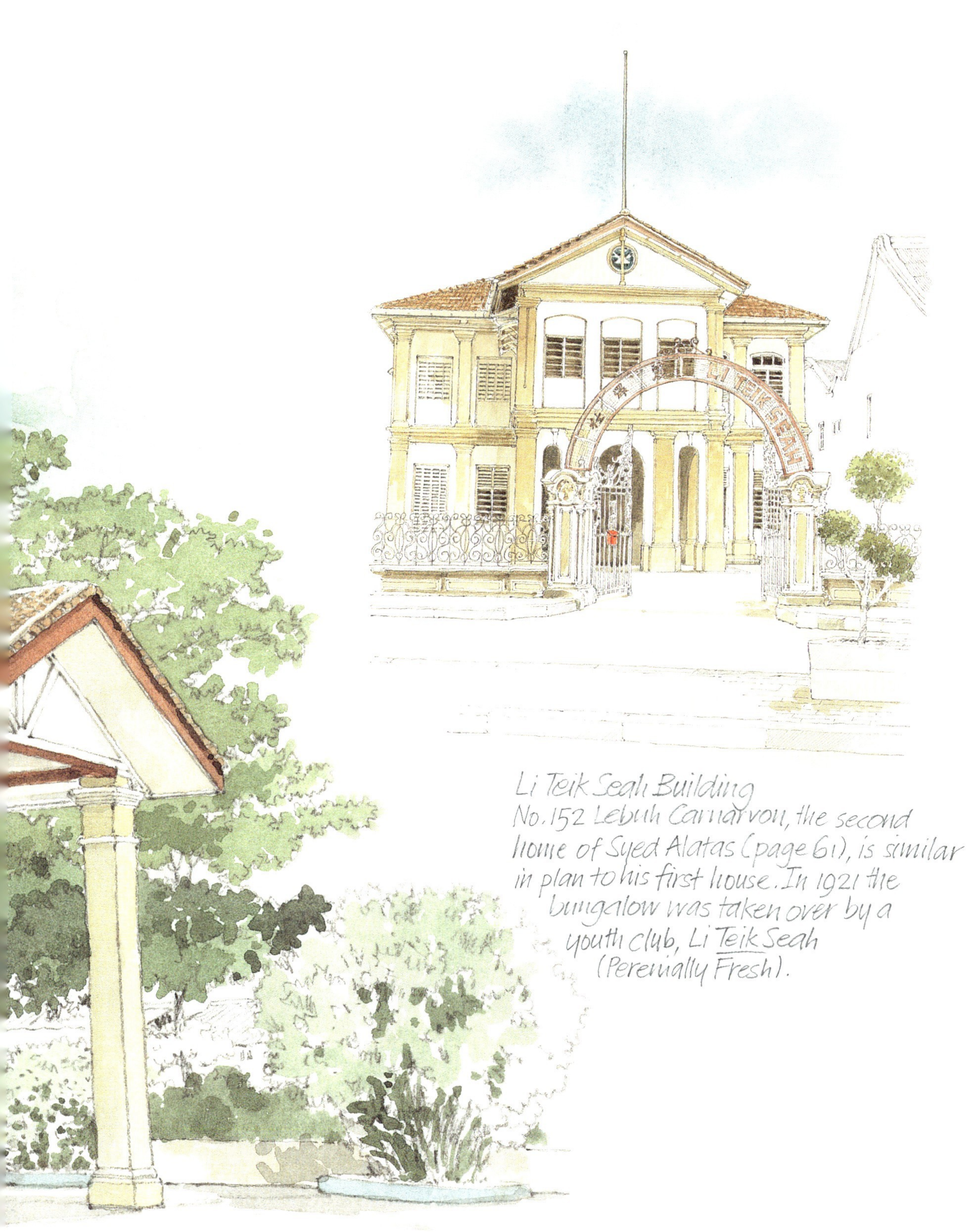

Li Teik Seah Building
No. 152 Lebuh Carnarvon, the second home of Syed Alatas (page 61), is similar in plan to his first house. In 1921 the bungalow was taken over by a youth club, Li Teik Seah (Perennially Fresh).

Syed Sheikh Al-Hadi's Residence
The house on Jalan Jelutong in brickwork with Chinese roof tiles and Palladian pilasters is now a temple run by white-robed nuns.

The corner balcony of a shophouse in Jalan Magazine is guarded by curved wrought iron railings. The pilasters and the consoles under the eaves and balcony are richly ornamented with vase and floral designs all highlighted in typical ochre.

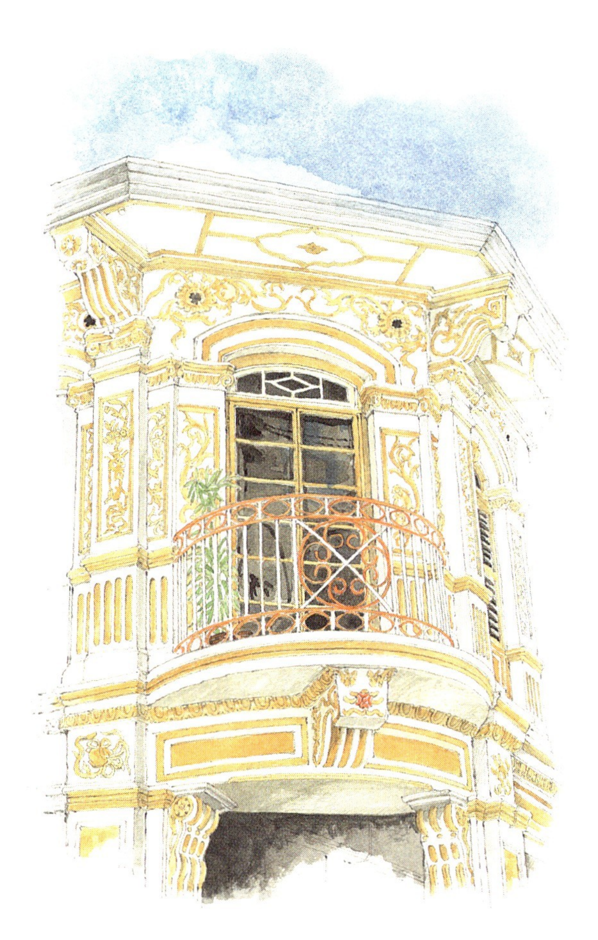

Kek Lok Si (Pure Land Temple)
Kek Lok Si's foundation stone was laid by the Thai monarch Rama VI, hence its name Pagoda of Rama VI, but completed in 1930 after his death. The octagonal base rises in decreasing multi-stages of tre-foil arcades and niches until the top two circular levels, and is crowned with a golden stupa, all in Thai-Burmese Buddhist style.

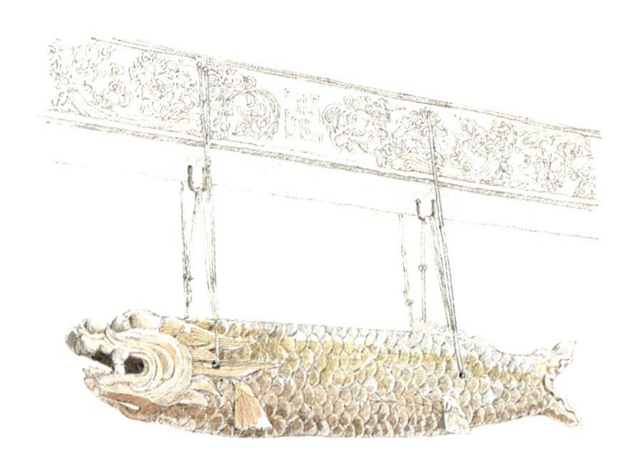

A hollowed-out wooden carp serves as a knocker in the Kek Lok Si. In Chinese culture, a carp with a dragon's head symbolises success.

Penang Buddhist Association
The centre for Buddhist studies, located on No. 168 Jalan Anson, was built in the late Straits Eclectic style by a group of Straits Chinese Buddhists in 1931. The interior's single vast hall has a vaulted ceiling over a central elevated altar with a seated Buddha and standing figures. The side walls have chapels built into them, and the floor tiles form lotus patterns.

The decorated entrance to the older part of the temple complex which comprises Halls to Kwan Yin, the Laughing Buddha and Gautama, the founder of Buddhism.

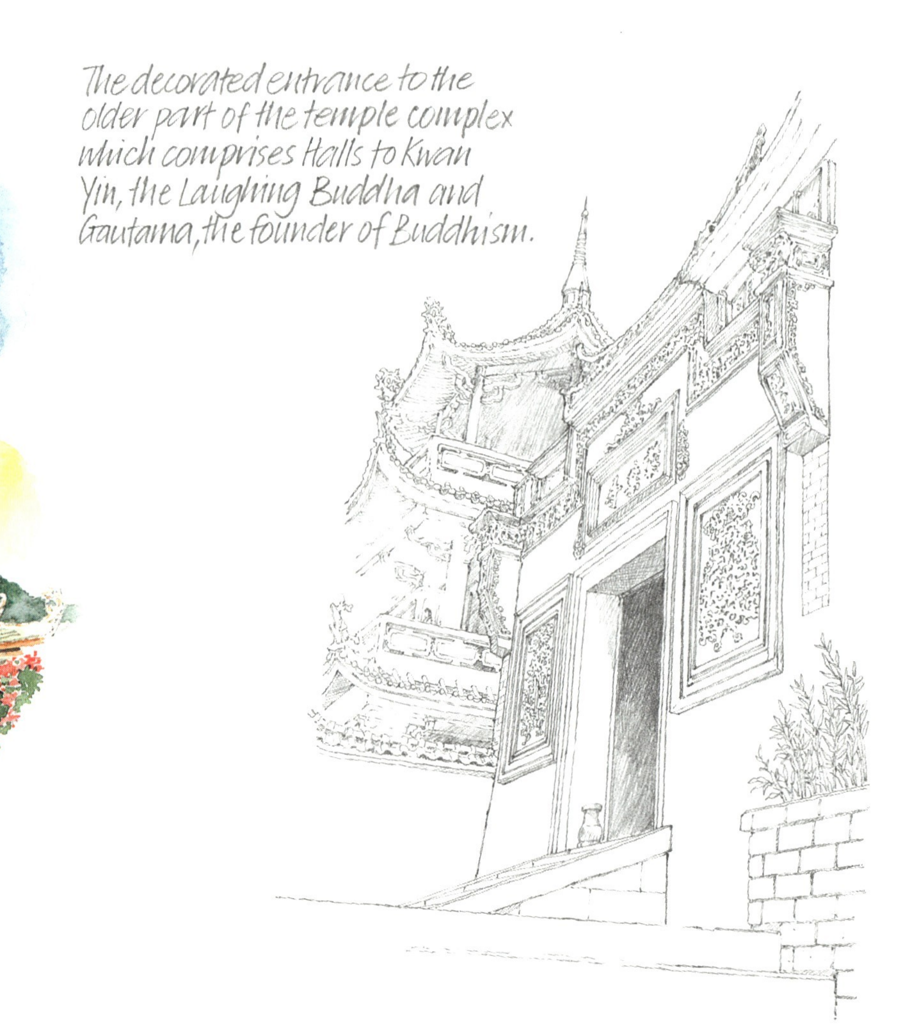

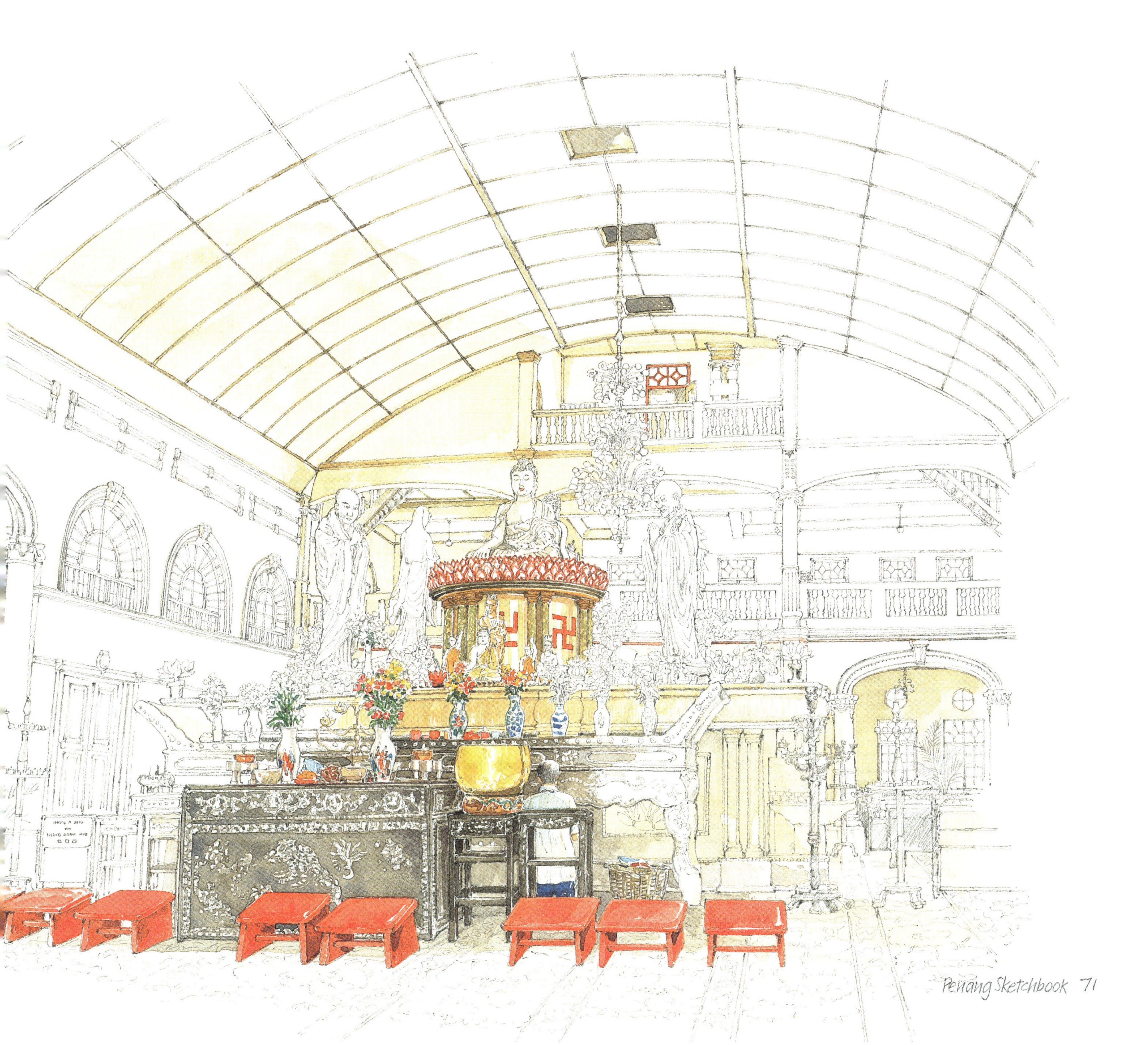

The front entrance of the Cheong Fatt Tze Mansion. A plaque with three Chinese characters referring to its celebrated owner hangs above the door.

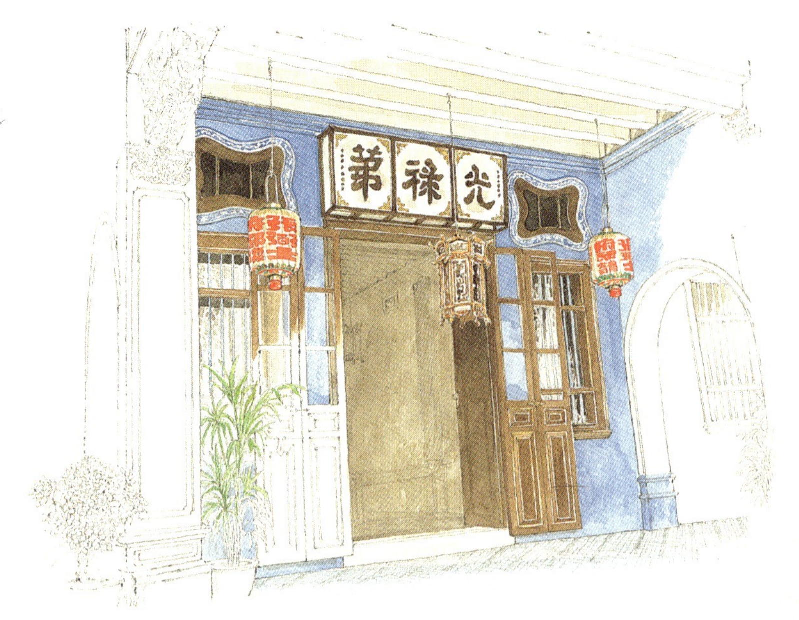

Light, filtering through the filigreed screens of wrought iron arches and balustrades, lights up the central courtyard of the grand mansion.

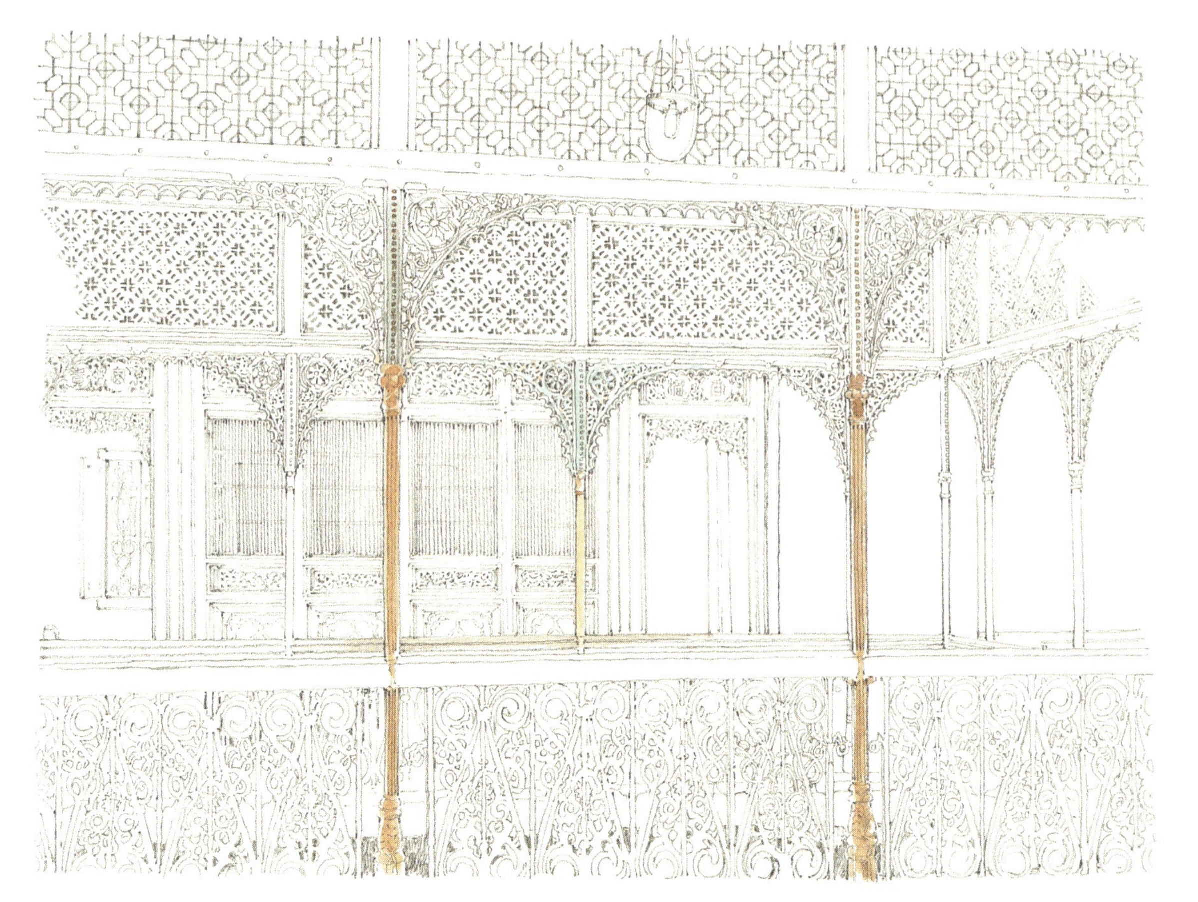

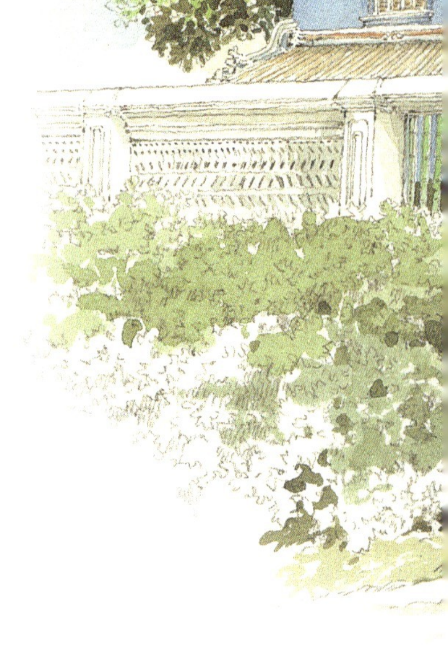

Cheong Fatt Tze Mansion

The eponymous Cheong Fatt Tze Mansion was the principal home of the illustrious Mandarin. The authentically restored mansion stands on No. 14 Lebuh Leith and is laid out in the traditional courtyard plan. The Chinese entrance gateway is placed at an angle observing favourable feng shui (geomancy) principles, and the four Chinese characters over the entrance doors inform passers-by of the owner's ancestry.

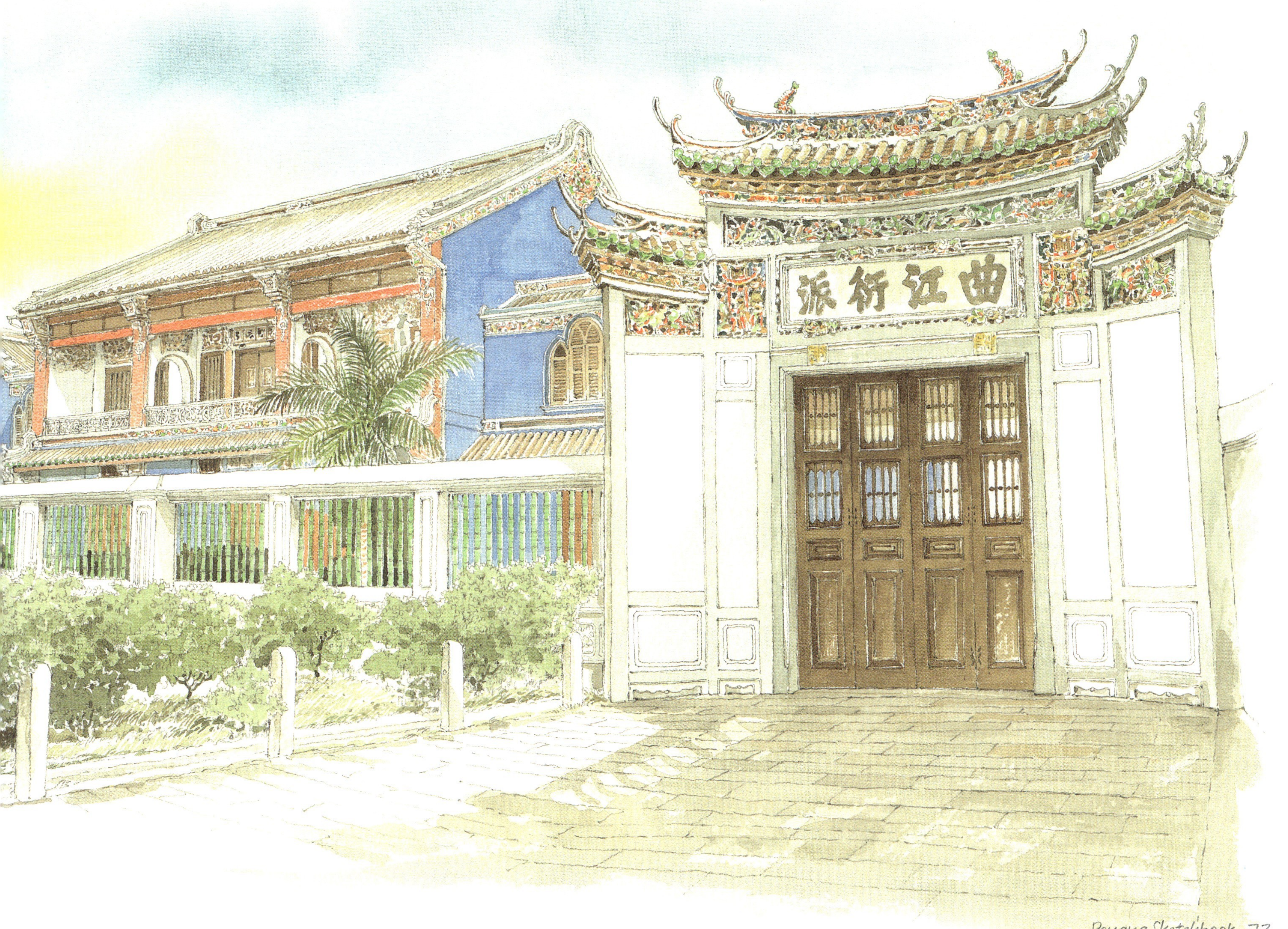

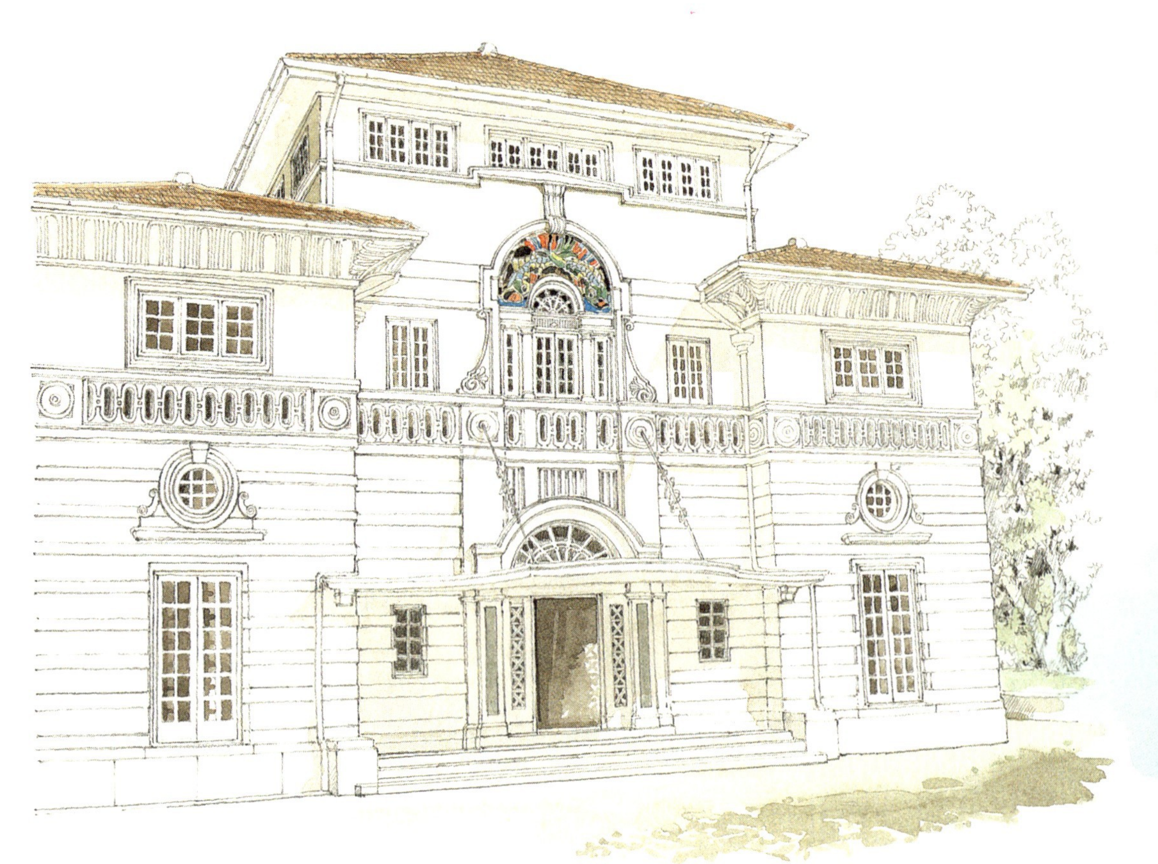

Leong Yin Kean Mansion
No. 32 Jalan Sultan Ahmad Shah was the home of an Italophile. It combines the classical with the freer Art Nouveau style. A grooved band with roundels separates the ground from the upper floors.

Woodville
The eclectic mansion on Jalan Sultan Ahmad Shah was built by millionaire planter Lim Lean Teng. The architect responded to Lim's request for a dome with the octagonal tower's oval dome. A fishscale, glass canopy replaces the usual porte cochere. A single-storey link joins the main house to a guest block on the left.

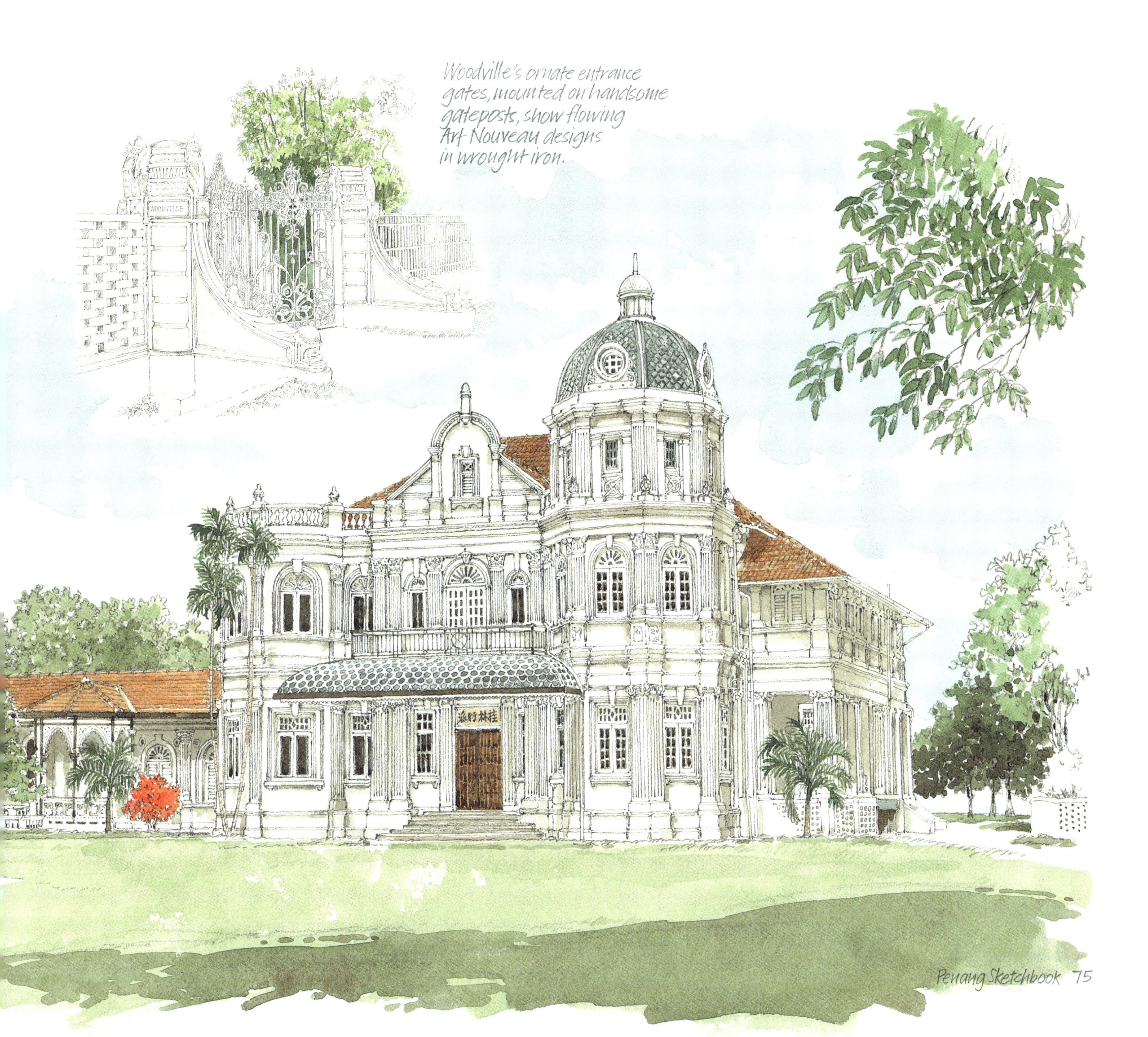

Woodville's ornate entrance gates, mounted on handsome gateposts, show flowing Art Nouveau designs in wrought iron.

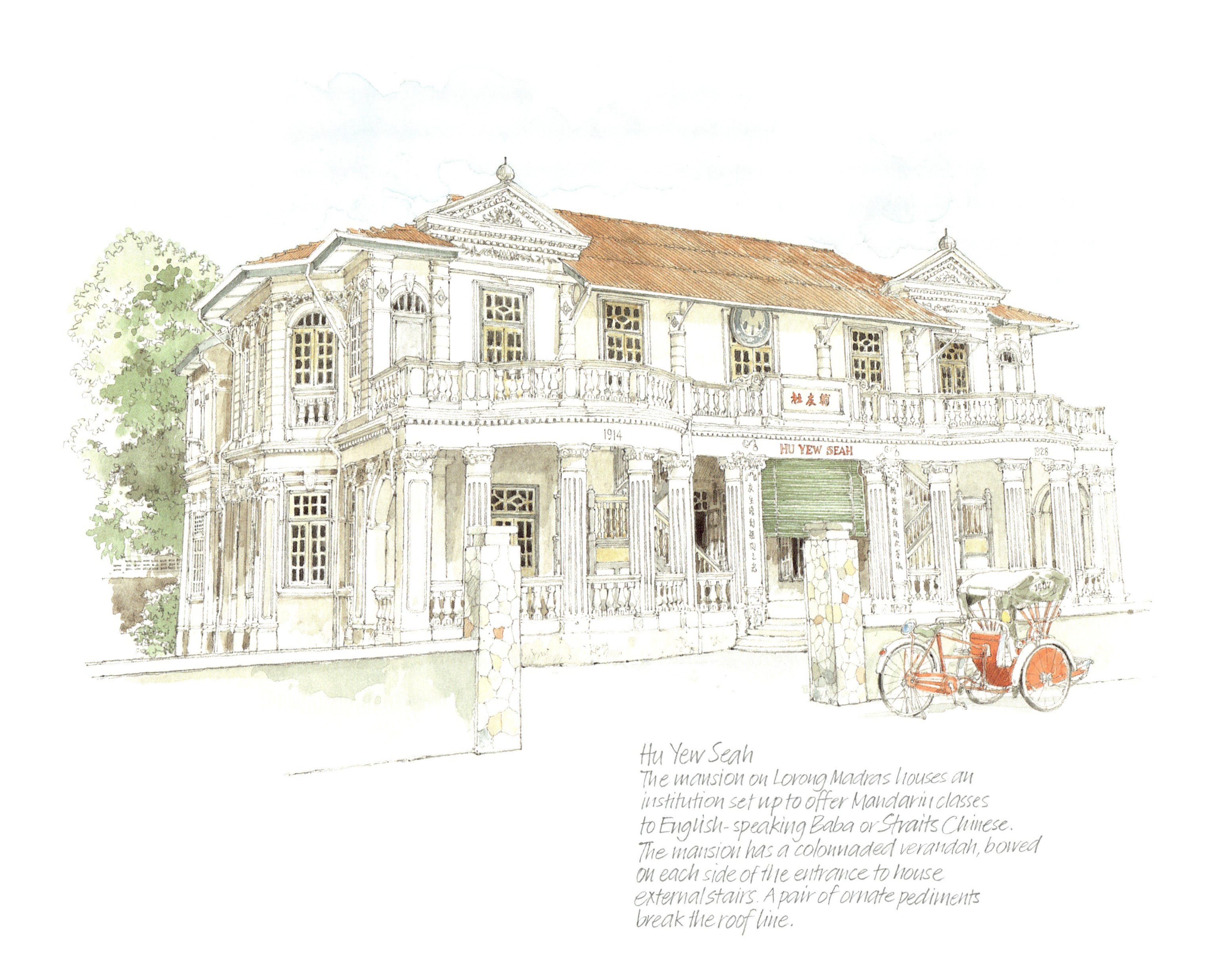

Hu Yew Seah

The mansion on Lorong Madras houses an institution set up to offer Mandarin classes to English-speaking Baba or Straits Chinese. The mansion has a colonnaded verandah, bowed on each side of the entrance to house external stairs. A pair of ornate pediments break the roof line.

Soonstead
No. 46B Jalan Sultan Ahmad Shah was built by millionaire planter Heah Swee Lee in the 1900s. The impressive mansion mixes neoclassical and baroque elements: the entrance is shaded by a glass canopy in a fishscale pattern; a heraldic crest and swags decorate the central pediment; and urns top the roof parapets of the two non-matching towers.

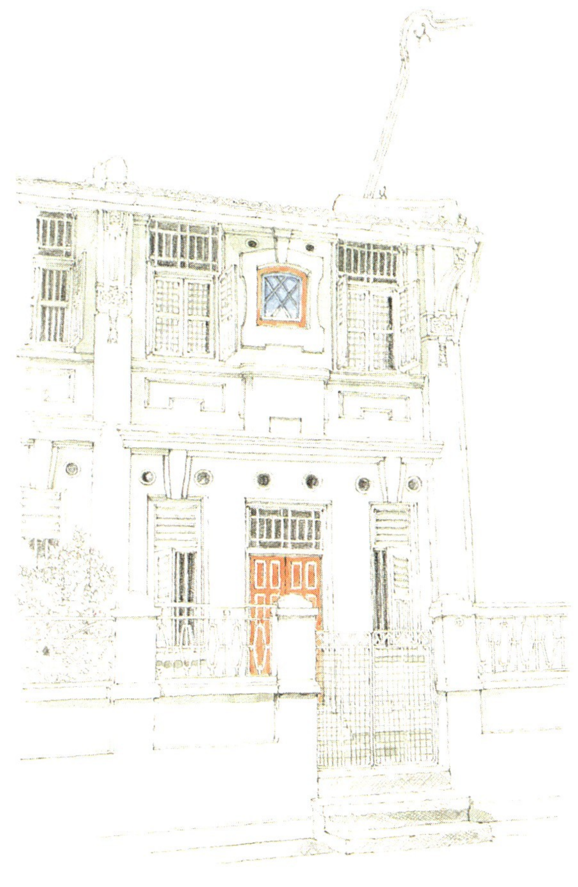

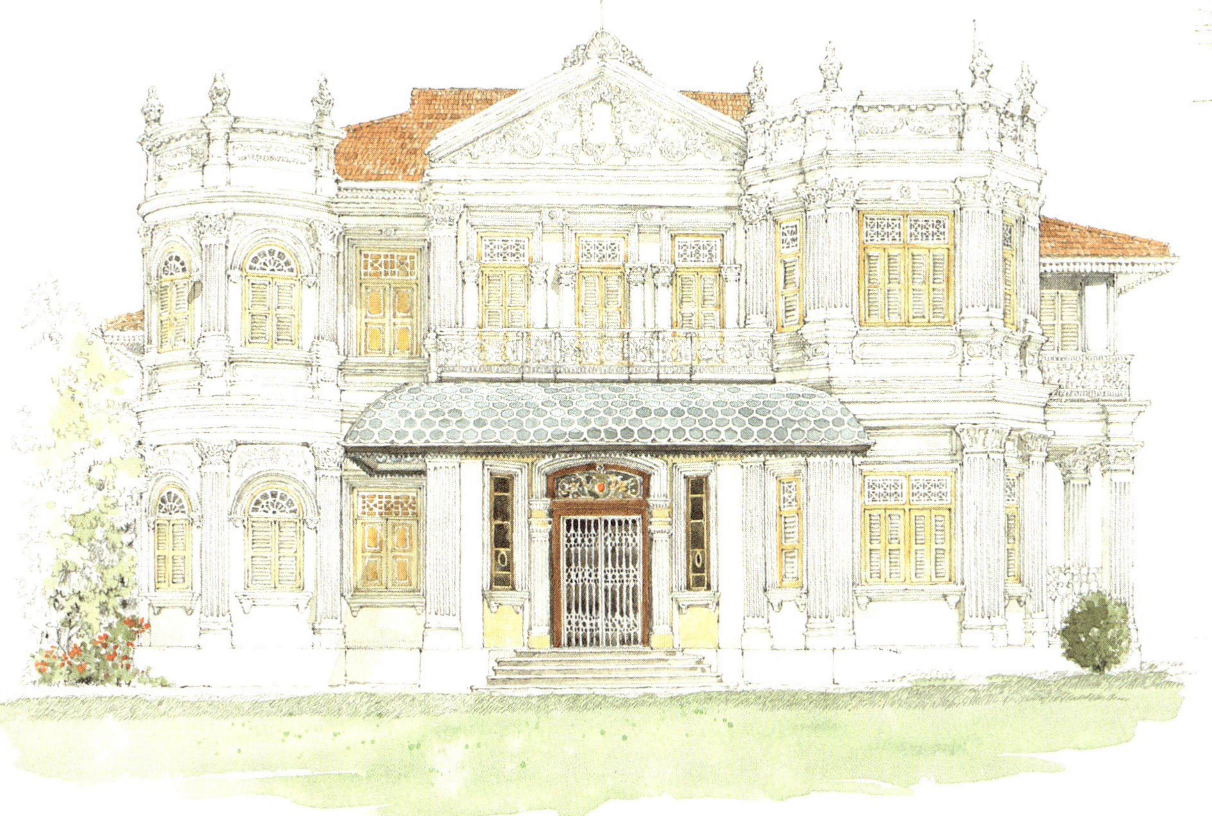

Nos. 12–18 Lorong Argus is a row of terrace houses in a quiet cul-de-sac behind the Cathedral of the Assumption (page 17). Eurasian Catholic families, descendants of the Catholics who fled Siamese persecution and were brought to Penang by Francis Light, reside here.

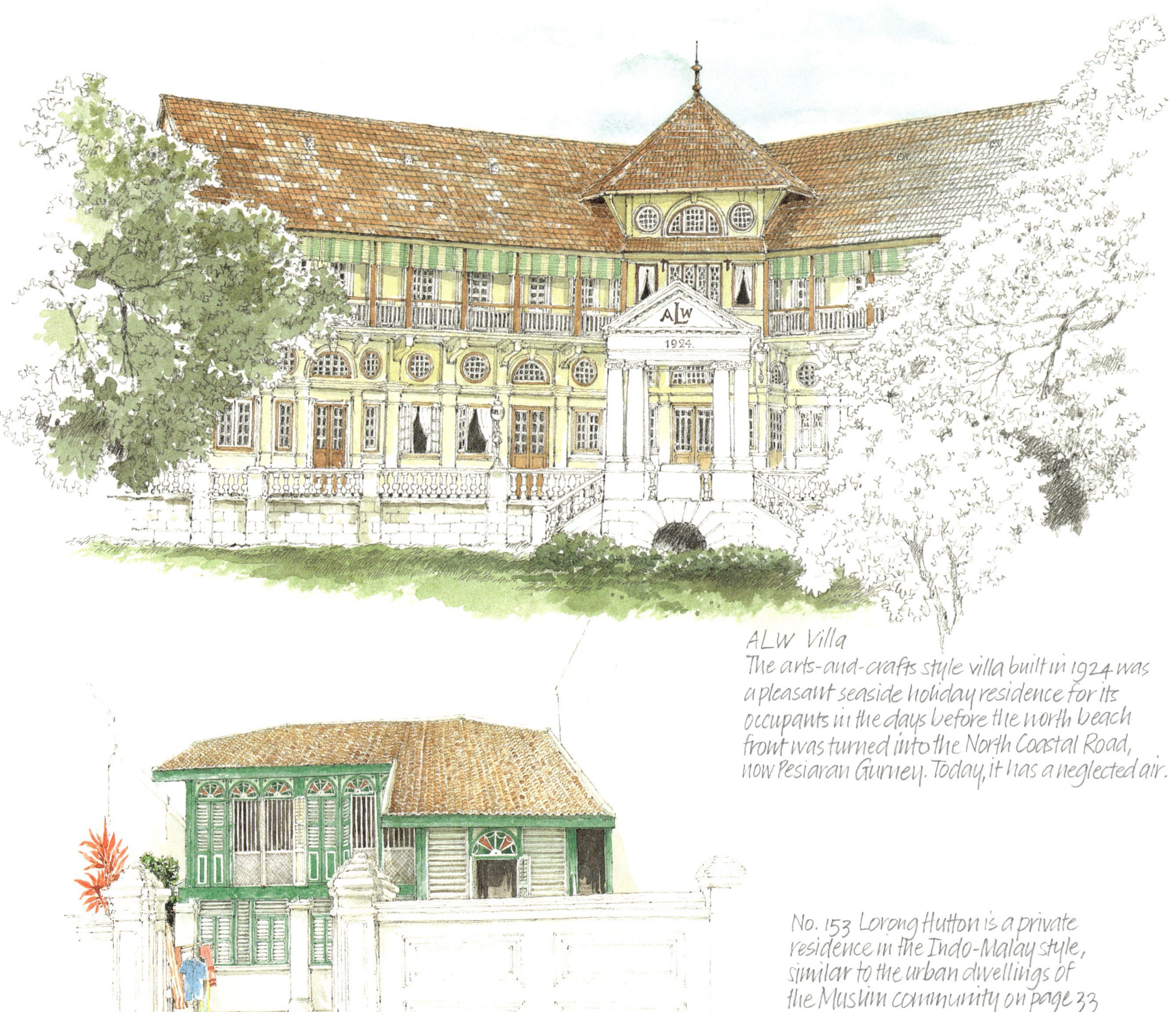

ALW Villa
The arts-and-crafts style villa built in 1924 was a pleasant seaside holiday residence for its occupants in the days before the north beach front was turned into the North Coastal Road, now Pesiaran Gurney. Today, it has a neglected air.

No. 153 Lorong Hutton is a private residence in the Indo-Malay style, similar to the urban dwellings of the Muslim community on page 33. The plastered brick boundary walls with moulded recessed panels and gateposts suggest an earlier affluence.

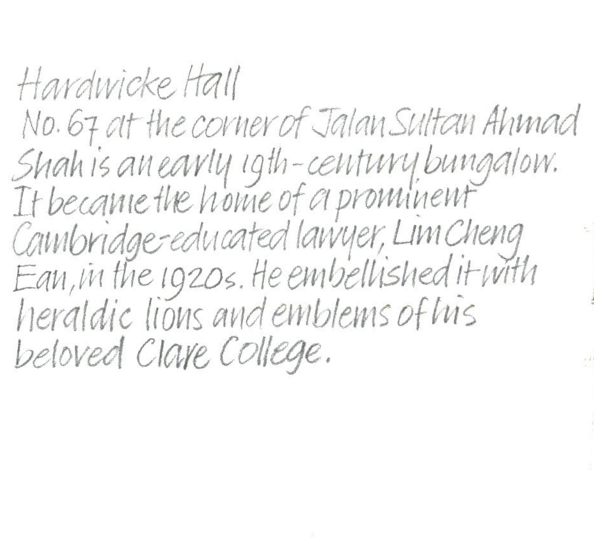

Hardwicke Hall

No. 67 at the corner of Jalan Sultan Ahmad Shah is an early 19th-century bungalow. It became the home of a prominent Cambridge-educated lawyer, Lim Cheng Ean, in the 1920s. He embellished it with heraldic lions and emblems of his beloved Clare College.

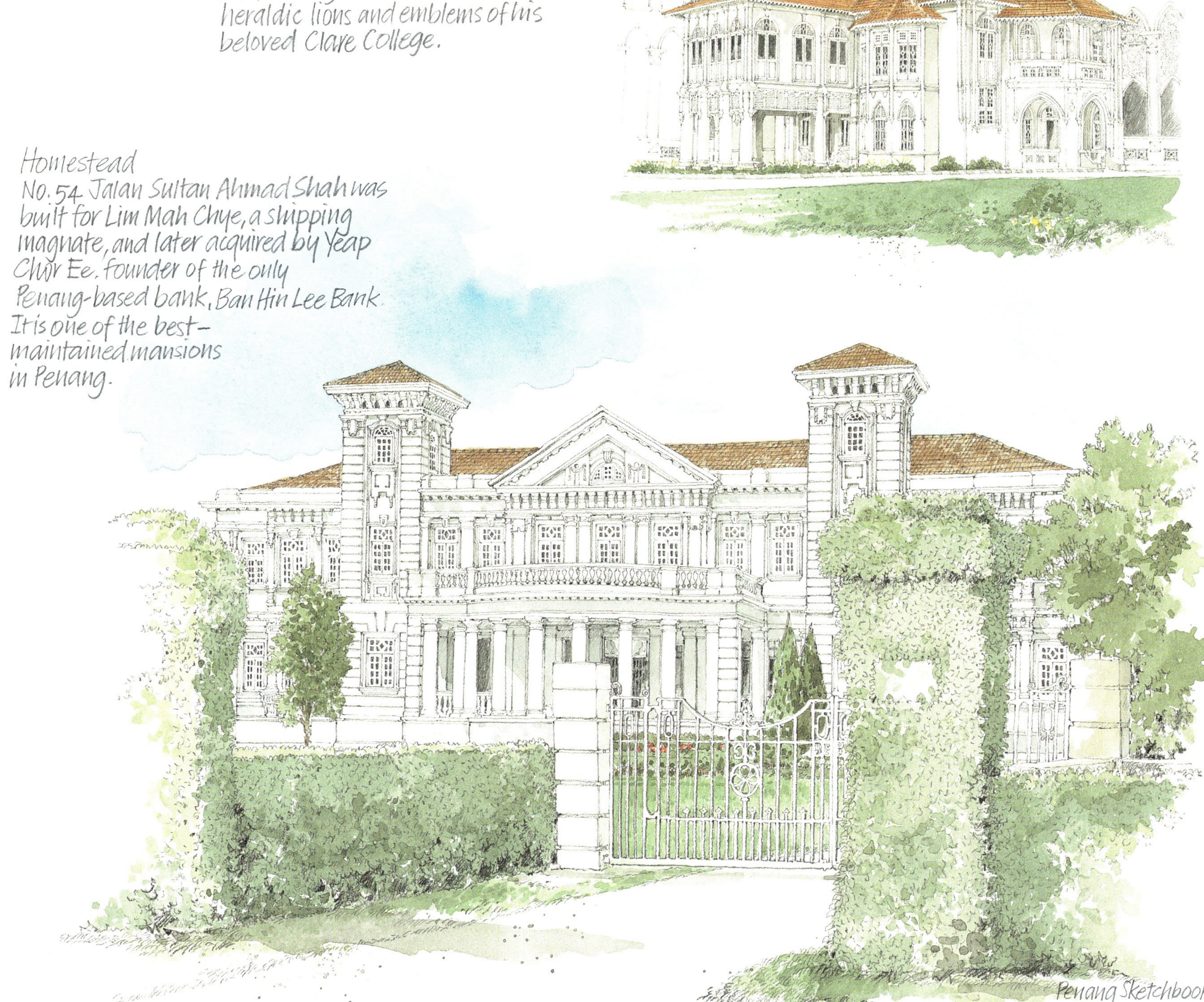

Homestead

No. 54 Jalan Sultan Ahmad Shah was built for Lim Mah Chye, a shipping magnate, and later acquired by Yeap Chor Ee, founder of the only Penang-based bank, Ban Hin Lee Bank. It is one of the best-maintained mansions in Penang.

The Waterfront

Penang's panorama is best viewed from the deck of a cross-channel ferry. The waterfront, though still busy, has declined since losing its free port status in 1974. Cross-channel ferries transporting people and goods across the water have replaced *sampan* (man-powered rowing boats). The handsome Western classical style buildings along Pengkalan Weld are reminders of Penang's heyday as the entrepôt for the produce of northern Malaya, southern Thailand and northern Sumatra in the early 20th century.

Pengkalan Weld, named after Frederick Aloysius Weld, Governor of the Straits Settlements, was created in the 1880s. The massive land reclamation, completed in 1904, culminated in Swettenham Pier, where ocean steamers used to berth. Today, the occasional visiting navy's vessels and big cruise ships dock at the pier. The earliest godowns are located here; Boustead built the first in 1893 on the newly reclaimed land. European trading houses had their offices and warehouses here, some of which still survive. One of the more colourful survivors of the old waterfront is the clan jetties, clan surname villages built over the water, which provide essential stevedoring services. In the 19th century the North Channel was the scene of their dragon boat races; this is revived today as competitive sports events in the Pesta Pulau Pinang (Penang Island Festival).

Although the city's orientation has turned inland, Penang's waterfront still recalls its beginning as a trading port and the days of sea travel linking it to port cities such as Colombo and Rangoon.

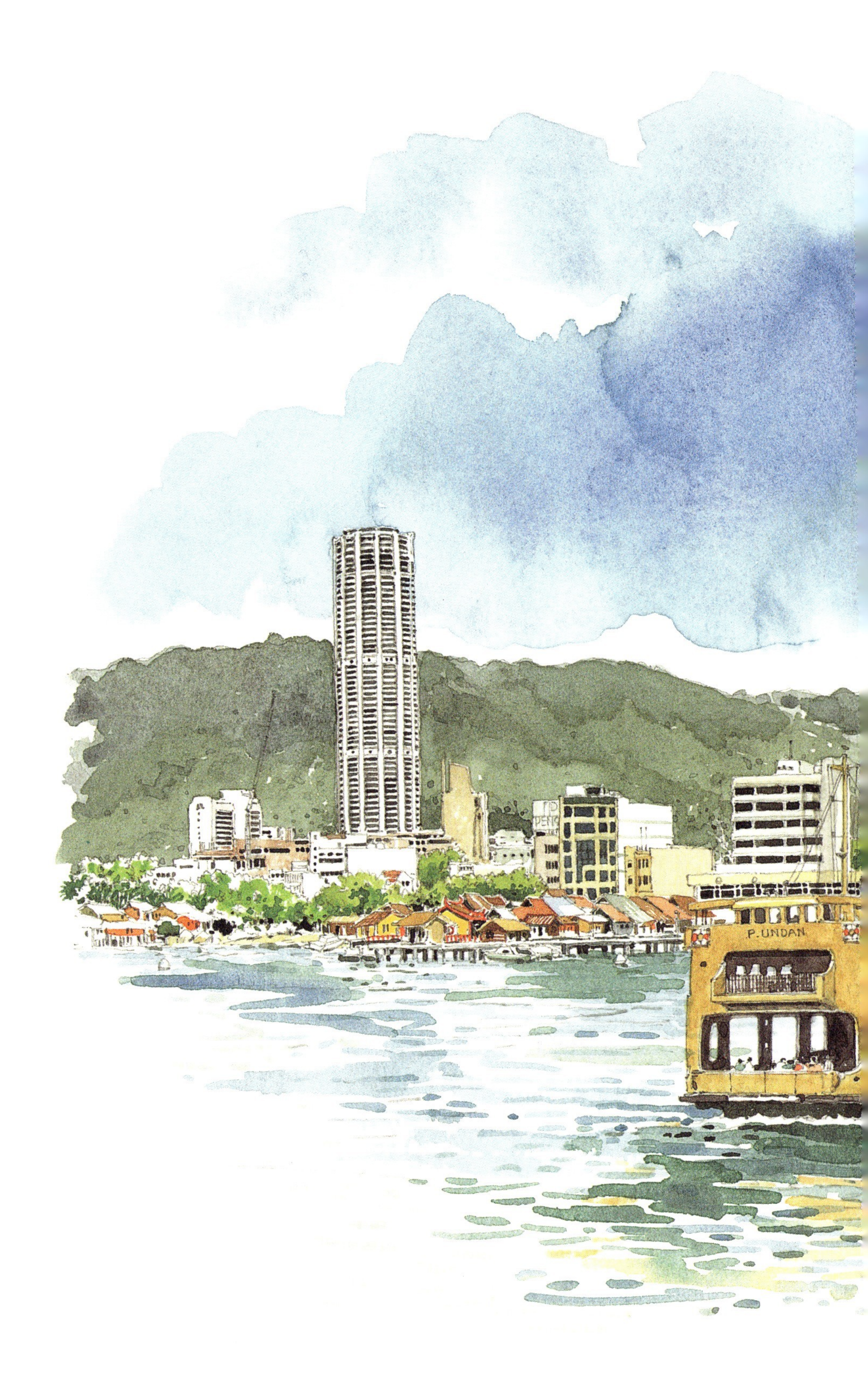

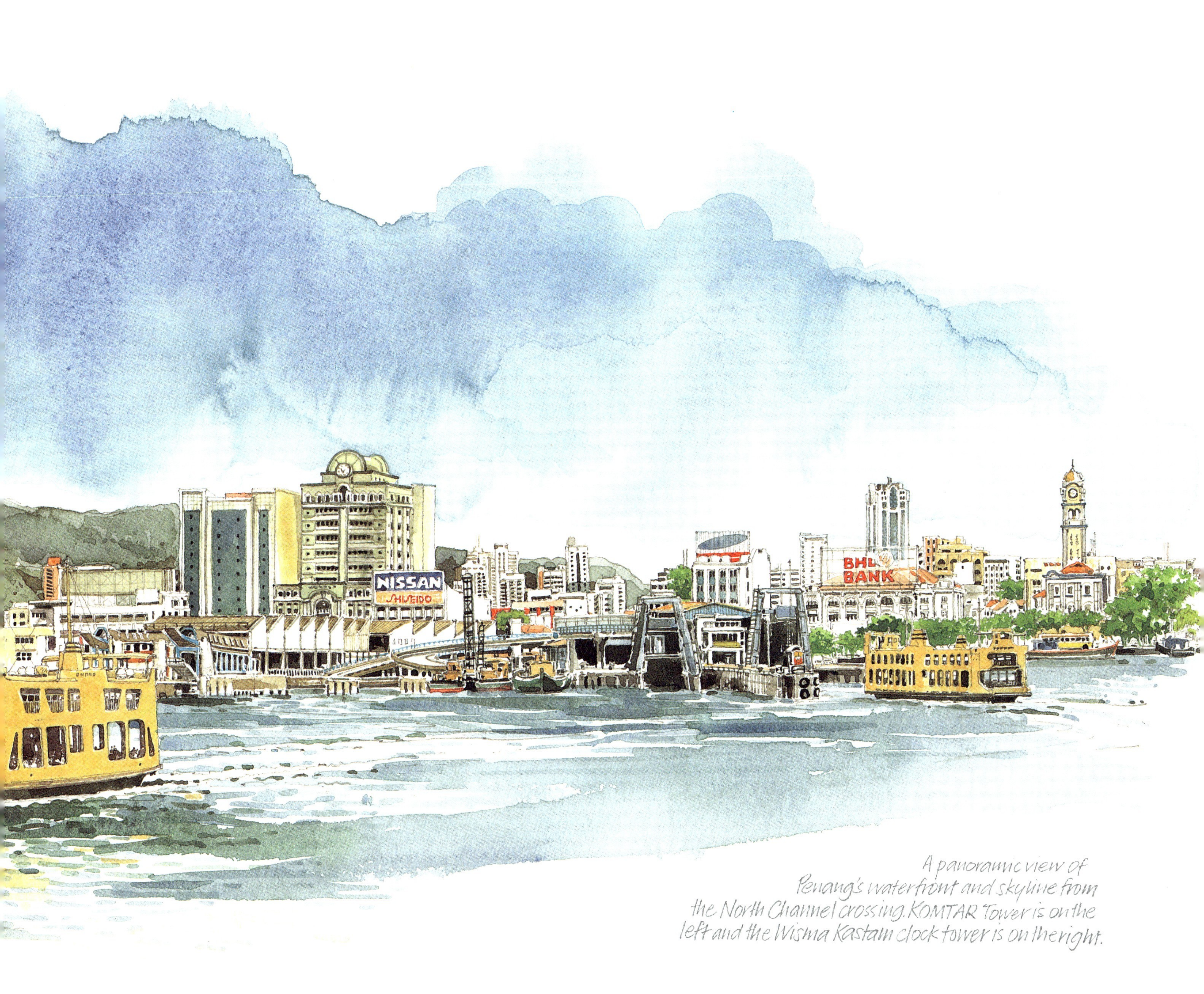

A panoramic view of Penang's waterfront and skyline from the North Channel crossing. KOMTAR Tower is on the left and the Wisma Kastam clock tower is on the right.

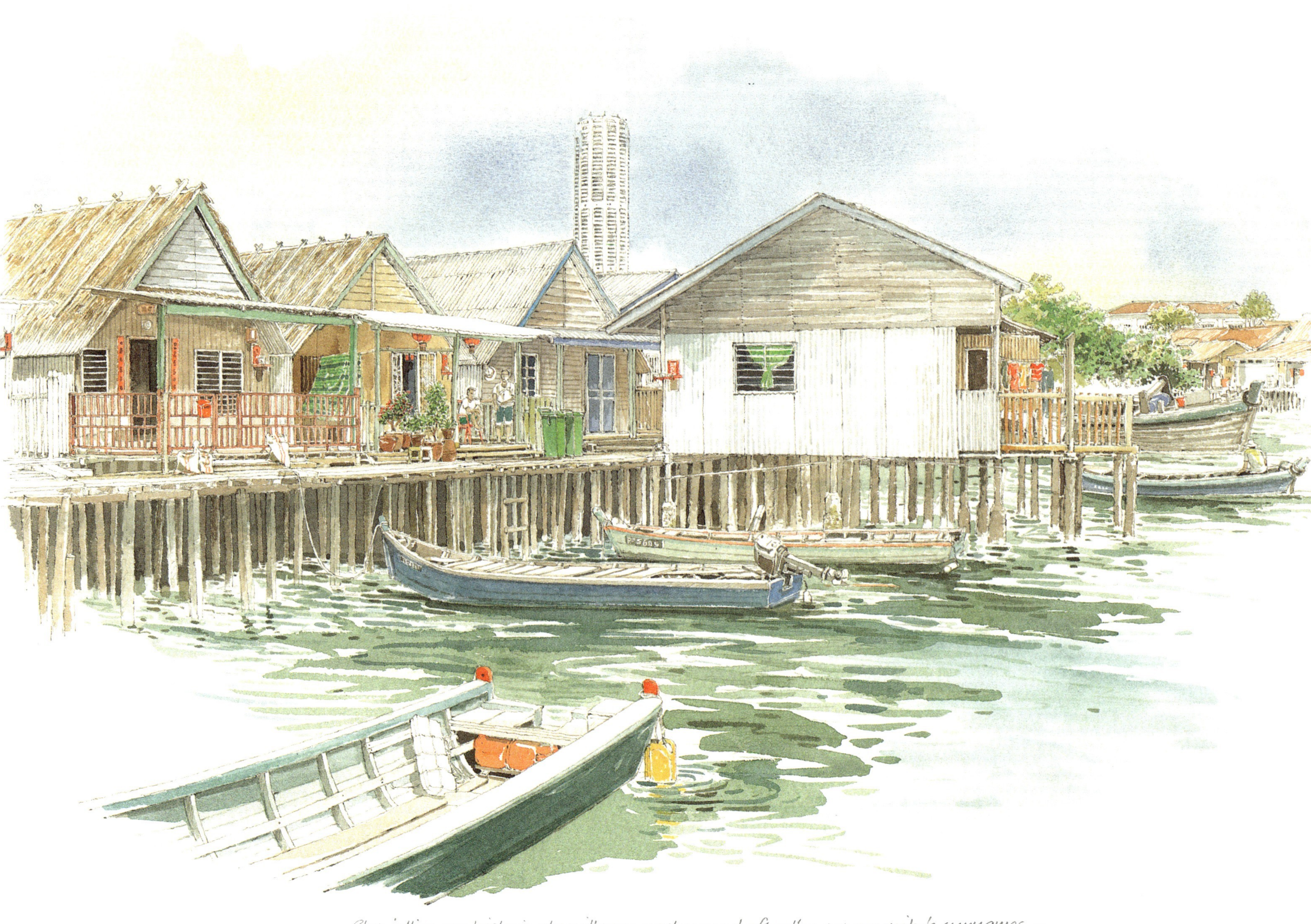

Clan jetties are historic clan villages, each named after the community's surnames – Lim, Chew, Tan, Yeoh and Lee. Wooden walkways on piles sunk into the sea link the timber houses. Fenced-in areas serve as entrance porches, and separate the public walkway from the house proper. Fishing, stevedoring and cross-channel ferrying are still carried out by the jetty communities. Chew jetty, the largest, offers boat rides.

Godowns between Lebuh Victoria and Pengkalan Weld with workers' quarters above. Long beams spanning across sturdy columns and two-storey pillars support the upper timber floor. Panels below the louvred windows are decorated with interlocking diamonds or plain vertical boards. Roofs are covered with Chinese clay tiles.

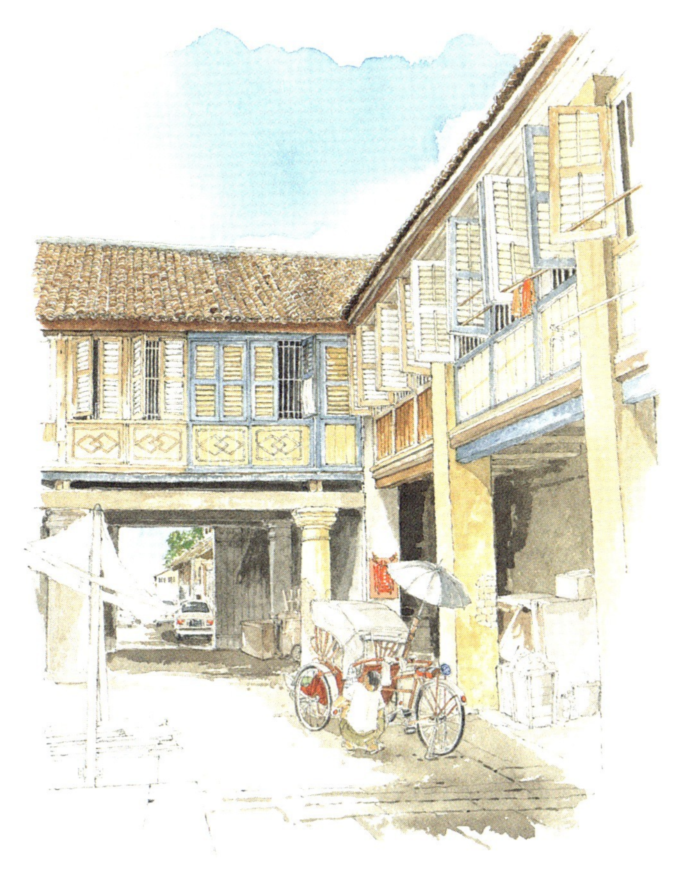

Koe Guan Godown's first floor was used to house immigrants freshly arrived from China. The walls are infilled vertical planks on low walls between short pillars in Tuscan Order. Birdcages are hung on poles slung between the central open casements to air them.

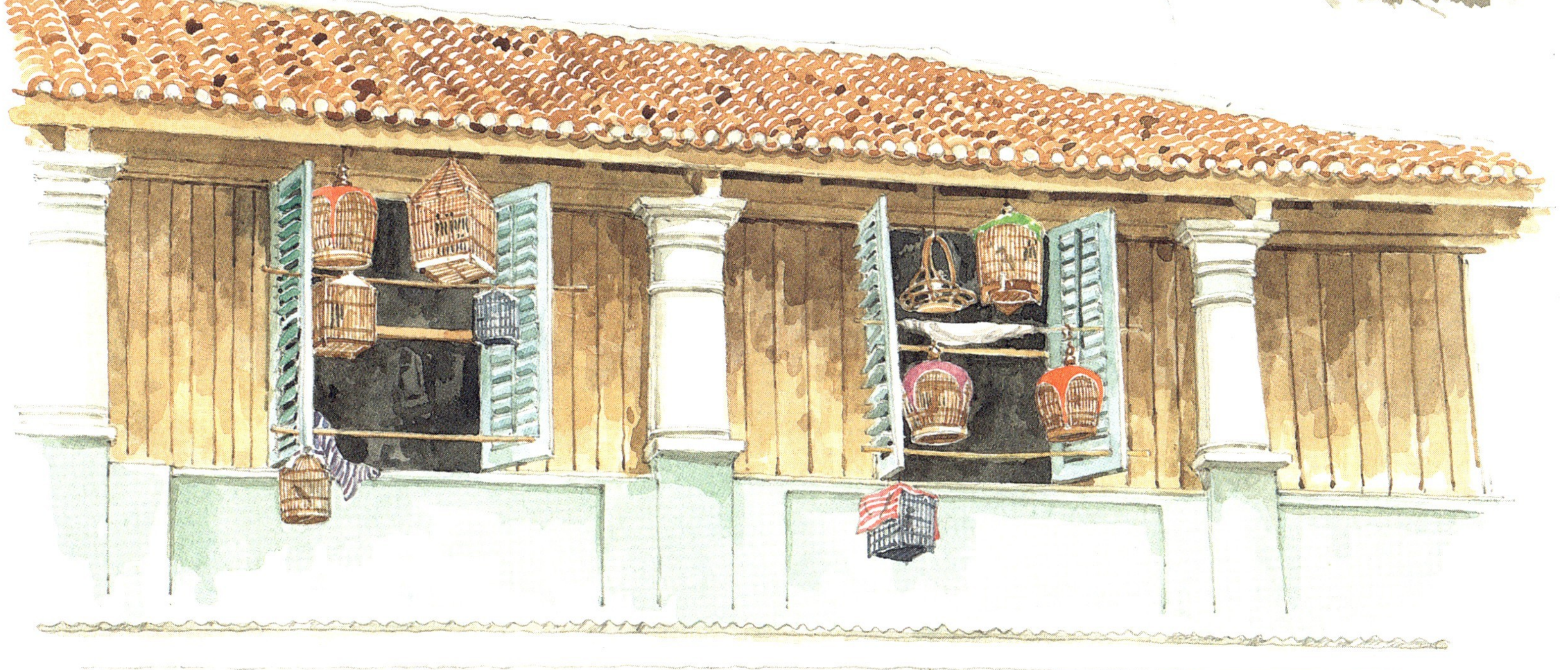

Wisma Kastam (Customs Building)
The former Malayan Railway Building on the corner of Gat Lebuh China is a landmark with its prominent domed clock tower. Its corner site allows for three finely articulated elevations. The long side has two bays, with half-round pediments at the roofline breaking the monotony. Giant Ionic columns frame the windows of the two upper floors. The ground floor arcade is treated with mock rustication grooves.

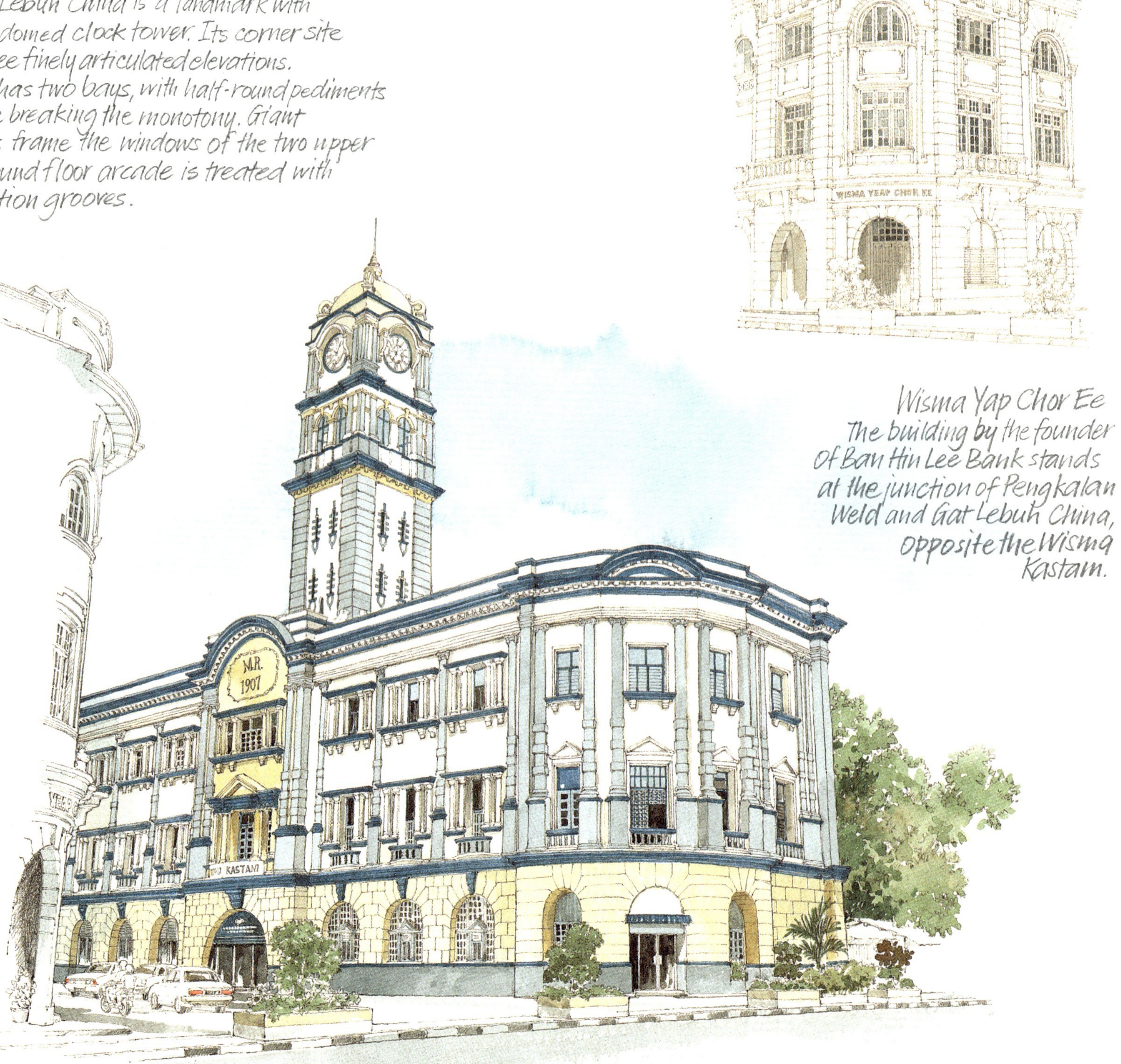

Wisma Yap Chor Ee
The building by the founder of Ban Hin Lee Bank stands at the junction of Pengkalan Weld and Gat Lebuh China, opposite the Wisma Kastam.

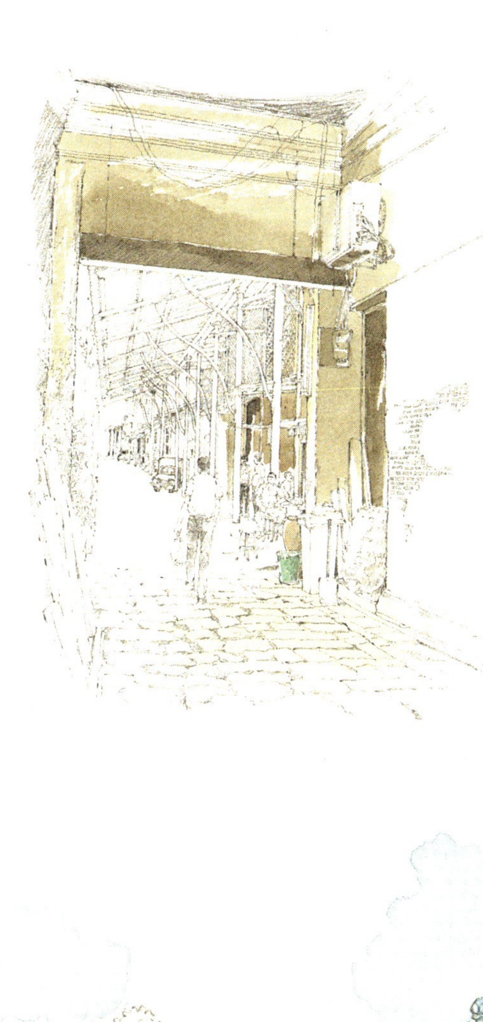

A narrow alley along the godowns built for European shipping and trading agencies, laid with granite blocks worn shiny from years of foot traffic by Indian stevedores pulling handcarts.

Former Paterson Simons Building
The freestanding building's neo-classical façade is tropicalised by metal window hoods from which hang additional chick.
The present owner's sign partly conceals the entablature carrying a balustraded roof parapet with spherical finials and screening a Chinese-style roof behind.

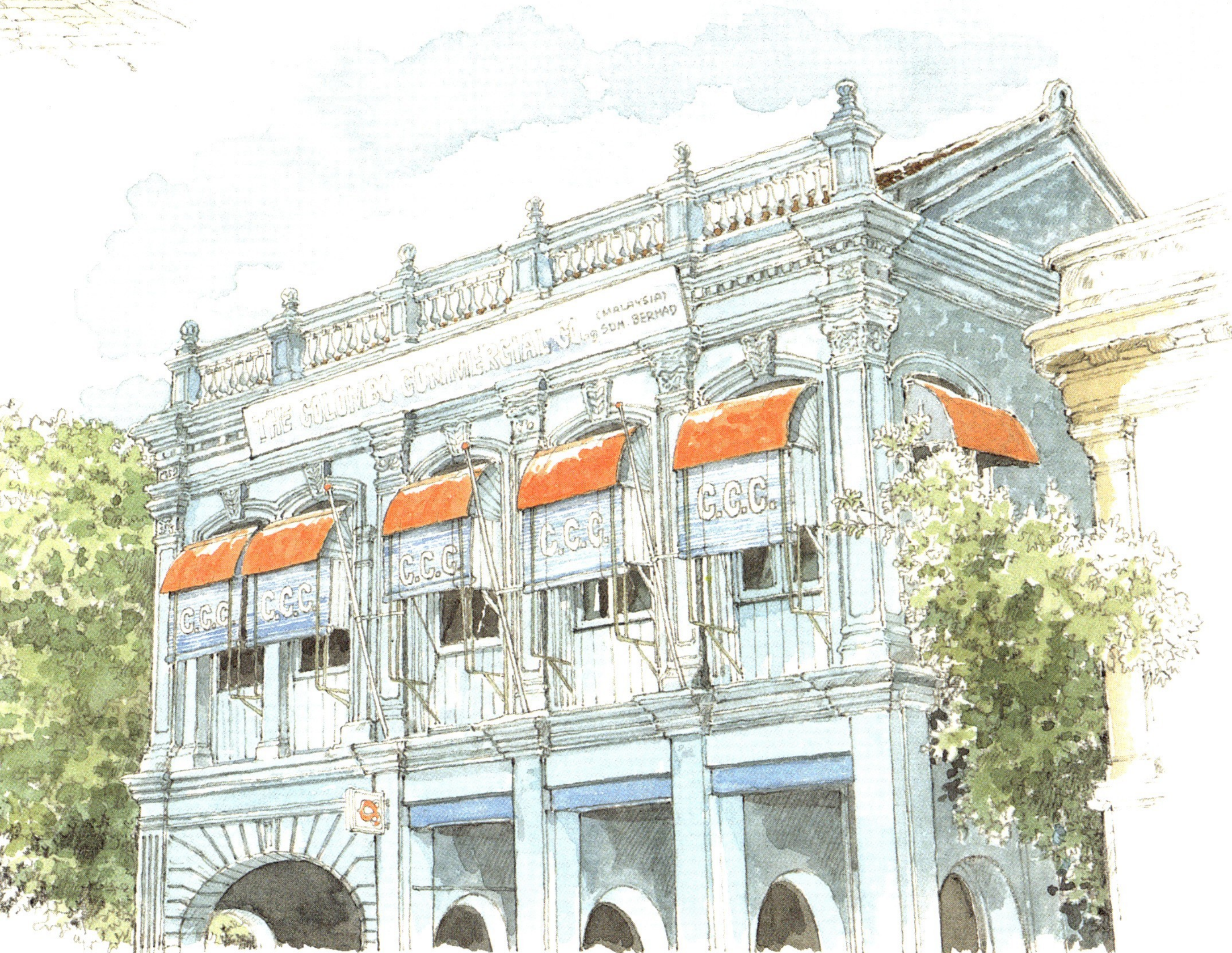

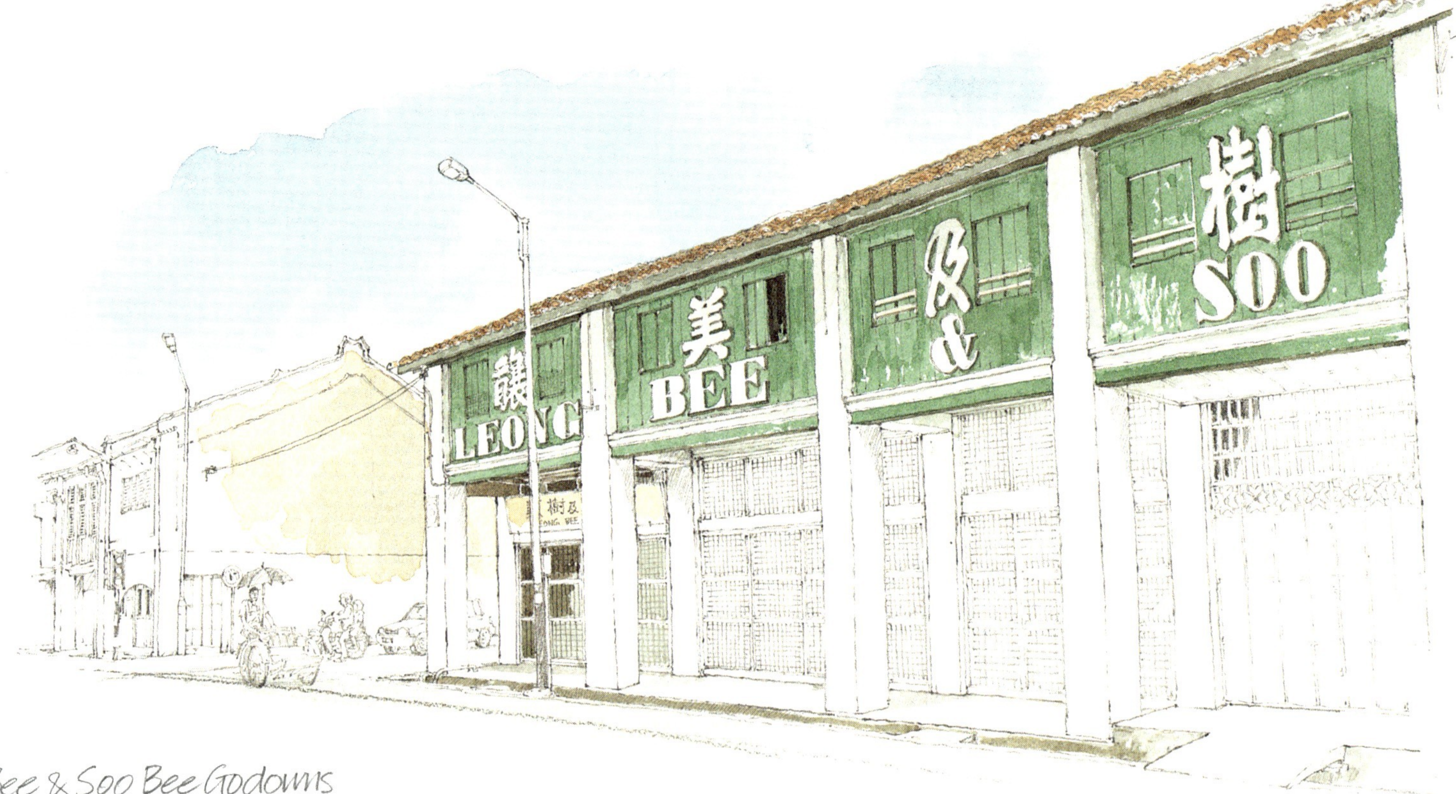

Leong Bee & Soo Bee Godowns
The godowns' sturdy brick columns form a five-foot way along Jalan C.Y. Choy. Bold, storey-height English letters and Chinese characters fixed on the first floor timber boarding to advertise ownership and function are now completely hidden behind the hoarding.

Anglo-Indian Godown
No. 21 Lebuh Penang was, until recently, the best extant example of a mid-19th-century Anglo-Indian godown. As with typical godowns, thick brick walls enclose ample storage space on the ground floor and sturdy pillars support a timber upper floor used for offices and quarters. Conversion to an electrical supplies outlet has marred its authenticity.

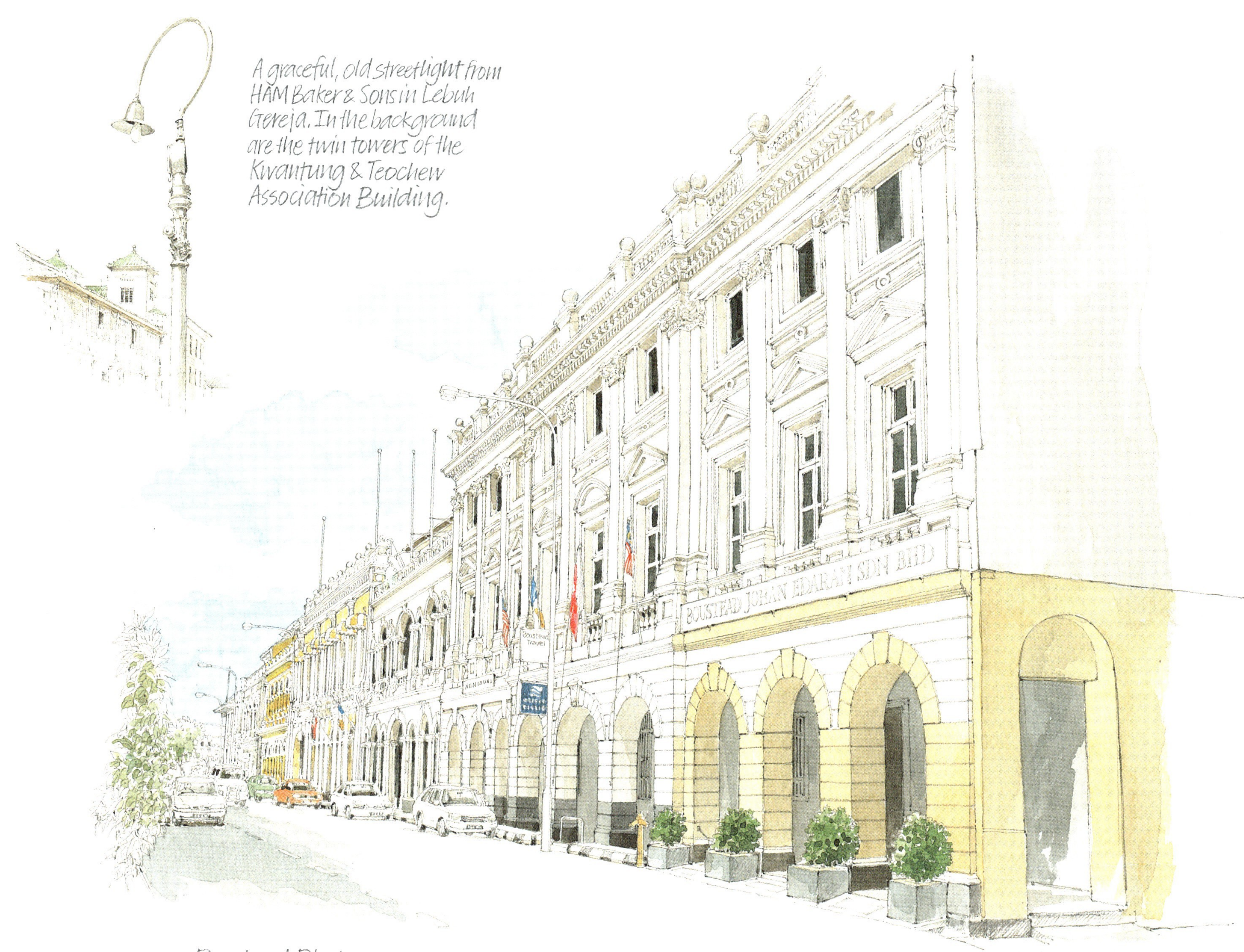

A graceful, old streetlight from HAM Baker & Sons in Lebuh Gereja. In the background are the twin towers of the Kwantung & Teochew Association Building.

Boustead Block

The classical style favoured by the colonialists was used with great effect in the waterfront buildings on Pengkalan Weld, creating an ensemble of unified, city street architecture of distinction. Boustead, a European shipping agency and import-export company, still has its offices in the first building.

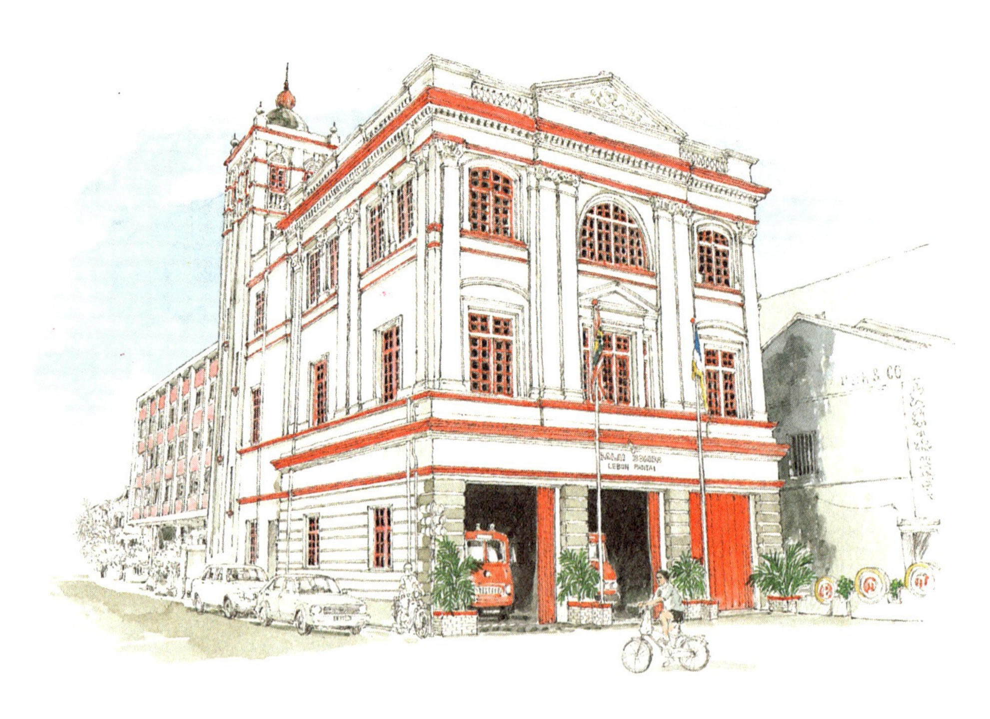

Balai Bomba (Central Fire Station)
The freestanding, three-storey building at the junction of Gat Lebuh Chulia and Lebuh Pantai has functionally large doors that open onto Lebuh Pantai. A low, domed tower for drying out long fire hoses stands at the corner.

Khie Heng Bee Mills
The mill on Jalan Jelutong has high walls accented by two-storey brick columns that form a five-foot way on the ground. The windowless first floor is completely blanked out by metal siding.

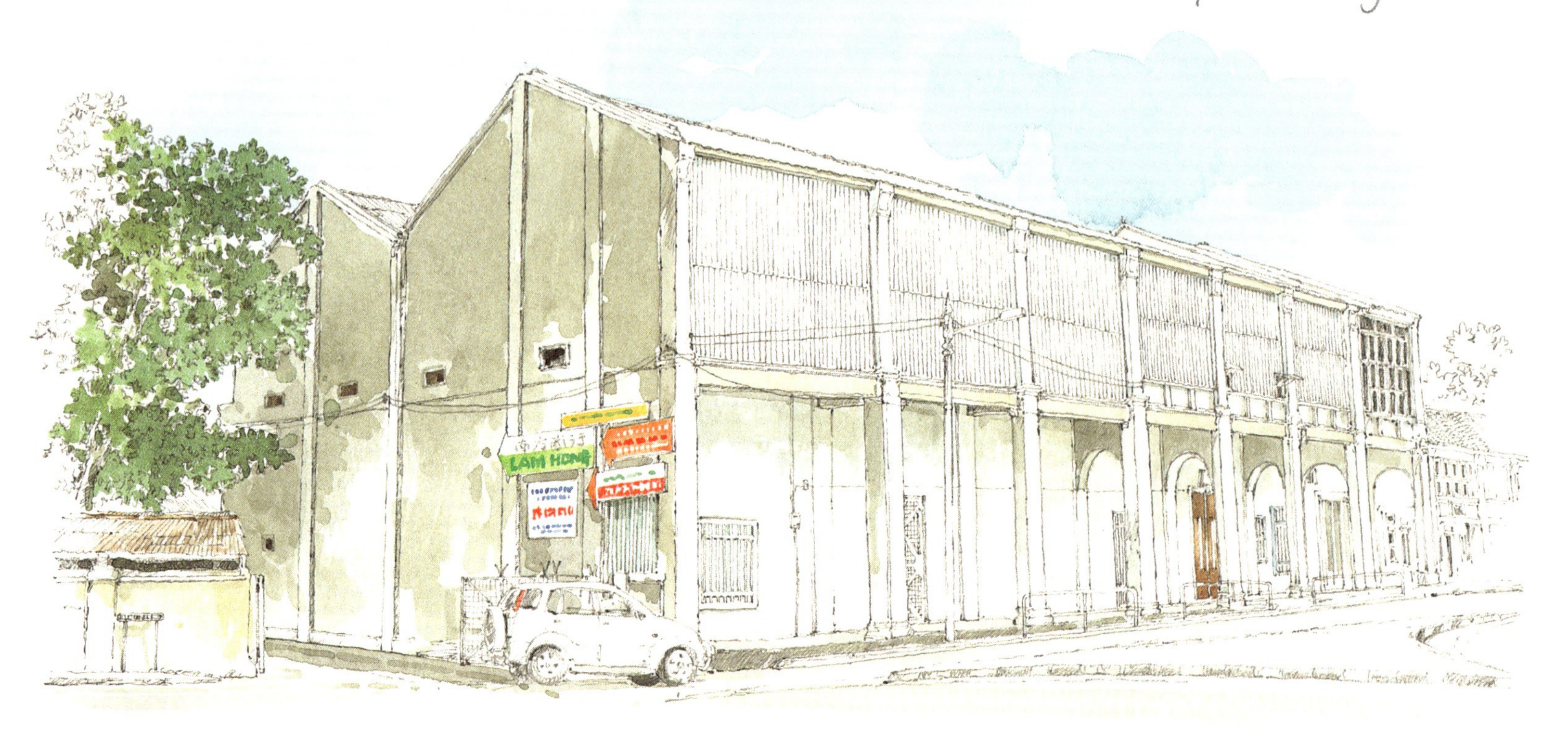

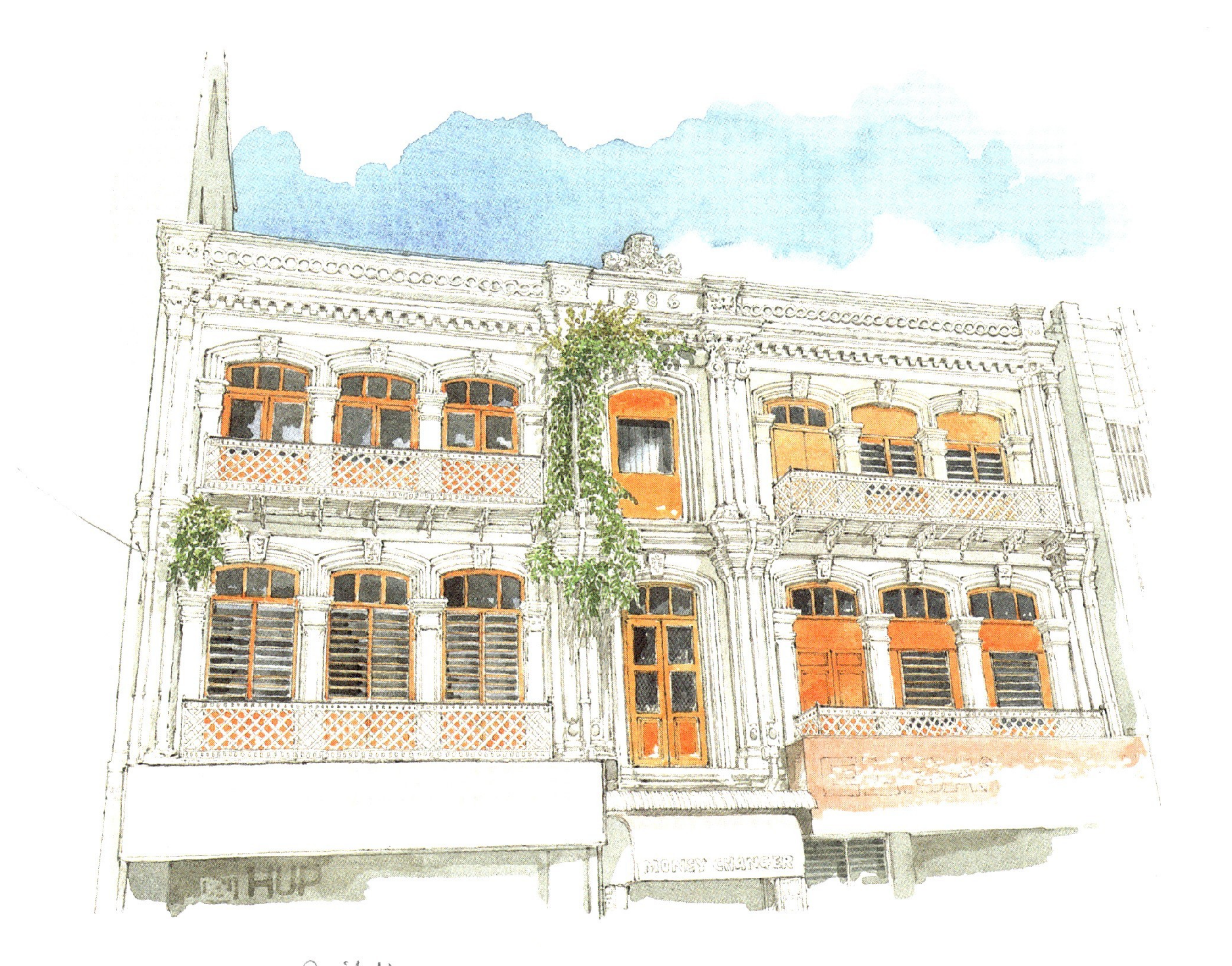

1886 Building
The building on Lebuh Pantai, formerly 'Goon Yen & Friends', a local-owned retail store run along Western department store lines, is reputed to be the oldest commercial building surviving in its original form. A central bay divides the upper two floors equally into three-window bays on each side. The full-height windows have cantilevered cast iron balconies in a fine network pattern.

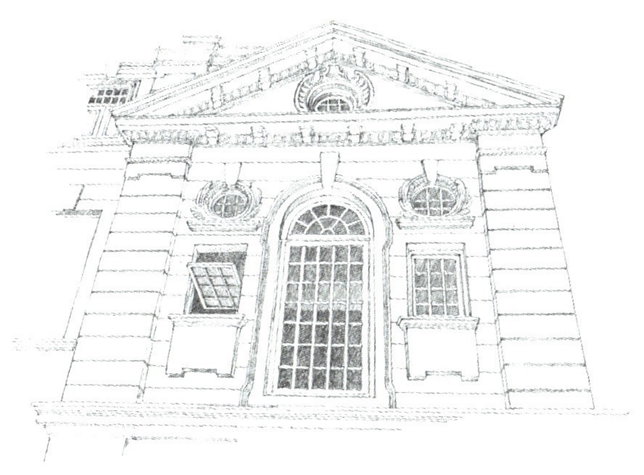

Detail of the pediment on the Gat Lebuh China façade of the 1923 George Town Dispensary.

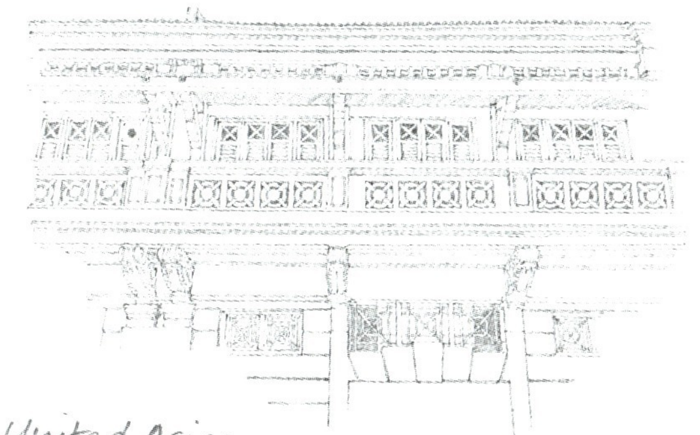

Bangunan United Asian Bank's (UAB) cantilevered upper floor balcony is supported by decorated console-type brackets. The balcony's fringe roof has simpler triangular brackets.

Gazetteer

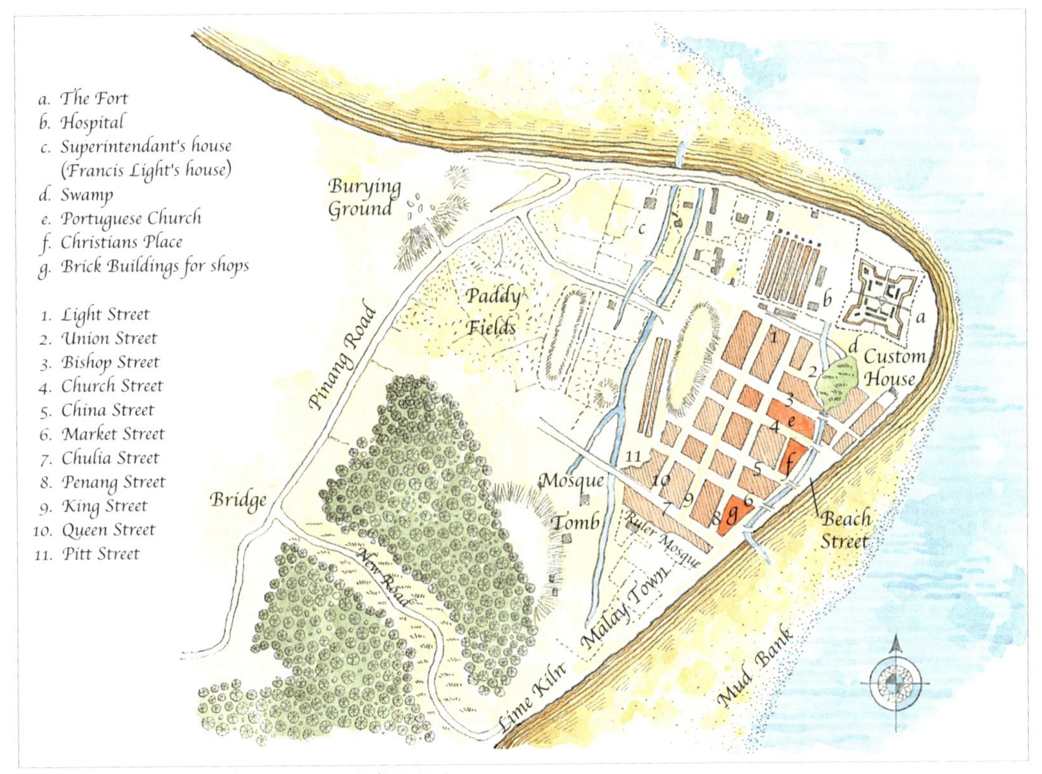

Early map of George Town based on Captain H.R. Popham's 1798 plan.

THE FOUNDING OF A SETTLEMENT

Page 8

Francis Light Statue, Lebuh Farquhar

The bronze statue was based on the likeness of Francis Light's son, William Light, as there was no picture of the founder of Penang. It was sculpted by F. J. Wilcoxson, cast at Burton's Foundry, Thames Ditton, and completed in 1939.

Protestant Cemetery, Jalan Sultan Ahmad Shah

Besides housing the tomb of Penang's founder, Francis Light (d. 1794), many other Europeans connected with the early settlement were buried here, such as Governors Phillip Dundas (d. 1807), William Petrie (d. 1816) and Colonel John Alexander Bannerman (d. 1819), who all died in office. There is also a group of Chinese graves in the cemetery dating from the 1860s to the 1880s—probably those of Christian Hakkas who came to Penang after the Taiping Revolution in China. Captain H. R. Popham's 1798 plan showed a 'Burying Ground', a mound at the edge of the early town on the northwest of Jalan Penang—at the same site.

Page 10

Penang Hill Railway, Ayer Itam

Considered an engineering feat at the time, the funicular railway, based on Swiss examples, was designed in 1922 by A. R. Johnson of the Federated Malay States (FMS) Railway. It was opened on 1 January 1924 by the Governor of Penang, Sir Laurence Nunns Guillemard. The 592-metre (647-yard) ride up or down the hill takes about half an hour. A timber carriage from the first train can be seen in the forecourt of the State Museum & Art Gallery, Penang (page 20).

THE CIVIC SPIRIT

Page 12

Victoria Memorial Clock Tower, Pesara King Edward

The 60-foot tower was donated by a loyal subject, philanthropist Cheah Chen Eok, in 1897 to commemorate the Diamond Jubilee of Queen Victoria's reign. It was completed in 1902 after the Queen Empress's death.

*Page 13 (map reference **c**)*

Government House, grounds of Convent Light Street

Francis Light's 'bungaloe' was built by Indian convicts after the settlement was made a penal station in 1789. It dates back to 1793. The Governor's Office and Council Chambers were housed here for some years. It was the seat of Penang's government in the early 19th century, and Stamford Raffles, founder of Singapore, worked here from 1805 to 1810 as Deputy Secretary to the Governor of Penang. The bungalow was acquired by the convent in 1859 and served as a novitiate in the early years.

Page 14

Francis Light Memorial

The memorial is built on the original 1-hectare (3-acre) Company's Square and its grounds have remained virtually intact. The memorial's marble plaque carrying the epitaph to Francis Light was erected by the son of James Scott, the founder's friend, and was first placed in St. George's Church. It was removed to its present location when the memorial was built.

St. George's Church, corner of Lebuh Farquhar and Jalan Mesjid Kapitan Keling

The two men most responsible for the founding of the church were Reverend H. S. Hutchings, the Colonial Chaplain, and Captain Robert N. Smith of Madras Engineers. It was built entirely by Indian convict labour and completed in 1818 at a cost of 60,000 Spanish dollars.

*Page 15 (map reference **d**)*

State Assembly Buildings (Dewan Undangan Negeri), Lebuh Light

Formerly the Recorder's Courts and Magistrate's Courts, these dignified Anglo-Indian buildings are typical of architecture in the early half of the 19th century in their use of classicism in a pure and unadorned form.

Page 16

Supreme Court, junction of Lebuh Light and Jalan Mesjid Kapitan Keling

The present building, completed in 1905 at the cost of 206,678 Straits dollars, replaced an earlier courthouse on the same site dating from 1809. Logan Memorial (page 17) stands at the western end of the park-like grounds.

Page 17

Logan Memorial

The memorial was erected in 1869 by the people of the Straits Settlements to commemorate the death of James Richardson Logan of the famed *Journal of the Indian Archipelago and Eastern Asia*. He stood for justice and championed the rights of non-European communities. He and his elder brother, Abraham Logan, fought through the press for the end of Indian rule, which led to the Transfer of 1867. This tribute is inscribed on a marble slab on the memorial: 'He was an erudite and skillful lawyer, an eminent scientific ethnologist and he has founded a literature for these settlements …'.

Cathedral of the Assumption, Lebuh Farquhar

The cathedral, formerly the Church of the Assumption, founded by Father Garnault at Lebuh Gereja, moved to its present site around

1857, where it occupied a temporary building. The present building was erected by Father Manissol in 1860. Its two wings were added in 1928 during extensive renovations, and the sanctuary was renovated in 1955 after the church was elevated to a cathedral.

Pages 18–19
Town Hall, Jalan Padang Kota Lama
The Town Hall was built around 1880. Its role was more social than administrative, and it had an assembly hall, a ballroom with adjoining supper rooms and a library. It was used to stage dramatic and musical productions. Postcards from 1910 show the Town Hall with a single-storey *porte cochere*.

City Hall (Municipal Council Building), Jalan Padang Kota Lama
The building of the magnificent edifice commenced in 1900 and took three years to complete, at a cost of 100,000 Straits dollars. The present 24 Municipal Councillors meet regularly in its panelled Council Chamber.

Page 20
State Museum & Art Gallery, Penang, Lebuh Farquhar
Reverend H. S. Hutchings founded the Penang Free School on this site in 1816. The present building was constructed in two stages, in 1896 and 1906. The older, symmetrical, eastern half was destroyed by World War II bombs and never rebuilt. In 1961 the Hutchings School, which had taken over the building from the Penang Free School, relinquished it to the government for conversion into a museum and art gallery. The museum opened in 1965. It underwent a major renovation in 1997 and reopened with the present displays. The ground floor shows Penang's major communities and their cultures while the first floor galleries tell Penang's history with rooms displaying the famous oils of Captain Robert Smith and the engravings of William Daniel.

Page 21
Eastern & Oriental Hotel (E & O Hotel), No. 10 Lebuh Farquhar
The E & O Hotel was a sister hotel to Singapore's Raffles and Rangoon's Strand, all associated with the legendary Sarkies brothers. The E & O Hotel was managed by Arshak Sarkies, the youngest brother. Sold and resold, the hotel has recently undergone extensive rebuilding and refitting into an all-suite hotel. The old Art Deco, four-storey structure built in 1929 by architect Messrs Brossard Mopin has been retained. Penang's oldest hotel might still be able to claim it has the longest sea front—244 metres (800 feet)!

Page 22
Convent Light Street, Lebuh Light
In 1852 three French Sisters of the Holy Infant Jesus Mission arrived in Penang to work among the poor. They were joined by Mother St. Mathilde, considered the founder of the Mission. The present 3-hectare (7-acre) site at the end of Lebuh Light was acquired in 1859. The convent expanded over the decades and a chapel, Sisters' cloisters, a nunnery, a novitiate, an orphanage, a boarding house and classrooms were added.

Page 23
ABN AMRO House, No. 9 Lebuh Pantai
The *Nederlandsche Handel Maatscappij*, founded in 1824 to promote Dutch overseas commerce, established its Penang branch in 1888 as the bank of the Netherlands Trading Society. Its functions were to 'advise like a chamber of commerce, finance like a bank and trade like a merchant'. The building was designed by architects Wilson & Neubronner. The contractor, Lee Ah Kong, completed it for a sum of $41,200 Straits dollars and the bank opened in 1905. Modifications were made to the tower design in the early 1900s. Old postcards of 1910–15 showed the corner tower capped with a dome and more elaborate supports above the roof cornice. Later, it became a flatter, cap-like roof with overhanging eaves. The building was carefully restored for the bank's centenary in 1988. The meticulous work was undertaken by ABN's Head Office in Amsterdam based on original documents from their archives. The original height of the banking hall with its mezzanine gallery was restored, revealing hidden mouldings; partitions were removed, showing the elegant Corinthian columns and cornices. The side elevation on Lebuh Union can now be fully appreciated.

*Page 24 (map reference **a**)*
Seri Rambai, Lebuh Light
The Dutch presented the legendary demi-cannon to the Sultan of Johore in 1605. It was captured by the Achehnese Sultan when the Johore capital was sacked in 1613, then given to the Sultan of Selangor in 1795. The Madras Native Infantry from the fort in Kuala Selangor seized it and brought it to Penang in 1871. Today, flowers placed on it by women regarding it as a fertility symbol embellish the Dutch East India Company's logo of heraldic lions and dolphins.

Fort Cornwallis, Lebuh Light
Named after the Governor-General of Bengal, the star-shaped fort was built at the tip of Tanjung Penaigre, where Francis Light landed. The name 'Tanjung Penaigre' comes from the hardwood *Penaga* tree growing there which Light ordered cut and cleared for the fort. Old postcards of 1900–1905 show the fort with many buildings for the military, surrounded by a water-filled moat, filled in since 1923. Today, only a gunpowder magazine and a chapel survive within the walls. The fort now serves as a landscaped cultural venue for visitors.

Page 25
Suffolk House, Jalan Ayer Itam
On his deathbed in 1794, Francis Light made a will bequeathing to Martina Rozells '... the pepper Gardens with my Garden house plantations and all the Land by me cleared in that part of this island called Suffolk ...'. All the materials for the house were imported from India and Burma—thin Indian bricks, terracotta, marble floor tiles and Burmese teak bearers. The floor plans are mirror images of each other and elevations are perfectly symmetrical. Light's 'pepper Gardens with my Garden house' were bought over in 1805 by W. E. Phillips and served as Governor's Residence for him and Colonel Bannerman, his father-in-law. In 1818 it became Government House. Subsequent modifications and additions were made after 1850 with a large roof over the original parapetted flat 'terrass' and jack roof. Conservation work is in progress to restore Suffolk House to Francis Light's 'Anglo-Indian Garden House'—the country's first and only one surviving of its kind in the country.

Page 26
Mariophile, Tanjung Bungah, St. John's Hill
The French Seminary of the Holy Angel, better known as College-General, moved to Penang in 1806 from Burma following the move of the French Catholic Mission. It was founded in 1660 and has a long history of training missionaries in Southeast Asia. The hill-top bungalow with its adjoining Chapel served as a retreat, and is still in use by the College-General which relocated its new seminary buildings to the foot of the hill in 1984 after its old complex, which was adjacent to College Square, was sold and demolished.

Page 27
State Religious Council (Majlis Jabatan Agama Islam Negeri), junction of Lebuh Downing and Lebuh Pantai
The building was once a part of an extensive complex housing the old government offices. It was built in 1889 and added to until the last extension in 1907. It now houses the State Religious Council, the Office for Islam Religion and a *syariah* court.

THE SOUTHERN INDIAN CONNECTION

Page 29
Nagore Shrine, junction of Lebuh Chulia and Lebuh King
The shrine, built in the early 1800s, venerates Syed Shahul Hamid, the famous Muslim saint of Nagore, southern India. The tradition of venerating city saints came to Penang with the Tamil Muslim traders of Tanjore. Feast days are observed by flying flags and distributing food. The alcoves on the side wall house shops.

Pages 36–7
Nattukkottai Chettiar Temple, Jalan Waterfall
Soon after the Chettiar community established itself in Penang in 1854, it bought the land in Jalan Waterfall to build a *chettinar*. The Nattukkottai Chettiar Temple, dedicated to Thendayuthapani, an incarnation of the Hindu deity Murugan, was built within the compound in the temple style of the Chettiars' homeland and consecrated in 1857. The best Burmese teak was used in its superstructure, and it has a magnificent *gopuram* (entrance tower).

Page 38
Mahamariamman Temple, junction of Jalan Mesjid Kapitan Keling and Lebuh Queen
The temple is the oldest Hindu one in Penang. Its founding in 1833 is corroborated by a notice of a consecration ceremony held a hundred years later in 1933, when the temple took its present form. The foundation stone was laid by Justice of the Peace V. Natesam Pillay. In 1979 major repair works were carried out by a sculptor and two assistants from the Academy of Sculptors, Mahapalipuram, southern India.

Page 39
Noordin Family Tomb, Lebuh Chulia
Mohamed Merican Noordin built the tomb for his mother using Indian masons. He too was buried there after 1870. Noordin was an early Muslim Municipal Councillor and was made a Justice of the Peace. The tomb's vestibule housed a school for the Muslim community which Noordin endowed for the 'learning of English, Hindoostanee, Malay, Tamil, Malabar and the Alkoran. Twenty dollars per month'.

Pages 40–1
Kapitan Kling Mosque, junction of Jalan Mesjid Kapitan Keling and Lebuh Buckingham
The mosque was founded before 1798. Later, Cauder Mydin Merican, as Kapitan Kling, was asked by the community he headed to build the mosque. The 19th-century title Kapitan (headman of the community) has a long history dating back to Melaka under the Portuguese. Kling, a term not used now, refers to Indians. The mosque has undergone various phases of extensions since the early 1800s.

Extensive conservation and development works continue today under the South Australian Heritage Consultants and Contractors Group (SAHCC).

THE CHINESE LEGACY

Pages 42–3
Khoo Kongsi, Medan Cannon
The well-established Khoos in Penang formed the Khoo clan association in 1835. In 1850 the association bought the land at Medan Cannon and converted the existing bungalow into the clan temple. All the Khoos in Penang belonging to Leong San Tong Dragon Mountain Hall can trace their lineage back to a common progenitor, Khoo Chian Eng of Sin Kang village, Hokkien province. A grand, new temple built in 1901 was mysteriously destroyed by fire, believed to be a casualty of hubris. The present, more modest one was completed in 1906 at a cost of 100,000 Straits dollars, with master builders, craftsmen and

materials from China. The ensemble of clan temple, association office, stage and terrace houses has retained the social organisation of a Hokkien clan village.

Pavilion Stage, Medan Cannon
The Pavilion Stage facing the Khoo Kongsi, an integral part of the temple complex, is unaltered from its 1906 original timber and brick structure. Its woodcarving, painting and *chien nien* decorations embody the highest standard of traditional skills.

Page 45
Cheah Kongsi, Nos. 8–8A Lebuh Armenian
Founded in 1835 by pioneer settler Cheah Yam, this was the earliest of the five great Hokkien clans. The well-endowed clan was run by generations of Cheahs, who originated from Sek Tong village in southern China. The mid-19th century clan temple and office buildings combine a courtyard plan with a porched bungalow plan and townhouse architecture. Its decorations are richly eclectic.

Pages 46–7
Lo Pan Hang (Carpenters' Guild), Lorong Love
Lo Pan is the patron saint of all builders, engineers and architects, carpentry being pre-eminent in Chinese architecture. He is a historical figure contemporary with Confucius (551–479 BC). He invented many basic tools used by carpenters today such as the right-angle rule, the compass, the nib and the straight thread *bak thau* (an instrument used to draw straight lines with an inked thread), and invested them with moral virtues. He was the 'Chinese Da Vinci', and was also attributed with the invention of the extendable ladder, the collapsible umbrella and the giant kite. Under the old guild system, the craft was passed down from master to apprentice. Lo Pan Hang was the first stop for all immigrant builders before they moved on to other parts of the country.

Kuan Yin Temple (Goddess of Mercy Temple), Jalan Mesjid Kapitan Keling
The temple was founded in 1801 by the pioneer Chinese from Kedah, Koh Lay Huan, alias Che Kay, and is shown on a 1803 plan. It is dedicated to Kuan Yin (the Goddess of Mercy), a Buddhist Bodhisattva, that is, one who has attained Nirvana but remains on earth to save lost souls. A second goddess, Ma Chor Poh, patron saint of sea voyagers, is also worshipped here. The temple is one of the edifices of the world's four main religions along the former Pitt Street—Buddhism, Christianity, Hinduism and Islam.

Page 52
Dr Sun Yat Sen's Penang base, No. 120 Lebuh Armenian
The building was extant in 1875 as a dwelling house or messuage, and was first owned by Cheah Joo Seang, a trustee of the Cheah Kongsi. From 1901 to 1911, Sun's *Tung Meng Hooi* party was headquartered here. This was where Sun, leader of the Chinese nationalist revolution, held the historic Penang Conference on 13 November 1910 and planned the Canton uprising of spring 1911. Though the latter failed, it led to the Double Tenth Revolution, the eventual overthrow of the Ching dynasty and the establishment of the first republic in Asia.

Page 53
Chung Keng Kwee Temple, Lebuh Gereja
The private temple, school and ancestral hall, built after 1893, was named after Chung Keng Kwee, who was made Kapitan China and sat on the Perak State Council following the Pangkor Engagement of 1874.

Hai Kee Chan Office-residence
The office-residence adjoining the temple was built after 1893 by Chung Keng Kwee on the site of the rival Ghee Hin secret society. The temple and office-residence are of great historic significance. Their ornate ceramic sculptured tableaux and gilded carved wood screens are of the finest Cantonese craftsmanship.

Page 54
Tua Pek Kong Temple, Tanjung Tokong
Tanjung Tokong (Cape of the Temple) has been there from earliest times as the Malay name of the locale testifies. Taking precedence over Penang's two other Tua Pek Kong temples (pages 50–2), the temple site's favourable geomancy has powerful significance. The Hokkien and Hakka dialect communities have disputed claims to this site for two centuries. Tua Pek Kong, literally 'Great Grand Uncle', is commonly regarded as the God of Prosperity and Protector of the Land. Penang's Tua Pek Kong was Chang Li, an 18th-century Hakka scholar and exile, who settled in Penang with two brothers or close friends. They brought with them the skills needed to build a new society. After their deaths, the last in 1796, they were buried at the temple. Their three tombstones can be seen on the grave mound behind the temple.

Page 55
Ng Fook Tong (Five Luck Villa), No. 407 Lebuh Chulia
Founded in 1819, it was one of the earliest Chinese schools in the country. It was formerly at the site on Lebuh Gereja that is now occupied by the Chung Keng Kwee Temple (page 53). The current building dates from 1898, and was built by the United Association of Cantonese Districts to serve as a night school.

THE SUMATRAN LINK

Pages 56–7
Mesjid Lebuh Acheh (Acheen Street Mosque), Lebuh Acheh
The mosque, also known as Mesjid Melayu (Malay Mosque) or Mesjid Jamek (Friday Mosque) is the oldest one in Penang. It was founded in 1808 by Arab-Achehnese Tengku Syed Hussain Al-Aidid, a royal claimant to the Achehnese throne, whom Light persuaded to move to Penang. The octagonal minaret design reflects the founder's Arab-North Sumatran origin. The mosque was a focal point of the Achehnese revolt against the Dutch in the 1870s war.

Page 58
Gudang Acheh (Achehnese Godown), junction of Lebuh Pantai and Lebuh Acheh
The building was in existence in 1805 as a gaol, hence its thick lower walls and small windows. *Gudang* (place where goods lie) comes from *gidangi* (Telugu), *gudao* (Portuguese) and *gedong* (Malay).

Page 59
Sheikh Omar Basheer's Residence, No. 69 Lebuh Acheh
Sheikh Omar Basheer was the *imam* (leader of prayer) of the Mesjid Lebuh Acheh (pages 56–7). The Basheer family arrived in Penang from Acheh around 1792, at about the same time as Tengku Syed Hussain Al-Aidid. Generations of Islamic teachers and *da'wa* (missionaries) have come from the Basheer family, and they have held the coveted positions of *qadi* (magistrate in Islamic law) and *mufti* (Muslim priest or expounder of the law). The two houses on the grounds of the mosque (Nos. 67 and 69) have survived from the early Malay Town south of Lebuh Chulia in Francis Light's early settlement.

Page 60
Sheikh Zachariah Basheer & Sons, No. 6 Lorong Lumut
The operational trading base of Sheikh Zachariah Basheer was set up in 1900 to trade in spices and other produce of the region. Sheikh Zachariah continued to lead the Lebuh Acheh Muslim community after the death of his father, Sheikh Omar Basheer, for whom he built the mausoleum in Kampong Melayu, Ayer Itam.

Page 61
Syed Alatas Mansion, No. 128 Lebuh Armenian
Syed Mohamed Alatas, an Arab-Achehnese, succeeded Che Long as the leader of the Red Flag secret society. He was a supporter of the Sultan of Acheh and smuggled arms from British India for the Sultan's anti-Dutch resistance. He married the daughter of a Chinese pepper trader, who was also a secret society leader, and the union strengthened the Red Flag-Khian Teik alliance. His second house on Lebuh Carnarvon (page 69) is in the Straits Eclectic style, and was a gift from his father-in-law.

THE STRAITS ECLECTIC STYLE

Page 63
Lebuh Campbell Market, junction of Lebuh Campbell and Lebuh Carnarvon
The municipal wet market was built around 1900 on grounds that were part of the 7-hectare (18-acre) lot granted to the 'Mohamedan Church for ever' (page 41)—the Kapitan Kling Mosque's burial ground. The graves were removed to a new cemetery in Jalan Perak except for one, a shrine known as Keramat Mustafa Wali and dedicated to the patron saint of poulterers, which still stands on the market grounds.

Page 64
Teh Bunga's House, No. 138 Lorong Hutton
This was the home of M. Z. Marican, alias Teh Bunga (flower tea), the son-in-law of Wanchee Ariffin, who was a descendant of pioneer Bapu Alauddin who came to Penang with Francis Light as a representative of the Sultan of Kedah.

Page 65
Lorong Bangkok Terrace Houses, Lorong Bangkok
The two rows of 40 terrace houses were built in 1928 by Cheah Leong Kah, a horse carriage repairer who later pioneered motor firms. One of the early Western-trained Chinese architects, Chew Eng Eam, was commissioned to build the terrace houses. Chew also designed the oldest Chinese restaurant, the boat-shaped Loke Thye Kee, in 1919, and the Majestic Theatre, which opened in 1926.

Page 66
Shih Chung School, No. 11 Jalan Sultan Ahmad Shah
Cheah Tek Soon's lofty residence is still known by locals as Goh Chan Lau (five-storey building.) In the 1900s, when Cheah's brother, Cheah Tek Thye lived there, it was called the Chinese Residency. In 1910 it became the Tye brothers' Raffles-By-The-Sea. Tea was served on the lawn opposite rival Runnymede Hotel. After World War II, it was taken over by the P'i Joo Girls' School and finally, the Shih Chung Branch School. Today, it is in a dangerously dilapidated condition.

Page 67
Cathay Hotel, No. 15 Lebuh Leith
Yeoh Wee Gaik's former mansion is now a 53-room hotel favoured by foreign and local visitors seeking a colonial ambience. The hotel was taken over by Loke Yean Peng in 1948. It has kept most of the original features of a heritage mansion including an inner courtyard and grand staircases.

Page 68
Syed Sheikh Al-Hadi's Residence, No. 410 Jalan Jelutong
A Malay of Arab descent, Syed Sheikh Al-Hadi's friendship with the Riau royalty enabled him to travel to Egypt. After his return he published Jawi magazines at his Jelutong Press in the 1920s. His novel *Hikayat Faridah Hanom* (The Story of Faridah Hanom), the first written in the Malay vernacular, was a bestseller and expressed his modernist Islamic view. The bungalow has since been taken over by nuns and converted into a temple.

Page 69
Li Teik Seah Building, No. 152 Lebuh Carnarvon
The second home of Syed Mohamed Alatas was a wedding gift from his father-in-law, Khoo Tiang Poh, a wealthy pepper trader and close associate of the Achehnese community.

Page 70
Kek Lok Si (Pure Land Temple), Ayer Itam
The Kek Lok Si, also known as the Temple of Supreme Bliss, is the country's largest temple complex and is spread over 4 hectares (10 acres) of rocky hill slope. Construction began in 1893 and was completed in 1905. The Five Great Sponsors were the Hakka tycoons led by Chong Fatt Tze. Three tiers of buildings comprise Halls to Kuan Yin, the Laughing Buddha and Gautama, the founder of the faith. A well-equipped monastery and nunnery are sited among terraced gardens with fish and tortoise ponds. The famous Pagoda of Rama VI, Ban Hood (Pagoda of Ten Thousand Buddhas), was named after the Thai monarch. It has remained remarkably intact.

Page 71
Penang Buddhist Association, No. 168 Jalan Anson
The association was founded in 1925 by Straits Chinese Buddhists who wanted to study Buddhism in its pure form free of Taoist beliefs and superstition. The Mahayana Pure Land Sect is followed, but the Theravada School is also encouraged. The temple was built by the association whose income is derived from residential properties developed in the 1930s.

Pages 72–3
Cheong Fatt Tze Mansion, No. 14 Lebuh Leith
This was the principal home of the illustrious Nanyang Mandarin industrialist, Hakka-born Cheong Fatt Tze (1896–1917). He left China as a poor immigrant in the 1850s for Java, rapidly prospered and expanded his business to Sumatra. In the early 1890s he moved his base to Penang. He represented Nanyang Chinese in both British and Dutch territories, and also served the Ching government first as Vice-Consul in Penang, then as Consul-General in Singapore. He was the director of China's first railway works and modern bank. He advised both the Empress Dowager and Yuan Shih Kai's Republican government.

Cheong built his Eclectic Style courtyard family mansion between 1896 and 1904. Though Chinese in layout it combined both Eastern and Western features—Victorian cast iron columns and balcony panels, Chinese gilded carved wood doors and lattice screens, Art Nouveau stained glass windows, gothic-style framed louvred shutters and the largest single example of *chien nien* porcelain shard decorations in one building. This rare historic mansion has been carefully restored by Architect Laurence Loh and won the UNESCO's Asia-Pacific Heritage 2000 Award for Most Excellent Project.

Pages 74–5
Leong Yin Kean Mansion, No. 32 Jalan Sultan Ahmad Shah
This was the home of the son of tin-miner Leong Fee, one of the millionaires of 'Hakka Millionaires' Row'. Leong Yin Kean's snug seaside palazzo incorporated the owner's taste for Italian mosaic and marble. The house was designed by Charles Miller of Stark & McNeil architects and built at a cost of a quarter million Straits dollars in 1926. Leong's daughters lived there until the 1980s. It was bought over by Datuk Keramat Holdings Berhad, renamed simply The Mansion, and restored recently.

Woodville, No. 70 Jalan Sultan Ahmad Shah
Jalan Sultan Ahmad Shah is known to locals as 'Hakka Millionaires' Row', and is where the rich and famous have their *Ang Mo Lau* (European buildings). Woodville's owner, Lim Lean Teng, a wealthy Teochew planter with vast estates in Kedah, built this in 1925. The architect was Charles Miller, who also designed Leong Yin Kean Mansion (pages 74–5).

Page 76
Hu Yew Seah, Nos. 41–5 Lorong Madras
Choong Thiam Poe, an early member of the *Tung Meng Hooi*, founded Hu Yew Seah to educate English-speaking Baba or Straits Chinese in their mother tongue, Mandarin. In 1927, the building was inaugurated by Nobel Laureate Rabindranath Tagore, the Bengali poet, who was much admired by the English-speaking literati in the region.

Page 77
Soonstead, No. 46B Jalan Sultan Ahmad Shah
Originally belonging to Heah Swee Lee, this mansion was later sold to Heah's in-laws and renamed. Heah was a Perak State Councillor. He donated the Penang Polo Ground, and became its first non-European member. Soonstead, like its neighbours, is set in extensive grounds.

Page 79
Hardwicke Hall, No. 67 Jalan Sultan Ahmad Shah
Khaw Joo Ghee of the famous Khaw family resided in the bungalow at the turn of the 20th century. He was followed by Lim Cheng Ean, an eminent lawyer, who served as the first Chinese Magistrate in Penang. As Legislative Councillor of the Straits Settlements, he championed vernacular education and freedom of the press.

Homestead, No. 54 Jalan Sultan Ahmad Shah
The mansion was designed by architect James Stark of Stark and McNeil originally for *towkay* (Chinese merchant) Lim Mah Chye in 1919. It was bought by banker Yeap Chor Ee who provided for its upkeep in a trust. His descendants still live in this well-kept, palatial mansion by the sea.

Pages 80–1
Ku Din Ku Meh Residence, No. 20 Jalan Penang
Kedah-born Ku Din began his career as Head of Kedah Prisons at the age of 14. The Sultan of Kedah appointed him High Commissioner of Setul in 1897 when parts of southern Thailand were provinces of Kedah under Thai suzerainty. In 1902 Ku Din took the title Raja of Setul and used the royal name Tengku Baharuddin bin Tunku Meh. He was fluent in Malay and Thai, owned ships and successfully traded in local produce. He married a Penang woman and had his trading office in this town house.

THE WATERFRONT

Page 85
Koe Guan Godown, Lebuh Pantai
The early 19th-century godown behind the Koe Guan Company office was originally on the waterfront before the reclamation of the land forming Pengkalan Weld. Immigrant coolies (cheap, unskilled labourers) from the company's boats from China were housed here before being transshipped to the tin mines of southern Thailand. The patriarch founder of Koe Guan (High Source), Khaw Soo Cheang built up his fortune from tin mining and trading after he arrived as a penniless immigrant in the 1810s in Penang.

Page 86
Wisma Kastam (Customs Building), junction of Pengkalan Weld and Gat Lebuh China
The Wisma Kastam, formerly the Malayan Railway Building, was built in 1907 to mark the completion of FMS Railway. Locals claimed it was 'the only railway station without a rail' as the trains were on the mainland. Passengers bought their train tickets, proceeded to the Railway Jetty at the end of Gat Lebuh China and boarded the Railway Ferry Steamers to Butterworth to catch their northbound or southbound trains. The building served as administrative offices with ticket booths and a station hotel with a Railway Restaurant, Bar & Grill.

Wisma Yeap Chor Ee, junction of Pengkalan Weld and Gat Lebuh China
The office building was named after its owner, Yeap Chor Ee, the founder of Ban Hin Lee Bank, the only Penang-based bank. Yeap built up his financial business by investing wisely and consolidating it during the rubber slump in the 1930s.

Page 87
Former Paterson Simons Building, No. 9 Pengkalan Weld
The building was developed by Phuah Hin Leong, who was born a Lim and adopted by a Phuah family. He was a legendary rags-to-riches early immigrant from China who started with 'a pair of oars' by ferrying passengers and goods across the Channel, and ended by owning 'a pair of mills'. Phuah invested in godowns and shipping offices along Pengkalan Weld and Lebuh Pantai, renting them to European trading houses such as Paterson Simons.

Page 89
Boustead Block, No. 1 Pengkalan Weld
Massive land reclamation in the 1880s culminating in Swettenham Pier in 1904 raised Penang to the status of a modern transshipment centre, a fulfilment of the East India Company's original objective. Frederick Aloysius Weld was Governor of the Straits Settlements when the project began and the man-made *pengkalan* (quay) was named after him. Boustead Block was the first building to be built on the reclaimed land in 1893. Boustead, which is still based here, smelted tin ore and exported the ingots with the Boustead imprint. Other trading houses and shipping agencies in the building were Schmidt & Kuesterman, Behn Meyer, Shiffman Heer and Paterson Simons (page 87).

Page 90
Khie Heng Bee Mills, Jalan Jelutong
The mill is one of the few survivors of the island's first industrial boom in the late 19th century. Sited north of the Penang River, the rice mills were part of the supporting food-processing industry. Rice was milled, boiled and loaded onto boats on the waterfront and sent to feed the workers at the mainland rubber plantations. Another process was the moving of copra and grain from the drying area across the road by an aerial tramway to the mills and godowns on the waterfront. Phuah Hin Leong bought the site to expand his rice and oil mills. Spread over 2 hectares (5 acres) at its height, Khie Heng Bee Mills was one of the largest industrial enterprises of Penang.

Balai Bomba (Central Fire Station), junction of Gat Lebuh Chulia and Lebuh Pantai
Fire-fighting in the early days was carried out by the police until 1909 when the first 28 locally trained firemen started a proper fire-fighting service. This fire station was opened the same year.

Page 91
1886 Building, Lebuh Pantai
Goon Yen & Friends were Chinese *towkay* who broke the traditional preserve of European-owned commercial buildings on the northern Lebuh Pantai. These were the first mixed-use commercial buildings with rental offices on the upper floors and retail outlets on the ground floor. The 1886 Building, though Chinese-owned, was run along Western lines. Its ground floor emporium displayed a range of goods which impressed even European customers, while upper floors were let out to offices such as Howarth Erskine Engineers.

Acknowledgements

The first time I ever set foot on Penang, the famous Pearl of the Orient, was in 1960 on a class field trip. I was left with an unforgettable impression of the city, Penang Hill, Kek Lok Si Temple and trishaws along the streets. When I became a fully-fledged artist I had a yearning to sketch buildings of a bygone era and it was natural for me to revisit Penang in my artistic pilgrimage. In fact Penang has became my most frequented location for creative inspirations, apart from Kuala Lumpur. After more than 18 months of effort, I am pleased to share my labours of joy. I hope they will inspire people to preserve and care for the historical remnants of the past.

I take this opportunity to thank my publisher Didier Millet and the dedication of the editorial and design team for producing another sketchbook of Malaysia. The author of this book, Chen Voon Fee, has again demonstrated his professional knowledge in facilitating our understanding of the distinctive features of local architecture and recognition of its historical value. The constant support of my wife and daughter and most importantly, the sponsorship of ABN AMRO Bank and EON has resulted in the successful publication of this book. For their support and contributions towards the Malaysian world of arts, my family and I extend our most sincere gratitude and appreciation. — ***Chin Kon Yit***

To the author Khoo Salmah Nasution, whose *Streets of George Town Penang* (Janus Print & Resources, Penang, 1993) has been my constant guide, and when gone astray, has pointed me in the right direction—*Ribuan Terima Kasih.* My thanks also to Henry Barlow for providing me with copies of *Early History of Prince of Wales Islan* by F. G. Stevens (JMBRAS Vol.Vll Part 3, 1929) and *First British Pioneer: The Life of Francis Light* by H. P. Clodd (Luzac & Co. Ltd., London,1948) on which I relied for the account of Penang's founding and early history. I also referred to *Twentieth Century Impressions of British Malaya* edited by A. Wright and H. A. Cartright (Lloyds Greater Britain Publishing Co., London, 1908).

Thanks to artist Kon Yit, your drawings have given me fresh insight into the richness and variety of Penang's irreplaceable built heritage, and Yin Yoong, for your patient advice on computer glitches and for being a cheerful companion on our searches in Penang. And to Didier, thank you for giving me the chance to do a second Sketchbook with Kon Yit, and on my initial suggestion—Penang. — ***Chen Voon Fee***

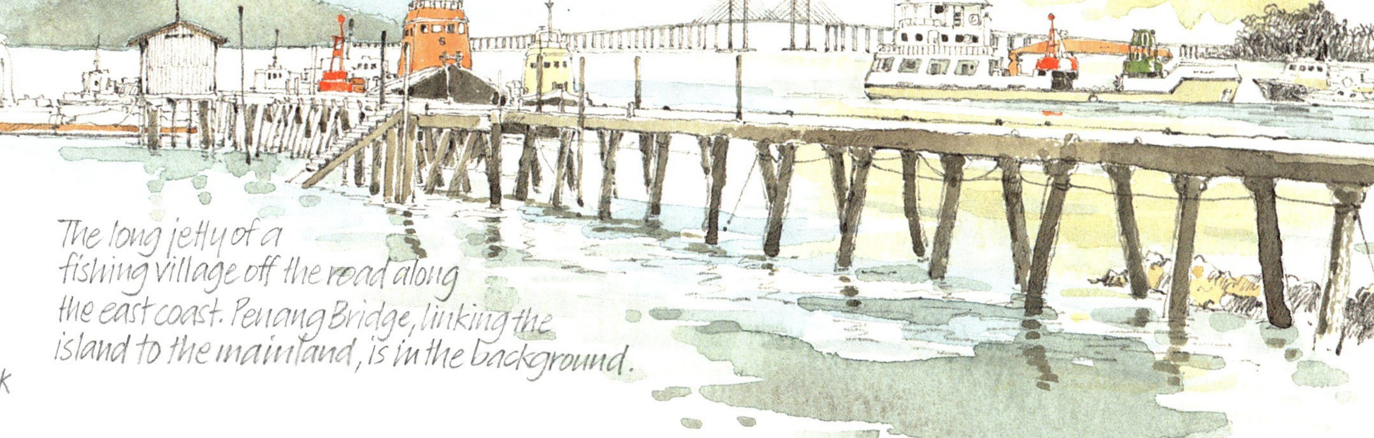

The long jetty of a fishing village off the road along the east coast. Penang Bridge, linking the island to the mainland, is in the background.

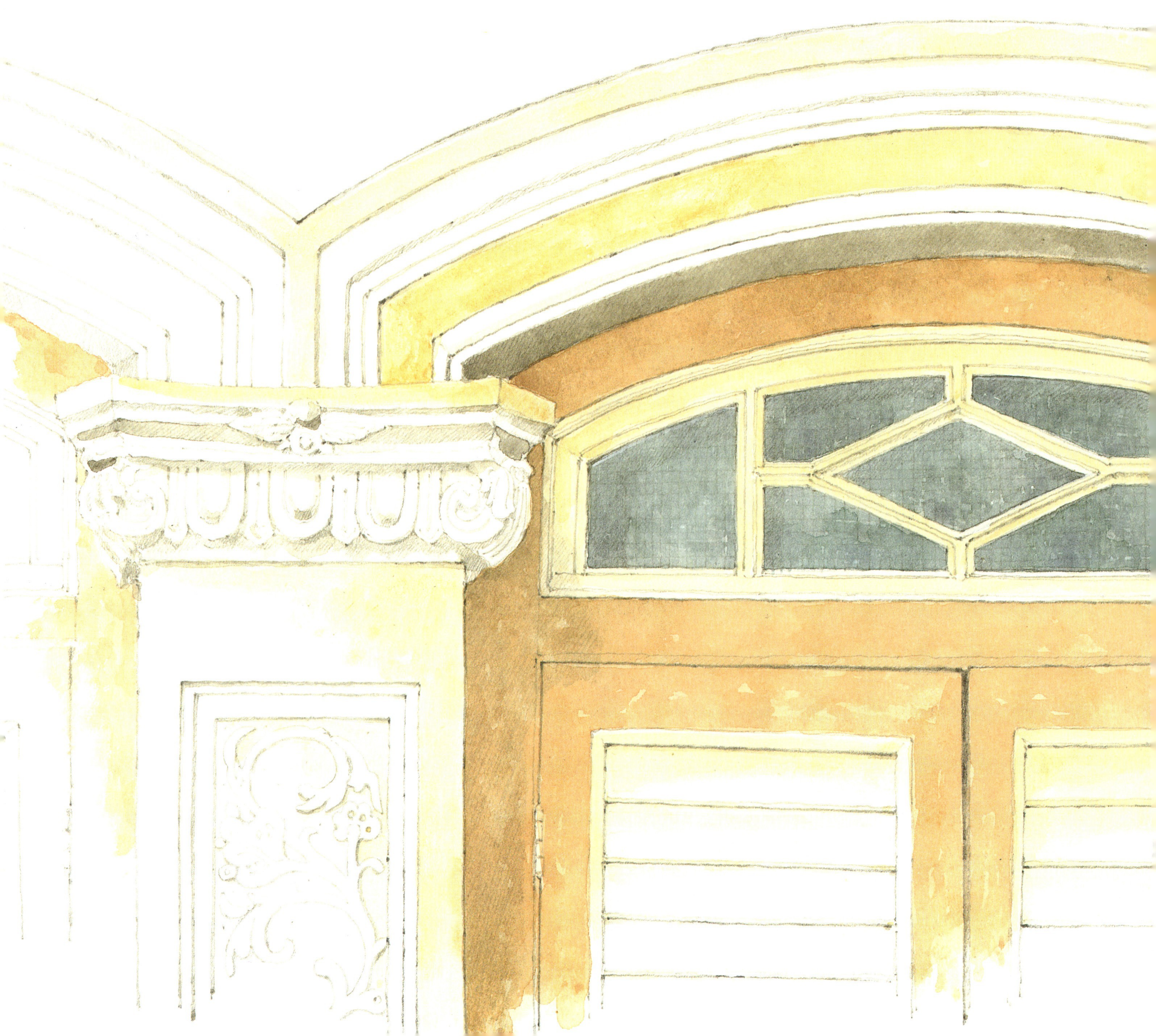